Rebel Read

The Prince of Speed

REDLINE BOOKS

Acknowledgements:
Motogp.com, Mortons Motorcycle Media, The Mick Woollett Archive, FIM/Good-Shoot, Stefan Knittel, Paul Blezard, Colin Seeley, Ken Jones, Malcolm Edgar, Tom Mortimer, Phil Morris, Peter Jones, Steve Wheatman, Phillip Tooth, Scott Matthews, Tim Parker, Mark Zanker, and Joan Caddick for making available Phil Read's medals, trophies, helmets and leathers at The Oswestry Road Racing Museum, also a special thanks to Nick Jeffery for his sharp-eyed proof reading and Mick Duckworth for his expert editing.

People I won't invite to my funeral:
Pat Frost
Tony and Sophie Smith
Phil Morris
Ben Shaughnessy
The MV Agusta Company
The Oxshott doctors
Geoff Duke
The TTRA
The Cobham Merc dealer
My golf partners
My ex-wife Angie
My daughter Esme

ISBN 978 0 9555278 7 6
Designed by Redline Books and printed in Malta

REDLINE BOOKS
www.redlinebooks.co.uk

Contents

'If your ship doesn't come in, swim out to it' Johnathan Winters

To all the people who have helped me during my decades of racing, to my friends, and to the brave riders we have lost, not forgetting my ever-supportive Mum, also a keen motorcyclist, I dedicate this book.

1 The lad from Luton

At 24, Phil is one of our most accomplished riders, yet so few know him off-track that he has remained something of an enigma. Obviously, as a professional road racer he takes racing seriously but not to the extent that it becomes an overriding obsession. In common with some other top-liners, notably Mike Hailwood, Phil becomes a ball of controlled nervous energy on the start line. But whereas Mike appears nonchalantly calm, almost flippant at times, Phil's attitude is tense and he seems to become oblivious to all around him. You may get an answer from him when he's in that frame of mind. But it's likely to be brusque, almost inaudible. Back in the paddock, between races, he cracks jokes with the best but the fact that his mind strays to the track will show through every so often. You may find that he has little time for people or things which do not directly concern him. So you wander off and mentally tab him as unapproachable, even rude.

HIGHLY STRUNG

This is unfortunate. If you suggest as much to Phil, he would be most upset. Highly strung, he overlooks points which may give a bystander entirely the wrong impression. Offhand, yes: but deliberately so—never. Away from the noise and bustle of the track, he is a different picture altogether. More at ease, full of boyish fun.

David Dixon, October 1963, *Motor Cycle*

At the end of 1963 the weekly magazine *Motor Cycle* ran a feature on Phil Read, the rising young star from Luton. It was written by staff journalist David Dixon and the one thing I remember he said was that I was an enigma. I didn't really know what that word meant so, probably for the first time in my life, I opened a dictionary to discover that I was 'a puzzling, obscure or mysterious person or thing'. Obviously, like a number of other people, David Dixon could not understand what made me tick. Well, if he was mystified then, he must have become more baffled as the Phil Read story developed over the years that followed.

All I can say is that if I am enigmatic, I've been that way since the day I was born in Luton on New Year's Day 1939. Maybe that's why it takes time for people to understand my thinking. I was born into a family already steeped in motorcycles and speed. Back in the 1920s, my mother had ridden around Luton on a 350cc New Hudson with hand-change and belt drive, which had to be bump-started. No doubt some people thought a young woman should have a more ladylike method of transport. But I wouldn't have liked to be the person who told her so. I can just imagine her reply - short and very much to the point. She was never one to mince words, and always let people know where they stood with her, like me perhaps? But please don't get the impression she was some kind of fire-eater, far from it. She was a kind, warm person and much of what I have achieved stems from her generosity - and her steely determination, which I seem to have inherited.

Dad's plane, a JAP-engined Aeronca C100, I understand it's now being restored at Fairoaks Airfield.

She had to be determined and self-sufficient, too. The outbreak of war in the year I was born took my father off into the Royal Air Force as a flight engineer; and it was not long after the end of the war in 1945 that my parents separated, leaving my mother to care for a very wilful seven-year old.

Unable, or unwilling, to go out to work and leave me in the care of relatives or neighbours, she built up from nothing a business that she could run from our home. Times must often have been difficult, but she made sure that I had all I needed even sending me to a private school in nearby Harpenden, where a natural disinclination to conform to authority became evident. Perhaps my teachers were lucky that I had not yet been to Imola, the Italian city famous for its racing circuit, where the local patron saint St Cassian was stabbed to death by the pens of his pupils. It might have given me ideas!

Psychologists would probably say that I suffered from not having a father at home and teachers at Harpenden would certainly have agreed. But I disagree. Naturally I would have liked to have had a father's help and advice, especially when motorcycles began to play such an important part in my life. Like my mother, my father was a great bike fan, and at one time they both had 350cc Ariel Red Hunters on which they went on their honeymoon and rode off on holidays. He raced on grass tracks, too, and I believe he was the first member of the Luton Flying Club to hold a private pilot's licence (PPL).

Whether or not he owned his own plane I'm not sure, but I do have very early recollections of a twin-cylinder monoplane being stored away during the war in the barn of my late maternal grandfather's farm, by then owned by my Mum Doris.

What I did miss was my father's engineering skill and knowledge once I had my own bikes. It would have been great having him there to show me the way, helping me with preparation and tuning. Instead I had to do it the hard way, working it out for myself, helped by Phil Irving's book, *Tuning for Speed*, but not always getting it right first time in my mid-teens.

I lived a happy, fairly carefree life then. My mother's enthusiasm and help in my ambitions more than compensated for my father's absence.

If I was in trouble as a youngster, I wasn't the only one. There was always a gang of us rushing about all over the place. We were lucky in having a park opposite my home on West Hill Road, although the park-keeper didn't think so. He was frequently at our front door, telling my mother what mischief her lad had been up to. It was always me; I was always the ring-leader. But did it worry her? Never. She knew what I was like, and she wasn't going to try to change me. I'm glad she didn't try, because there would have been a fair old battle raging in our home had she done so. Anyway, I think she found it funny that her son was upsetting the keeper of the park, which when she was a girl had been where her father kept cattle and she had ridden on top of hay wains at harvest time.

Our other great haunt was a disused grass tennis court my grandfather had built behind the farmhouse. It was there that my mother had learned to play well enough to represent Bedfordshire, which she also did at hockey. Skill at tennis was something else I seemed to have inherited from her. I showed enough promise for my mother to send me to a professional coach, but when I was 13 a new interest came to surpass all others, even a pretty brunette called Ann West, with whom I travelled on the bus to school each day.

Left to right

Mum and Dad's wedding with Granny Read on the far right

1942 Mum with me at her farm, West Hill Road, Luton

August 1941 Granny Read on the left

Dad's MSS Velo, the first bike I ever rode

Dad, on the left, a very keen cricketer

The new fascination was a 1930 250cc hand-change Matchless motorcycle purchased with Christmas present money for the princely sum of £3.15s 0d, after I had beaten down my old friend John Bates, from his original asking price of £4. Riding came naturally to me and a place to ride created no problems as I could tear round and round that disused tennis court. Better still, because it had been built on the side of a slope, there were two banks for me to scramble up and down. The fact that there was a row of large poplars in the way never bothered me. They added to the excitement, just as they had provided some added thrills when, as a ten-year-old, I had climbed to the very top of a 100ft tree to look out over all of Luton, including the giant Vauxhall car works three miles away.

With that old Matchless, I really was the leader of the pack. Now, it was my friends' mothers coming to the front door, complaining to my mother that their children's clothes were torn and dirty from riding her Philip's motorbike. Well, I had to let them ride it sometimes, didn't I? After all, I needed people to stand guard in case the police appeared on those occasions when I sneaked out on to the public road to see what speed I could get out of it. The only way I could reward them for being watchdogs was by letting them ride the bike, but only around the tennis court, of course.

There was more to that bike than riding it, though. Lovingly, I would strip it down to the last nut and bolt, clean it, and rebuild it. It was my Meccano set. Perhaps I should have been surprised when, having taken it apart the first time and put it together again, it started without any difficulty. But I wasn't. I almost knew instinctively that I had done everything properly; it seemed that I had inherited my father's engineering skills.

Life was not always centred on that old Matchless. Other sports, like cricket and football as well as tennis in the park, kept me occupied and many summer evenings were spent cycling through the country lanes around Luton.

We'd go off, a gang of us, boys and girls, pedalling up and down those narrow lanes, sometimes going over to Luton Airport to watch the small planes landing and taking off, nearly always coming home late and exhausted. They were good times. The evenings were warm and long, the countryside was all corn-coloured or green, there were few cars to worry about then and no jets roaring in and out of the airport. It was silent except for the birds, and they were as happy as we were. Moreover, I had won the affection of Ann West, despite rivalry from my mates and others.

As well as changing schools in 1954, I also went to my first motorcycle race meeting, the excitement of which was heightened by travelling pillion on my father's 1938 Velocette MSS. From time to time he would come around to see how I was, and it was just prior to one of these visits that he suggested a trip to the 'Hutch', the Hutchinson 100 races at Silverstone. You can't imagine how excited I was at the prospect of going to a real race meeting with all the great names. I dashed across the park to see Brian Setchell, a racer in his mid-twenties who lived in the same avenue as my aunt and uncle.

'I'm going to Silverstone,' I managed to gasp. And when I got my breath back, I barraged him with questions. Who would be there? Would Geoff Duke be racing? Would I see Surtees? (John Surtees was then the rising young British star).

Poor Brian. Ever since I had discovered he raced, I had pestered him for information and watched closely as he prepared his 350cc AJS 7R, asking why he did this and that. Yet he was always patient, even helpful. Now he wiped his hands and went into his parents' house for that week's *Motor Cycle* so I could learn more.

Riccione, on the Yamaha in the wet 1970, Pasolini on my right, Agostini on pole nearest camera, Grassetti on my left

The ride to Silverstone was uneventful. My father was to have a much more memorable return journey from the 'Hutch' the following year on the back of my KSS Velo! But the racing itself really turned me on. Like most youngsters I naturally thought I could do just as well, if not better, though deep down I knew I had a long way to go to match the likes of Duke and Surtees. I knew that racing was the life for me and I knew, sitting up there in the stand at Silverstone watching my heroes, that one day I could reach the top. Already the ambition was burning inside me.

Before I left the circuit that afternoon, my ambition was fired even further. Much to my joy, my father suggested a trip to the pits to chat to some friends he had among the riders.

My elation was rather soured, however, by one rider who shall remain nameless. Unlike my friend Brian, who did all he could to encourage me, this guy was very off-hand, ignoring me completely while he and my father talked. I just stood there, probably looking pretty calm, but inside I was seething. All the time they were talking I was thinking, 'I'll "do" you one day, mate,' in other words, beat him on the track.

Many years later I was telling the story to someone who couldn't have known me all that well, because he asked whether I ever did 'do' that rider. Of course I did, and I was still some way off 20 when I did. There are certain things you don't let lie, not if you're Phil Read.

I remember, still quite vividly, another episode from my early racing days. There was a certain rider, a Norton privateer called Bob Anderson from Bedford, who really used to get under my skin. Tall, good looking and ex-public school, he would turn up at the circuit with his bikes immaculately prepared, while I, like most of the other riders, was madly getting everything together at the last minute, barely having time to wipe the oil from my hands before getting into my leathers and racing. His arrogance upset me, although I've since come to realise that such attitudes can be just as much part of racing psychology as the signs of a person's real character. Taking him as a role model, I set out to promote a similar image of efficiency and organisation.

Some years later when I was riding for the Yamaha factory team, our new 250 fours were a handful to ride at a winning speed and we struggled with their handling. I wrote to Bob and asked if he would like to try to help us improve them at the 1966 Dutch TT. By then Bob had switched from bikes to cars, did well in Formula Junior and graduated to Formula 1. It came as a great shock to hear in 1967 that he had been killed testing a Formula 1 car at Silverstone. A terrible waste of a great riding and driving talent.

After that first trip to Silverstone, I couldn't wait until I was old enough to get my licence at 16, and have my own Velocette so that I could get out on the road. Sadly, the old Matchless had to go, it wasn't fit for the road anyway and was sold to my previous next-door mate, Peter Briars, for a £5 profit. That was quite a business, too; getting the Matchless from my home to his. Neither of us had a licence, so it was a case of riding through the back lanes in the dusk from Luton to near Harpenden, with a few of us keeping an eye out for the police.

As soon as I was 16 I took my test, and passed first time - just. My bike was now a 350cc KSS Velocette, carrying on the family tradition of favouring these once-great British machines, that had carried such heroes as Alec Bennett, Stanley Woods, Bob Foster and Freddie Frith to Isle of Man TT victories. What I overlooked at the time was that they were racing on closed circuits: I was roaring around public roads looking for other riders to take on.

Nor did a near-miss with the local law bring me to my senses. I was tearing around the outskirts of Luton one evening when I noticed a police car sitting in a side road. Perhaps they had been warned about me, I don't know, but when I looked back over my shoulder to see whether they were following or not, my heart skipped. There was this black Wolseley burning rubber round the corner. My first thought, believe it or not, was to stop, my second was to go like blazes. I did the second, following the tightest route possible, cornering the way I had dreamed I would when I was racing in my imagination against Duke and co. Only this was for real, and my licence was at stake. In what was a very short time, yet seemed like ages, I reached West Hill Road and my mother's garages. I cut the engine and glided into the relative security of the garage, slipped off my jacket, and, making sure the coast was clear, walked up the road to home. My mother, who had probably never seen me without a bike since I passed my test, thought I had crashed. 'Where's your bike?' she asked, as soon as I came through the gate. I told her.

'You won't give me away, will you?' I pleaded. 'If they come here, tell them I haven't got a bike any more. Say I sold it.'

'Calm down, calm down,' she said, 'Of course I won't give you away. Now go upstairs and wash, then come down for tea.'

What a marvellous woman and a fantastic mother. In her eyes I couldn't do much wrong. But that brush with the law gave me a bit of a fright, as well as providing some excitement and a taste of what it would be like to be racing on the roads. There were some other close shaves, too. On one hair-raising moment, at an intersection, a car drove out without seeing me and I also recall a nasty skid on some loose chippings. After these scares, I decided to do my speeding in the place designed for speed, the race circuit. Not everyone agreed with me. Brian Setchell, for example, had noticed with increasing apprehension the way I tore around the roads.

'Racing? Forget it for a year at least.' A year! The way I was riding I might not last a year. And even if I did, I would be lucky to keep my licence. Racing was the obvious answer to my need for speed, especially now that I had left school to start my apprenticeship with a local firm of engineers, who, as my mates loved to remind me, made mangles and washing machines. But they made other things, too, and I started on £3.10s a week. Obviously I was going to need some help if I hoped to exchange the KSS for a machine more suited to racing.

Good old Mum! With her assistance I was able to order a new 350cc BSA Gold Star from Bert England's Dunstable shop. I was sad to part with the Velocette, though. It was my first real motorbike, in that I was legally allowed to ride it on the roads, and those years of tradition meant a lot to me when I rode it. When I was in Florida for the 1976 Daytona 200, I was loaned an MSS to ride between the hotel and the track. It was quite an experience, riding a Velocette single again, and boy how those memories came flooding back.

It made me realise, too, how sensible my decision had been to quit fooling about on the roads and take to the track. At least on the track everyone is heading in the same direction, with a first aid post on every corner, and there was prize money for being fastest. Racing on the road, even if there's no one else involved and you're only trying to push the speedo a few notches higher than you've ever been before, inevitably it leads to trouble and often to serious injury, or worse.

Ridden carefully, a bike is a great means of transport; it gives you a feeling of freedom and excitement that travelling in a car never does, and challenges your ability to ride fast and safely. But if you want to be a Valentino Rossi or a Casey Stoner, don't live out your dreams on the road. Book a track-day, ideally where professionals are on hand to advise. It's the same when you're riding home from a meeting - and this applies to car drivers as well. There's this great temptation to imitate your heroes.

The Velocette was both my first and last true road machine for many years. I did ride the Gold Star on the road when I first bought it, and for a time I used to ride it to meetings I competed in. Principally, though, it was a machine for racing, the one on which I served my apprenticeship.

BSA supplied Gold Stars to special order and mine took its time to turn up. As a result I had to adjust my plans. The original intention was to race in the Clubman's event at Silverstone Saturday races, but that had come and gone by the time the Goldie arrived. However, it was worth the wait. Fast with good handling, altogether it was a beautiful sports motorcycle of the period.

Only a couple of hundred yards down the road from the dealer's, the engine cut out and just would not start again. Red-faced, I pushed the bike back to the shop, where the mechanic quickly spotted the problem. The high-tension plug lead was shorting out on the cylinder head. With the problem rectified by an insulated plug cap, I climbed back on and headed home with my new pride and joy.

My mother and I, with some advice from Brian, had chosen a brand new circuit not too far from my home as the venue for my racing debut at the first meeting on 13 May 1956. This was Kirkby Mallory, now better known as Mallory Park and home of the Leicester Query club, to which my father had belonged for some years. I mention that because I'm sure it helped get a start, something not always as easy as it might appear to be to someone outside the sport.

Before I could go circuit racing, the Gold Star had to be stripped and several hours were spent taking off all non-essentials such as registration number plates, lights, the silencer and centre stand. I stood back to survey my handiwork, then a horrible thought occurred to me. How was I going to get the bike to Mallory? I didn't have a van, or a trailer. I would have to ride it there. Back on went everything deemed absolutely essential for road riding but I didn't bother with the lights, reckoning that I would be able to do my road work in daylight.

When the great day dawned, 13 May 1956, I was already at the circuit, having ridden there the previous day. I slept in a tent while my mother slept in the Triumph Mayflower car in which she had followed me up with the tools and camping equipment. It was a nice car, but not designed for sleeping. Yet there were no complaints from Mum, who was as excited as I was when I set about preparing the bike for the meeting. I'm glad she was there, because someone else might not have understood the way I went all quiet while I was waiting for practice, my stomach feeling all knotted up. Out on the road I had never felt afraid, or worried, but this was something new, a strange nervous tension. So much depended on me doing well. I expected it of myself.

That first ever practice is something I'll never forget, if only for one of the most heart-stopping slides I've ever had in my life. Somehow I stayed on, more by good luck than good riding, and with my second-hand leathers (bought from sporting dealer Monty and Ward) several sizes too big for me, I flapped my way round the circuit, gradually getting a better feel for my bike and the circuit.

At Mallory Park in my second year of racing a 350cc BSA Gold Star

Me, wearing silver and red helemt, with Dan Shorey and old school friend Hayden King, seated on my Norton

But if lady luck had ridden on my shoulder during practice, she left me to my own devices in the qualifying heat. Although down in the programme as a reserve, I was allowed to ride, only to slide off at Shaw's Hairpin. My mother's heart nearly stopped when someone shouted up to her, 'Phil's crashed,' but she said she felt really relieved and proud when she saw me fighting my way back through the field. Oh yes, I had kept the engine running. I hadn't gone there to quit. Furious with myself, I had remounted and rejoined the fray. However, there were only two laps left, and I could do no better than to finish 13th, just one place away from qualifying for the final. I cursed my luck, but nonetheless felt happy with my performance. I hadn't disgraced myself too much.

That day, more than 57 years ago now, still stands very fresh in my memory, whereas numerous other races since have faded into obscurity. I remember, too, that my helmet had the now-familiar Read styling, although it then had silver stripes on a red background. For most of my career, the style has been white stripes on black background, based on Luton Town football club's colours. I can't claim to have originated the design, as it was copied from the helmet of the great Bill Lomas, a talented road racer from Milford, Derbyshire who won the 350cc world title on a Moto Guzzi in 1955 and 1956. I am told Bill approved.

That first season saw me race in about seven meetings, getting to know the circuits, the riders and a few of the pitfalls. I was also sorting out the bike and developing my riding technique. One thing is sure, I couldn't have been starting out at a better time, for in those days it was possible to ride against the best on the British racing scene early in your career. I enjoyed every minute I was out there on the track, though others might have felt differently. Nowadays, when I look at some of the short circuit aces, I'm glad I'm not out there. With more money in their pockets, today's youngsters can avail themselves of some mighty potent Japanese machinery long before they have the experience to handle it, and even club meetings can be too hairy for comfort these days.

Just as I was beginning to look better with every outing, so too the bike was looking more like a racer, with aluminium rims and full 'dustbin' fairing of my own design. Something must have gone astray in the execution, though, because that fairing kept cracking during races. I was also well aware that riding your racing bike to a race meeting is not the most ideal preparation either for yourself or the bike. My second ride-to-race trip to Oulton Park convinced me of that.

I had set out for the Cheshire circuit with my good friend Eddie Carter, who would act as my mechanic on and off for several seasons. We were both on bikes, me on the Goldie, but we were late setting off and had trouble finding a cheap place to spend the night. We couldn't go on past Crewe because the Goldie had no lights. So Eddie and I decided, with great reluctance because it would cost us both a week's wages, to book into the Crewe Arms.

It took a bit of courage just walking in there to see if we could have a room, but somehow we egged each other on, did all the necessary signing of registers, and went out to look after the bikes. The porter, who had eyed us rather quizzically when we entered, followed us out.

'Your bags, sir?' he asked me. Smart sod! I'll give you bags, I thought and looked at Eddie. He could see what I was thinking, and nodded. Without saying a word, we unstrapped my toolbox from the back of his bike and handed it to the porter.

'Room 16,' I said, and then turned back to the bike. I had to. If I'd looked at the porter's face a moment longer I'd have burst out laughing. As it was, as soon as he disappeared, Eddie and I doubled over in hysterics. It was almost worth a week's wages.

The racing at Oulton Park was no laughing matter, however. In fact it was something of a disaster for me. Mind you, the opposition was red hot, with people like Bob McIntyre, Alastair King and Derek Minter all there. Another rival was Mike Hailwood, a year younger than me and making his debut. He didn't have to worry about paying hotel bills, of course. He arrived in his father's chauffeur-driven Bentley!

Because of the high standard of racing, I felt well pleased to be holding something like ninth spot in the heat, and was just about congratulating myself on qualifying for the final when the exhaust pipe broke off. As if that was not bad enough, worse was to follow because I think that every one of the closely bunched riders behind me ran over it. It was flattened beyond repair, putting paid to my day's racing. Not only that, it also left me with the problem of getting home.

It's in situations like that that the motorcycling fraternity comes into its own. There is always someone around to lend a hand and no sooner had I walked forlornly back to the paddock than another rider, Dennis I think his name was, came over with the offer of his exhaust pipe to get me home to Luton. Thanking him as best I could, I bolted his pipe onto my bike and set off with Eddie in tow, a bit too slowly for my liking, because it soon became obvious that we were not going to make it before lighting-up time. There was only one thing for it: Eddie was left to travel at his own speed while I roared off towards Luton. Even then, I would never have made it, except for the help of a Vincent rider who turned up just when it was getting dark. He waved me to tuck in behind him, and covered me until it was time for me to turn off the A5 towards Luton. Thinking back, that Vincent really moved, because there were times I was struggling to keep up with him. He had another 650cc to play with, mind you, but he knew how to ride that big machine. When he went off with a wave and a roar it was nearly dark, I turned off the A5 to ride the last five miles home through the dark lanes which fortunately I knew well.

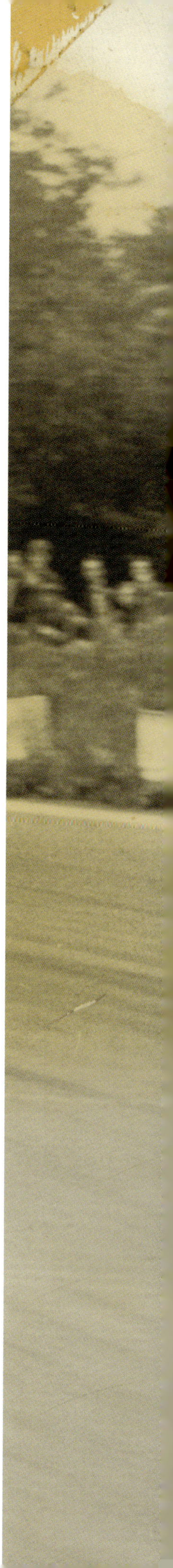

Mallory Park on the Gold Star again, braking hard alongside another 'Goldie'. My leathers, bought from dealer Monty & Ward for £18, were too big for me.

At Snetterton on my 350cc Goldie with a full fairing hand-made in aluminium

When I think about it, I must still have been taking the Goldie out on the public road, because one outing brought me into contact with another Gold Star rider, Chris Percival. Chris hailed from nearby Dunstable, and as well as his Goldie, which was strictly his road bike, he raced a 125cc Puch. Moreover, he had a van - at least his father did - and with this new-found luxury I travelled with him and was able to race at the final three meetings of the 1956 season, Castle Combe, Crystal Palace, and Brands Hatch.

It was a good year, my first season in racing, and having use of a van gave it a great ending. Sleeping in the van, waking to the sound of bikes and the smell of bacon and eggs cooking, it was a wonderful life. I made new friends and met some truly amazing characters who were only too keen to help a young rider. I lived for the weekends, and during the week in the factory, I secretly made bits and pieces to add to my race bike. It's been said that many a Luton engineering shop has gone bust as a result of motorbike-mad employees, and I'd agree with that. Still, my employers seemed happy with me, once I had stopped using their yard as a lunch-hour race track, and I was happy there.

Only one thing blighted the enthusiasm of that first season. I lost my girlfriend. It seemed to Ann that when I wasn't away racing, I was stuck in my garage-cum-workshop improving the bike or over at Brian's talking bikes. I guess she was tired of playing second fiddle to a piece of machinery, however beautiful it was. So out came the ultimatum: either give up racing, or give up her.

I'm not being funny when I say there was no choice: racing was in my blood. Ann was a very pretty girl of whom I was very fond, but there was no way she could replace the thrill, the sheer joy and excitement of racing a bike. Besides, we were still young and pretty innocent. So Ann went her own way.

I must have been upset, though, enough for my mother to try to cheer me up. She was old enough to have seen it all before, and she was, and always has been, an excellent judge of character. 'Don't worry,' she said. 'She'll be back one day, just you wait and see.' And so she was. A month or so later, I was down at the workshop, playing about with the Goldie, when the door opened. I looked up, and there she was. For once, the bike took second place and it was the end of our innocence.

Looking back on that first season, I see now how I might have avoided a lot of pitfalls. Instead, without anyone looking over my shoulder to guide me, I walked straight into them, and learnt by climbing out of them again. Time and time again I kept saying to myself, 'If only I had someone to guide me, I'd be progressing much faster.' Not that there weren't people around willing to help; it was more that I wanted someone there of my own, a father in other words. The fact that he was not there made me even more determined to do it myself - and to do it successfully. In the event I became regarded as something of a loner, a description that could not be further than the truth.

Me with my mother's Triumph Mayflower

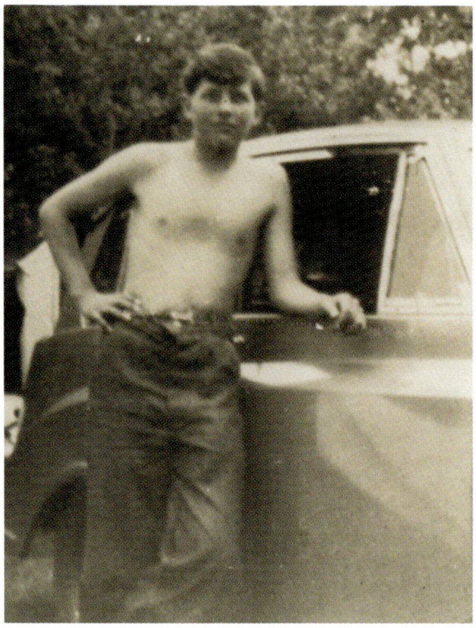

One thing that having a father around could not have prevented was failing my driving test in a car. I just couldn't believe the examiner when he said I had failed! I'd been driving cars and things on private property since I was a schoolboy. As it turned out, perhaps that examiner knew a thing or two. Next time round I got my licence, and with it came the use of my mother's Triumph Mayflower. But one night, after seeing Ann home, I went a bit too fast into a bend, rolled, and the car was a write-off. This time, I thought, I would be for it. But no, once again Mum came up trumps, and instead of banning me from using her car again, she offered to use the insurance money to buy a van for my racing. Twenty years later she still hadn't replaced that car; but had reverted to her first love of motorcycling on the 70cc Honda I gave her. We once tried to give her a car for Christmas, but she turned it down flat.

'It would be very nice, I'm sure,' she said. 'But I think I would prefer to keep my bike. For one thing, it takes up less room in the garage and I can ride on the pavements.' What an amazing woman she was!

Most of the 1957 season was raced, with mixed fortunes, on the Gold Star. But towards the end of the year I had the chance to buy the Geoff Duke 350 BSA special, considered to be the fastest Beesa in the country at that time, being sold by Frank Rutherford. Built for Duke by the factory it was probably only equal in performance with an average Manx Norton, but looked too good to miss, so I sold my Goldie and scraped together enough cash for the Duke bike.

Certainly it looked a good investment after one successful outing at Mallory, and I was looking forward to another good run in the supporting 350cc race at Silverstone. Even a rainy day and the wet track failed to dampen my spirits. Having never raced in the rain, a spot of water did not raise any horrors, but I was soon to learn that a wet track needed to be treated with careful respect.

From a poor start I had pulled through to third spot, passing none other than Bob King. The leading pair on Manxes, Tom Thorp and John Lewis, were only a hundred yards ahead, and I reckoned that a couple of laps would bring them within range. What I didn't take into account was the deteriorating condition of the surface, and while I was making a big effort around Stowe corner, the back wheel slid round, flicking me high into the air. Down I came with a mighty thump, sliding along the tarmac. I suppose I was lucky because all I suffered was a broken wrist. However, that was enough to bring my second season to an abrupt end.

During the winter that followed, I first met one of those great characters of motorcycle racing, the late and sadly-missed Peter Ferbrache. What a guy! During World War Two, at only 18 or so, he'd been flying missions over Germany as tail-gunner in an RAF bomber squadron. He was frightened when he raced in Germany, very worried he'd be recognised, by whom I can't think!! And the tales he told! Most weekends, 'Flue brush', as we called him, would call round to West Hill Road and the pair of us would go off together, usually to test his pair of Nortons. Not that I was allowed to ride them; at least, not on the first few outings. Nonetheless, I always took my leathers along, just in case, and finally one weekend my patience was rewarded. Pete let me try his 350 Manx. What a machine! Braking, handling, acceleration, it had the lot at a level I had never experienced before. I really put it through its paces, feeling exhilarated when I brought it back.

On the 350cc Duke BSA Special

Mum on her Honda 70

I'm looking pleased with the 350cc Norton Manx I bought from Peter Ferbrache with help from Mum.

'Well?' he asked.
'Incredible,' I replied. 'What a machine!'
'You interested in it?'
'What do you mean?' I stuttered, staring at him.
'I'm putting it up for sale. Interested?'

Interested! Was I ever? And the cunning old fox knew I would be. Talk about being taken for a ride! But I didn't mind. It was the kind of bike most young racers dreamed of owning. All I needed was the money. Back home to Mum, and after talking over the pros and cons she said she would help out. The Manx was mine, and I couldn't wait for the 1958 season to start. Not only did I have my own van, I now had a real racing bike. At last, things seemed to be moving in the right direction although I still had a long way to go to catch up with Mike Hailwood, whose father provided him a full equipe of machinery to contest the 125cc, 250cc, 350cc, and 500cc classes.

The season started well for me at Mallory Park, with a heat win, third place in the final, plus fourth and sixth in the unlimited capacity races. 'Flue brush' had done me well with the engine, which proved to be splendidly reliable all season, when I really threw myself into racing. Ann was busy studying to be a schoolteacher, and with my mother helping me with the paperwork to obtain starts and sponsorship, I was able to devote most of my non-working time to the bike.

It can't have been too much fun for the neighbours, or indeed anyone living around that neighbourhood. On one side of the park there was Phil Read working on his bike, on the other, Brian Setchell. Actually, Brian lived in a rather secluded private road, on which he could test his racer, but also living in that road was the Chief Constable. His presence didn't deter either of us, though, and it became something of a competition between us over the years to see who would get his bike ready first for the weekend's racing.

If Brian heard the Manx or the Beesa suddenly burst into life and roar up West Hill Road, he knew I was ready. Similarly I could hear whenever he had beaten me. It's a wonder property prices around that area didn't drop.

More success followed the Mallory meeting, and before too long the Norton began to pay its way. It had to, I was still only 19 and the money I was earning during my apprenticeship was abysmally poor. There were wins at Castle Combe, Silverstone, and Brands Hatch, and then I decided it was time to take the next big step forward and race in the Manx Grand Prix, in the Isle of Man in September.

Whatever my feelings were years later about the Isle of Man and the Mountain Circuit in particular, the very mention of the Island in those early days was enough to make me tingle. I had already made my first trip to Mona's Isle the previous year, as a spectator at the Golden Jubilee TT races of 1957.

What a week that was! We were crammed eight to a room in a back street boarding house, all intoxicated with the enthusiasm and spirit of the sport, roaming about looking at the bikes and seeing who we could spot. It was on that trip that I made my much-recalled blunder. We had all crammed into a van, about a dozen of us, and gone up to Windy Corner to watch the Junior TT race. You can just imagine what it was like, a whole crowd of people waiting impatiently for the first riders to appear. I was one of them, and when a bike flashed into, and out of, view, I was left speechless by its speed for a moment. Then I turned to my mates and said, 'Wow, who was that?'

'You idiot!' one of them gleefully told me, 'That was the travelling marshal. The racers aren't here yet.' In my excitement I hadn't noticed that the bike didn't carry a number.

When the race bikes did arrive, it was worth the wait. Stars like Bob Brown, Bob McIntyre, John Surtees, and John Hartle on amazing bikes like Gileras, Moto Guzzis, MVs and works Nortons. It was incredible; noisy and so exciting. I just couldn't put how I felt into words.

That night, when the others were full of the race and Bob Mac's flying victory at a record average of 94.99mph on the 350cc factory Gilera, I just sat there, silent, spellbound. There was no way I could express what I felt. I just knew I would have to get out there and do it myself one day.

My brace of Manx Nortons outside my home in Luton

Even greater treats were in store on the Friday, when we watched the eight-lap Senior race at the bottom of Barregarrow. Seeing John Surtees going through there on the MV Agusta was both breathtaking and frightening. What a spectacle, John flat on the tank, knee out, wobbling over the track and just missing the kerb. He must have known what he was doing, because he took the same route every lap, but the spectators were never quite so sure. As soon as someone shouted, 'Here's Surtees!' we all leapt from our vantage points on the wall and stood behind it. John had good reason to go as fast as he could. Ahead of him, and increasing his lead all the time with four ton-topping laps, was McIntyre the Flying Scot on his way to a TT double and, incidentally, winning me a two-bob bet that he would be the first rider to break the magic 100mph barrier.

My own first appearance in the Island in the following year was a completely different affair. Indeed, at one time it looked as if I would have to give the Manx a miss altogether, thanks to British Railways, who had somehow succeeded in losing the new crankshaft flywheels I had ordered for the Norton. Suffice to say they found them …on the eve of my departure for the Island.

Still, I managed to rebuild the bike in time for a few laps around the circuit before official practice started. I needed those laps, too. The bends, so famous and familiar from photos, were a completely different story taken at speed. You swept into them, often unable to see the line out, held your breath, and came out unscathed, elated and exhilarated. I remember being surprised, too, that the course was so bumpy. Little wonder I had trouble keeping the front wheel down!

In those days it was mandatory, as a newcomer, to ride in what was known as the Snaefell Race to qualify for the Manx Grand Prix itself, and, after lapping within the qualifying speed on my first official practice lap, I took a third place in the Snaefell Race to grab myself a start in the next day's Junior Manx GP. I finished a satisfying 17th at an average speed of 84mph and that night, I felt I had good reason to be pleased with my performance, having raced nine laps of the Mountain circuit in just 24 hours.

Those performances in the Manx and throughout the season did not go unnoticed. Towards the end of the year, I was approached by Geoff Murdoch, then the Esso representative, with an offer to sign with them for 1959. And at around the same time, Malcolm Edgar, then competitions manager with Mobil but later to fill the same role for Castrol, made contact. The result of these sponsorships was that I was able to afford a brand new 350cc Manx.

Actually, let's put that another way and say that I was able to order one. Such was the demand for these great bikes, and so short was the supply, that the 1959 season was already under way when I received mine. And that was only after a non-stop telephone campaign to Norton sales chief Bill Smith. It didn't worry me whether he was at work, in a meeting, at home, or at a circuit, I always managed to track him down. If he was reluctant to let me have a Manx when I first placed my order, he must have been relieved when he finally allotted me the bike and got me out of his hair.

Part of the trouble, I suppose, was that Norton did not make a lot of money from producing Manx Nortons. It used to be said that for every Manx made, the company made only six pounds. Imagine it, six pounds profit for what was a masterpiece of engineering and people wonder what went wrong with the British motorcycle industry. Of course, Norton reaped enormous benefits in advertising the success of their racing bikes and that was the reasoning behind production of the Manx.

On the start line for my first Manx Grand Prix in 1958, two years later I would win the Senior MGP at record speed.

At Cronk-ny-Mona in the 1959 Senior Manx Grand Prix

June 1959, Biggin Hill, 350cc Norton

However, I digress, and this is not the time to go into the whys and wherefores of the old industry. What is important is that I managed to get my hands on a new Manx. I had also managed to add a 250cc NSU Max to my equipe, if it could be called that. For some time I had been aware that riding just one bike was a serious handicap. A second machine would give more practice, in another class, and more racing. The trouble was that the bikes I really wanted I couldn't afford, so in the end I settled for the German-made NSU, persuading myself that it looked like being a reasonably competitive two-fifty. It might have been, too, except for a tendency to pull valve heads off their stems. First time out on it, at Snetterton, I very nearly won. The main opposition came from a rider on a genuine NSU Sportmax, whereas mine was just a modified roadster. That Sportmax was really fast down the straight, but I stayed in the hunt by out-braking it and passing on the bends. Then this character would go rushing by on the straight. Talk about infuriating. Even though I was enjoying the dice, I was getting madder and madder that his extra speed was more than a match for my better cornering, and after the race, which he won, I stamped over to his van. 'Look, boy,' I said, staring him straight in the eye. 'When you've learnt to ride that bike of yours you'll get famous.'

Who was he? None other than Bill Smith, the genial dealer and prolific racer from Cheshire. I don't think he's forgiven me for that cheeky remark to this day.

That first race apart, though, the reliability of the NSU was poor, and after a number of embarrassments I sold it in June 1959 to help pay for a 500cc Norton. That bigger Manx was a disappointment at first, slower than my 350 Manx and nowhere near as impressive at handling. If my efforts in the senior class were leaving me unhappy, at least I was able to hold my head high in the 350 races.

One of my best outings was at the early season Mallory Park meeting, where the 350cc Manx carried me to a morale-boosting victory over none other than Bob McIntyre. Slipping and sliding, I overtook Mac, only to lose the lead to him again after a mistake at the Esses. Back I came at him again, roaring past to take the flag and leaving Bob to settle for second place. Maybe he had been expecting me to crash. I don't think he was too happy, and who can blame him, the safe, experienced star beaten by a wild youth.

I used to be known as Pip, a shortened form of Philip, but in the early days I was on the grid at Mallory when a spotty young reporter came up to me and asked me for my first name. I said Philip and he said: 'Okay, so it's Phil Read'. He was Robin Miller, who went on to a career as a publishing magnate and a knighthood.

The arrival of the 500cc Norton coincided with Clubman's Trophy Day at Silverstone, an event for which I had high hopes. But the 350cc race started without me on the grid, as I had been caught up in the petrol queue and was unable to get out of the paddock in time. And as if that wasn't bad enough, the 500 packed up when I was down in sixth place. Little wonder I thought that bike had a jinx. Maybe it was built at Norton's Bracebridge Street factory on a Friday afternoon.

Left to right

Rounding Ballacraine on my 500cc Norton in the 1959 MGP

Flat-out down a very bumpy Bray Hill on my 350 in the 1959 MGP

Brands Hatch on a cold Boxing Day with Dan Shorey leading the pack

On the Steve Lancefield Manx at Brands Hatch in 1963

However, things came together as the weeks rolled by. I took a week off for a holiday, Ann was able to come round more with schools on their summer vacation, and after the hassles over the Manx and the disappointments with the NSU I began to relax. My racing improved. There was a third in the 350 and fifth in the 500 at Castle Combe, and even better than that was a fourth in the 350cc race at the Silverstone Hutchinson 100, ahead of Derek Minter and Geoff Duke. Was I chuffed?

Soon it was time for another crack at the Manx Grand Prix, but that year the Island's 'little people' were against me. I improved ten places on my 1958 performance, finishing seventh at 87.38mph in the Junior race but in the Senior, clutch trouble dropped me back to thirteenth at 89.13mph, after putting in a 94mph lap. Bear in mind that fairings were not allowed in the Manx in those days.

Back on the mainland there were places at Aintree and a crash causing concussion in the final meeting of the season at Mallory. I also made a decision that was to radically improve my whole racing career. I decided to get an expert to tune the machines and the man I went to was the pre-war Brooklands racer and brilliant technician Bill Lacey, who also did Mike Hailwood's bikes. I couldn't have made a better choice.

In 1960 the results came thick and fast: more than half a dozen wins in good company, plus many good podiums. By the end of the season I had taken second place behind Mike in the 350cc and 500cc ACU Star road racing championships, as well as a double in the ACU Clubman's races at Oulton Park. Even more importantly, I won the Senior Manx GP, at a record-breaking speed of 95.38mph with a record 97.09mph lap en route. I had retired in the Junior, luckily right by my Ramsey signalling point, where my team was being well fed on cream teas.

The 1960 season hadn't been without mishaps. In the 500-mile race for production machines at Thruxton I rode a BMW flat-twin for the importer MLG. Going into a corner I dug one of the projecting horizontal cylinders into the track: it flung me off and I was knocked out. I woke up in Andover hospital and decided

The 350 trophy, Oulton Park April 1960

I didn't want to be there, so set out to find Ann who was staying in the town. I got dressed, but couldn't find my shoes anywhere so went without them. I climbed out of the window and managed to get to where Ann was staying, but then an ambulance came and took me back to hospital. It turned out to be a good thing because I had a haemorrhage that night.

Then it was time to make another major decision. Just two weeks after the successful trip to the Isle of Man I was due to finish my five-year engineering apprenticeship. At twenty-one, I had a trade under my belt and an engineering qualification, plus the chance of a secure, reasonably well-paid job in the same factory. It looked more than likely that the next few years would see Ann and me get married.

That might have been how others saw it, but I had different ideas, wanting to look beyond Luton and a 9 to 5 existence. That wasn't what life was all about, I told myself. The important thing was to race motorcycles, and if I carried on with my weekday job, my race preparations and fitness would undoubtedly suffer. However, I didn't discuss this with anyone, deciding to wait until the end-of-season Mallory Park meeting before reaching any decision. After Mallory, where I had cleaned up in both classes, there was no doubt in my mind. The following Monday, I gave my notice at work. My boss was shocked.

'You want to give up a good job here to race bikes? You must be mad!' he said. 'You could soon be earning twenty pounds a week.'

But it was no good explaining I had earned well over £1,000 from the recent TT. They would never have understood, not the way things were in 1961.

My mother, bless her, gave me plenty of encouragement; in fact she was convinced I couldn't fail, simply because I was the son of two keen motorcyclists. Others were more sceptical. Anyway, it was too late. I had decided, and that was that.

June 1962 with Ann

At 21 years old I had determined to become a professional; to race motorcycles and not join the rat-race.

2 Professional racer

FORGOTTEN HERO

Seven-times GP world champion* and still riding and racing. So why has British motorcycling given Phil Read MBE the cold shoulder? *Bike* met him at Cadwell Park to find out

Words Gary Inman Photography Fly Tipping

Seven GP world titles. World championships in 125, 250 and 500cc classes. Title wins on underdog machinery. 121 GP podiums. Against-the-odds, era-defining GP titles for Yamaha. Sounds a lot like Valentino Rossi's CV doesn't it? But those are just some of Phil Read's achievements. And now the 70-year-old legend has come to Cadwell Park to show us the fast way round.

On the surface it's difficult to fathom why Read isn't Britain's biggest* motorcycle hero. Or at least one of them. Instead he's the forgotten man, on the sidelines, and two generations don't even know why. At a blustery Cadwell, one of the canteen ladies asks him for an autograph for her husband, and a few of the trackday riders pose with Read for photos and chat. But mostly he's left alone. The MV F4 1078 he'll ride later attracts more attention.

But Read is the real thing. Giacomo Agostini has an incredible haul of 500cc victories: 68 wins between 1965 and 1976. Yet when Read became Ago's team-mate at MV Agusta in 1973, and the pair were on similar machinery, it was the Englishman who won. And Ago wasn't past his prime. He had another 500cc world title in him. Read backed up his first 500 title with another the following year, muscling the long-in-the-tooth MV to the last ever four-stroke title until the MotoGP class. The inline four should've been outgunned by the swarm of Suzuki and Yamaha two-strokes being piloted by Ago, Barry Sheene, Jack Findlay...

Read, again on the MV, scored more points than Agostini in 1975's ten-round championship, but only the best six of each riders' finishes counted. Read scored 96 overall, but his best of six rides was a total of 76 to Ago's 84.

But, when compared to his contemporaries, Read's star has faded. Agostini and Sheene attained rock star, almost mythical, status: thanks, in some part, to their successful marketing. They became millionaires. The Prince of Speed turned up to meet us in a down-at-heel van having spent the previous day as star guest at an Enfield Bullet dealer's ride out. The mighty have fallen.

Read began his GP career racing clip-on to clip-on with Mike Hailwood in the era of the pudding basin helmet and European manufacturer domination. He bowed-out of GPs just as knees

* Actually Read won eight world titles including a TT F1 title

97

Since that momentous decision to leave Brown & Green, where I had served a five-year engineering apprenticeship, to become a professional and race for my livelihood, much has come my way. A great deal of it has been good, some not so good, and some very emotionally upsetting.

Luckily I'm still alive, in reasonably good condition and thankful for every day, which I still try to make worthwhile.

Looking back now I can surely say, to quote Frank Sinatra, 'I did it my way'. If I had my time over again I'd surely do some things differently, change a few things for the better, be more patient and lateral-thinking.

I challenged the authorities on circuit safety and about riders' poor financial returns from racing. I upset team-mates and factories and generally made myself unpopular saying what I felt needed to be said for the benefit of the sport or to improve machines and teams' performances.

Because of this I earned myself the nickname 'Rebel Read'. I'm not upset by this, as I believe I have true principles and always knew when it was right not to keep silent.

Anyway, the name has a nice ring about it, and it was good publicity for a while. I suppose I should even be grateful to the motorcycle press for coining it, for there were probably people calling me much worse things before the Rebel tag stuck.

However, I was never a rebel without a cause. I defied authority - race organisers and the FIM - because I believe riders must be treated with respect, not like performing monkeys. Motorcycle racing is a serious and important sport to millions of people; it requires the help and co-operation on all sides to maintain its momentum and TV appeal, not to mention preserving riders' lives.

When I first entered the professional ranks, many GP organisers considered riders as an inconvenient necessity for making money. They were indispensable in the championship events being presented, but their requirements, both financial and in terms of facilities and safety, were the lowest priority. At some circuits, spectators had better lavatories than the riders and mechanics.

To me, this seemed not only ridiculous but unfair. Organisers had us over a barrel. If we wanted to race, we had to race on their circuits regardless of their condition or the paddock facilities offered. Most private riders needed all the appearance fees they could get in order to compete in the 'Continental Circus' and factory riders needed to race for championship points. The organiser's stance was 'take it or don't race'.

Geoff Duke was banned for six months in the 1950s by the FIM for supporting a riders' strike for more money at the Dutch TT. Perhaps if we had been better organised, with a united riders' union in the 1960s and 1970s, these problems would have been resolved earlier. But riders are a unique breed. We're in this great sport because our life and passion is to race motorbikes around the world, win or lose. To go out there and pit our skills, courage, nerve, and our machine against the next fellow's. And because of that, we tend to work alone and even team-mates find it difficult to get along for the benefit of a team. For the last two decades or so we've had the professional International Road Racing Teams Association (IRTA) and sports management company Dorna to ensure a fair return for MotoGP riders and teams from the circuit owners. Circuits must now pay millions to run a MotoGP. A few years ago I read in the Belgian press that the Francorchamps circuit owners had agreed to pay Bernie Ecclestone's FIA £12 million per race plus 5 per cent for each of the following years that Formula 1 raced at their event. Not only that, I understand he required them to spend millions to improve poor spectator facilities.

Did standing up to the power of officialdom, in an attempt to bring a little democracy and intelligence to our sport, as I knew it, really make me a rebel? I think not. Formula 1 drivers such as Graham Hill and Jackie Stewart did a similar thing in motor racing. They weren't branded as rebels, but were seen as professionals trying to improve safety in their particular sport, standing up for their rights and the rights of their fellow competitors; the people who make the sport what it is. That is just what I tried to achieve.

In the mid-1960s top riders began to realise the fantastic appearance fees available at the season's early International events staged by motorcycle clubs on Italy's Adriatic coast. After the end-of-season Italian GP in 1964, an event organiser offered 3000lire (about £2,000) for the Yamaha team to race at two of their events the following year. I had just been paid a mere 400lire for the Grand Prix event. I grabbed their pen and signed the agreement.

This helped set the standard for most International events, which encouraged factory riders to make great efforts to bring their factory machines by paying at least ten times more than GPs.

After the first qualifying session at the Czech GP on the Brno circuit, I was one of many riders to notice an unprotected stone wall on the outside of the last medium-fast corner. I went to talk with the race organisers to ask for straw-bale protection to be placed in front of this killer wall. They told me they could do nothing more to give us better safety. I rounded up many riders who all agreed not to ride again on the circuit until these requested bales had been put in place at this dangerous section. Most didn't ride in the next qualifying session and within a couple of hours the straw-bales arrived. We had won a victory to make our point for safety to be taken seriously and from then on the FIM started to take notice and better ensure our minimal protection where possible at road circuit GPs.

One thing I learned from a very early age is that you must always be honest to yourself. 'To thine own self be true', Shakespeare wrote in *Hamlet*, which I was supposed to read at school but never did. There are times, though, when being true to your convictions will upset someone. It's regrettable, but to my mind it's also necessary. If your convictions are deep, true and sincere enough, they will stand examination and criticism.

Another thing I learned early in life, and it was rammed home forcibly in my first years of racing, is that if you want something badly enough, you have to make sacrifices to attain it. Motorcycle racing can be a cruel and hard sport, although on the other side of the coin, the riches to be gained are great, not just in terms of wealth, but the travel, the companionship, the excitement, and most important, the satisfaction. They're all things I'm grateful for and wouldn't have missed for the world. That's what always made the thought of retirement so hard: having to bid farewell to all the things I really loved about bike racing: the smells, the speed, the challenge, and the sense of danger every time you wheel your bike to the line. Those last seconds before the flag drops feel like an eternity, yet it's a new experience every time. You're out there, just you and the machine and you're going to win. The others are there to be beaten. I never really retired and in recent years I have found the same excitement and challenge from historic racing on Yamaha TZs, my replica 500cc Duke BSA and a fantastic 500cc Moto Paton twin, winning some great races on them all. They were not easily won and sometimes saw me dragging my knee on the track, which would have been unusual in my GP days.

Yet deep down, I know that the sport itself and the fine people really make it worthwhile along with the motivation it gives me. Back in my early days I would have settled for five pounds start money when little was being offered to top riders to help apprentice wages. I had a reply from Freddie Wallis senior of the Leicester Query Club, organisers of racing at Mallory Park, asking me who the hell I thought Phil Read was.

Five pounds, indeed! I should have known better than to expect a bit more start money just because I'd won a few races, even if one of them was the Senior Manx Grand Prix. A few years later they offered me thousands to race a factory MV Agusta at Mallory Park to thrill 80,000 fans packing the stands.

Back in 1961, what did surprise me was the lack of sponsors waiting to sign up this likely lad from Luton. I'd returned from that Isle of Man victory half expecting to find a queue of would-be sponsors lining up down West Hill Road. I was sorely disillusioned, I can tell you. But I did receive an invitation to have tea with the Mayor of Luton.

It's not in my nature to back down, and if no one wanted me to race their bikes, well, too bad for them. Read, the independent one, would race his own bikes. In those days I had little confidence to search a sponsor myself. Perhaps if I'd had someone working on my behalf or had a manager, things might have been better, who knows?

The same was true of trade contracts with the oil, petrol, chain, tyre and plug manufacturers. In 1961, there was still a fair amount of money floating about to tempt a rider into signing for a certain product, but rather than tout myself around I was happy to accept free goodies and bonuses paid out for a win or place. I think, though, that I was under contract, and receiving a retaining fee from the petrol and oil people in 1961. That was thanks more to Malcolm Edgar of Castrol and Geoff Murdoch at Esso, than to my own efforts, I must add.

Sad to say, that situation, whereby race tyres, chains, plugs, oil, and petrol were given away, was ruined for everyone in the end by the greedy few. Now, unless you are among the handful of top-class riders, you have to pay for these commodities. Fortunately, things have improved in other ways for the professional rider. Start and prize money may still not be all that brilliant in Britain, but generally it is a much happier story on the Continent.

Petrol and oil companies seem to have gradually become more generous, but in the mid-1970s, just after my four years with the MV Agusta team, it was the helmet manufacturers, cigarette and oil companies, plus big business organisations who were investing large sums of cash to boost their products and promote themselves through GP racing. Without this, motorcycle racing would not have become as big and popular as it undoubtedly has.

Not that there was a lack of interest in 1961. Crowds were big in Britain, 50,000 on average over three decades and the Continental grands prix were even better supported with some crowds of over 300,000 at eastern Bloc circuits like Sachsenring and Brno. Back in the 1950s Grands Prix at Solitude in West Germany could attract hordes of over 450,000, who sat beside the track with no protection against crashes.

One reason why crowds were coming back in the Sixties was that young man with whom I'd clashed in the past, Stanley Michael Bailey Hailwood, Mike the Bike. Only then, with so much depending on my own success, did I begin to feel that my racing career was being impeded to some extent by Mike, off the track as well as on it. The reason was that we both used the tuning services of the great Bill Lacey, and it was becoming increasingly obvious to me that Mike's machines were taking priority over mine. Whereas the previous season my engines were ready on time, I was now being asked to wait longer than originally promised. It was infuriating. For that 1961 season, I had bought two new Nortons, with the help of Esso and trade bonuses won during 1960. With Bill Lacey tuning them I had begun the season with high hopes. Yet I came to feel, to be blunt, that Hailwood's engines were treated to that little extra bit of attention, even at the expense of my own. Obviously, Stan Hailwood, Mike's father, known in the paddocks as 'Stan the wallet' wanted nothing but the best for Mike, and he had the cash and the power to do it. Any potential rival was treated with disdain, and any conversations between me and Stan were so brief as to be non-existent.

I was bloody annoyed, and seeing Mike in the paddocks before a race, laughing and joking by his big transporter and his dad's Bentley while I was all knotted up inside, really got me wound up. Mike didn't know it, but there were times when it just needed one of his seemingly harmless, jesting remarks, like, 'Remember, I'll be passing you on the right,' or, 'Okay, last lap to count,' from him as we went to the grid to make me feel I couldn't beat him. Of course, I would then go and do something stupid, like trying to leave him standing at the start and make a mess of it, so Mike would win yet another race in his relaxed style. It all comes back to race track psychology, Mike was a natural, able to conceal his nerves from the other riders.

Winning the 1960 Senior Manx GP at a record speed of 95.38mph, felt wrapped round the frame under the primary chain caught stray oil from its drip-feed. Today's historic racing machines use an oil-free belt primary drive.

Don't think I'm knocking Mike, though. He was one of the true greats, a terrific rider, a wonderful sporting character, a brave, fearless man and a lot of fun. But back at the beginning of the 1960s, hustling for races and better start money, trying to improve your own bikes on a limited budget, it was disheartening to have a man like Mike about. His bikes were always so much better than ours. They were given the whole works; special frame, special forks, lighter wheels, lightweight bits and pieces on the engine. He was probably saving about twenty pounds in weight, and that's a big help. And if he blew up an engine, one of his two full-time mechanics would simply wheel another bike out of the transporter. It was pretty depressing sometimes for us mere mortals with limited funds, I can tell you. If Mike hadn't been such a great guy and a fantastic rider, it would have been really easy to dislike him.

I suppose I even have to give old Stan his credit. He was ahead of his time with his Ecurie Sportive, the forerunner of the big racing teams we see so often now. It was good for the sport, helping to upgrade the off-track image of road racing in the public eye. As far as paddock presentation and life-style went, the Hailwood outfit was years ahead. When Mike was sleeping in caravans or hotels, the rest of us were in tents, or living and working in the back of Ford Transits. By the mid-Sixties, when some of us were lucky enough to be able to afford caravans, Mike and his Honda team-mate, Jim Redman were living in hotels, but they also had paddock caravans and were driving Ferraris. It was one-upmanship, if you like, but ultimately we all benefited from the path Hailwood paved in our sport.

I was told by Redman that they met Enzo Ferrari at their Rimini hotel. After they had test driven his car, Enzo agreed to sell them two Ferraris for the price of one. Nice one lads!

The biggest difference today from that Hailwood and Redman era is that most top-line GP riders, earning the sort of money they do, are more inclined to invest it, rather than throw extravagant parties or eat out at plush restaurants after the races. That contrasts with top British riders who buy flash cars, planes, helicopters and boats as soon as they have some success. Investment is sensible and can secure a future life style, yet there are times when I think back to those Ford Transit days when we tended to live, work and play together. I can't help feeling there was more fun and camaraderie then. We were all in the same boat. It was a new, exciting life shared by us all. Okay, we were all looking for that door-opening factory ride, but the 'family' feeling was stronger when we had great fun after the races, win or lose. Nowadays, the rival GP teams, whether factory or sponsored riders, tend to stick together in their little groups both on and off the track, and even though I'm by nature a very independent person, that change in the sport at MotoGP level makes me sorry for what they are missing.

Still, in retrospect, I had little to grumble about concerning my own conditions in that first season as a privateer. I had those two new bikes, lightened and improved and fully tuned where possible, and I even had a new van, a Bedford Dormobile, made possible by some of my trade sponsors who together had coughed up about £2,000 for my racing season. Yes, that was a lot of money then. Thanks to my mother I had a good double garage in the coach-house of her old home farm to work on my bikes, and the Lacey-tuned Nortons brought me my fair share of success in early-season meetings. Consequently, I set off for the Isle of Man and the TT in good heart.

15

Leading the great Gary Hocking on his 350 MV Agusta, at White Gates during the 1961 Junior TT, Gary finished second to me after the MV dropped a valve to run on only three of its four cylinders. Lucky me!

Victory! With Mum, a very young Barry Sheene and his sister Maggie

That trip, my first to the Island as a TT racer, was not without its lighter moments, one of them concerning the prototype 500cc Norton Domiracer twin. When Norton engineer Doug Hele offered me a ride in practice for its first circuit test, I jumped at the opportunity, if nothing else, it gave me another chance to get accustomed to the Mountain circuit and saved wearing out my own Manx. In the event that was just about all I did get out of it and I was lucky not to come off much worse than I had bargained for.

The first practice lap was not impressive, the machine suffering from what is known as 'megaphonitis', which meant that power was inconsistent at lower revs. To make matters worse, the usable power band was just a couple of thousand revs with only four gears. When I opened the throttle at Creg-ny-Baa the power came in with a bang, flicking me sideways and into the grass bank. A footrest was broken off and the fairing was pretty damaged too, so I pulled that off and set off at a more leisurely pace back to the pits. The open-mouths of the waiting crew was unforgettable. I told them the bike was so fast that the fairing had blown away in the draught.

After that little experiment I decided to stick to my own Nortons for the racing and it was on the smaller of these Lacey-tuned beauties that I achieved the impossible, a TT win at my first attempt. I could scarcely believe it; in fact, I didn't even know I had won when I crossed the line at the end of the 350cc race. But what I also didn't know was that Hailwood, on an AJS 7R, had been forced out with gudgeon-pin trouble after taking over the lead when Gary Hocking's MV four went sick.

To someone uninitiated in the ways of the TT, that may sound a bit strange. But the TT is not a race in the normal sense, in that everyone starts together and first to the finish wins. In a TT you start at ten-second intervals, in pairs in those days, and you race against the clock as much as against the other riders. That's why I didn't realise I was winning, though I could tell by the way spectators were grinning and waving as I raced through those last few bends that I was doing well. It's a good thing I didn't know. I'd have probably done something silly, like fall off with excitement.

What a moment! Junior TT winner on my own bike in my first pro season, the first British rider to win a TT race on a British machine since 1954; my first world championship points. No wonder I was over the moon - and my mother was there with me to share the joy.

Things were looking good in the Senior, too, until I locked the front wheel at the Gooseneck on the last lap and put paid to my chances of catching Australian ace Tom Phillis in third place. Tom was riding the Domiracer I had tried in practice, but on the last couple of laps it was beginning to slow, and I already had him in my sights when I went down. He held on to third, while Mike Hailwood went on

Leaving Parliament Square
during my 1961 winning ride

A neat-looking jump over
Ballaugh Bridge 1961 Junior TT

to win to make it a Norton double, and Bob McIntyre was second. What a great ride that was by Mike, a fitting climax to a week that saw him notch an amazing hat-trick of TT victories. He took that Norton 500 round the Mountain at an average speed of more than 100mph for six laps, the first over-the-ton average on a single cylinder machine. We didn't know it at the time, but his win would be the last Senior victory by a British bike for 31 years and mine would be the last ever in a Junior TT.

Mike's other wins were on Hondas, giving the company its first TT victories in the 125cc and 250cc races and beating established works riders. He certainly grabbed the headlines, but I had my fair share of press coverage and went home well pleased. I'd had a third ride that week, on a 125cc Bultaco owned and prepared by Frank Sheene, but the bike developed mechanical problems on the first lap and I missed two full laps before we sorted things out. I spent some time trying to chat up his pretty 16-year-old daughter Maggie, now Mrs Paul Smart. I remember Frank's young son Barry, who seemed always to be under my feet when we were working on the bikes. The little swine also had a go at my much-prized blue toolbox, managing to paint out the 'ip' of Philip Read before I sent him running with a cuff around the ear. In later years, that same Barry Sheene would seem to be trying to rub my name out of the record books.

Just one last thing about that memorable 1961 TT. That year, there were some other Japanese machines in evidence besides Hondas and Suzukis. They came from a factory called Yamaha which made, among other things, the greatest musical instruments, boats and snow skis. In view of what was to happen later, I couldn't have picked a better time to win a TT.

Racing Frank Sheene's 125cc Bultaco during 1961

Leading Dan Shorey at Brands Hatch in 1961, both on 125cc Bultacos

1961 125cc Dutch TT, where I finished fourth on an EMC

Hardly had I time to unpack my bags after my Island trip than I was getting ready to set sail again; this time with my fiancée, Ann West, to the Continent, for the Dutch and Belgian world championship events. Winning the Junior TT had won me a reputation beyond the British circuits, and much to my surprise and delight, the organisers for these events were eager to sign me. In addition, I could look forward to better start money than I'd been accustomed to, mainly due to the influences of Dr Joe Ehrlich, whose 125cc EMC two-stroke I was going to ride. Dr Joe carried a lot of weight in European racing circles at the time and managed to extract quite large sums for his machines and his riders.

Nonetheless I learned a hard lesson through him. During practice for the Dutch TT, his bike was not going anywhere near its full potential, but Dr Joe put pressure on me to improve my times to earn a better grid position for the race itself. Fool that I was, I tried too hard, went well over the limit, and crashed. It taught me a useful lesson, that a bike can go only to a certain limit, and the rider who tries to force it beyond that point is putting himself, his career, and the bike in jeopardy. Finishing the race is a first principle in the hunt for world championship points.

My first European race on the Saturday was the 350, in which I was racing my own Norton, as I would later in the 500. The 125 event was sandwiched in between these. My practice laps with my own bikes had been much happier affairs than on the EMC, with the result that I was on the second row of the 350 grid, the best of the privateers. I shared the line with Paddy Driver, also on a Norton, and the inimitable Silvio Grassetti on a works 251cc Benelli. With two rounds of the world title race gone - the West German and the Isle of Man - I was lying second in the table to the Czech ace, Franta Stastny, on the works Jawa.

I don't mind admitting I was nervous. Even worse, I was feeling a bit sick, mainly because conditions were much more humid there than I had ever encountered before. Still, things like that disappear once you're out on the grid, although I couldn't help but be conscious of the enormous crowd. Colourful, noisy, and full of holiday spirit, those 150,000 fans epitomised everything I had heard and read about Continental racing.

Considering all these things, I was lucky to get off to such a good start. But I could see there was quite a difference in racing on these circuits from scratching at home. It was all so much faster. I didn't think I was wasting any time, yet at the end of the first lap I was more than a hundred yards down on Gary Hocking's MV, with Bob Mac (Bianchi) and Stastny separating us. In the next few laps the Czech began to pull away even further from me, while I dropped back a place behind Ernesto Brambilla, brother of Vittorio, the Formula 1 driver, on another Bianchi. Up front, Hocking and Mac were dicing it out, with Gary getting the better of the duel. Some way back I was holding on to fifth place to earn myself another six points and stay in the championship chase.

Racing my 350cc Norton on Silverstone's wide-open spaces, I'm wearing stylish Italian goggles, it must have been sunny!

I improved a place to fourth in the 125 race, and then it was the 500cc event, the big race the fans were waiting for. It was incredible; you could feel the tension wrap itself round you as you lined up on the grid. And the noise, with great sections of the crowd chanting the names of their favourite riders. It made meetings at home seem like a church service in comparison.

Once again I finished fourth, and again Hocking's MV proved too good for the rest. Mike the Bike was second, with McIntyre, who had pushed me out of third place midway through the race, third. Actually, I had dropped to fifth, but managed to scratch back past Frank Perris in the closing stages; some years later he would be my team manager at John Player Norton.

I was happy. Both my bikes and I had proved worthy in world-class conditions. I had gained my first taste of the Continental courses I knew I would have to conquer. Ann and I really managed to enjoy ourselves at the post-race party, though I found myself fascinated by how other riders chatted up the local girls. We danced and drank the night away.

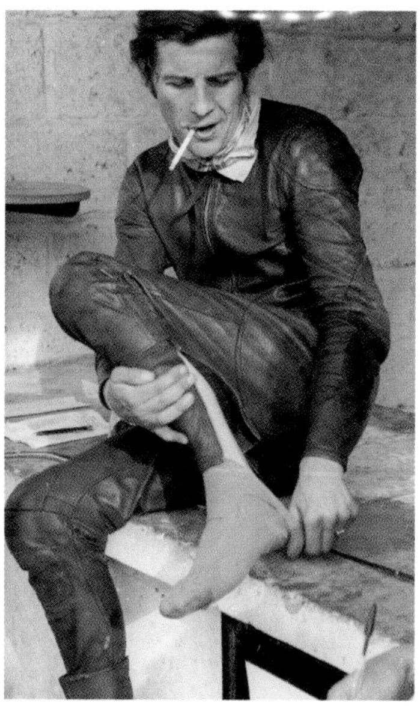

Afterwards, as I was walking back to the paddock, a rider I'd become quite friendly with caught me up. We chatted for a while, about the races and our bikes, and then he said, 'I hoped I'd see you some time. Thought I should tell you that you're starting to make yourself unpopular in certain quarters.'

'In what way?' I asked, knowing quite well that I'd already trodden on a few toes, but nothing out of the ordinary. Not for me, anyway. 'Oh, just things you say,' he said vaguely.

'Well, come on. You can't just say that. Give me some examples.' By this time we were at my van. I leaned against it, waiting.

'Ummm. Well, look, it's nothing personal, you know,' he went on. 'I just thought I should tell you, warn you. Not to get on the wrong side of people.'

'Look', I said. 'Either tell me what I'm doing wrong or let's forget it.'

'Well, what I'm thinking of is the TT.'

'The TT?', I said. 'I didn't do anything wrong there except win.'

'Yeah, well that's just it. You see, when you got the trophy and you made your little speech, you thanked everyone except Bill Lacey.

Now people are going around saying what a miserable, ungrateful bastard you are. 'Oh hell! So that was it.'

'Everyone knew, you see,' he carried on, 'that you were pissed off because Mike's bikes got more attention than yours. Well, we all know that anyway; that's the way it is. After all, Bill's an old friend of Stan; they've known each other for years. Why shouldn't he help Stan?'

'No reason at all,' I replied angrily. 'But he could have given me a bit of help when I needed it. You know yourself how badly my 350 was running. In the end we had to pack cardboard under the springs to stop the valves bouncing. But do you think I could get Bill Lacey to come over and have a look at it? No. He was too busy with Mike's bikes.'

'So you didn't thank him?' 'That's right', I said. 'I didn't thank him.'

The next morning we set off down through Holland to Belgium, and Spa-Francorchamps. Racing wasn't until the next Sunday, so there was no great hurry and we took our time. More than once I thought to myself, 'This is the life!' as we rolled along past windmills across flat, countryside, then into the hills of the Ardennes and finally to Spa. We sat at an outdoor cafe drinking beer and waved at other riders we saw driving into town. It was just like being in a circus with vans and the occasional caravan continuing the jaunt around Europe, putting down somewhere for the weekend show then moving off to the next venue.

Helmet showing the Guernsey crest

Wearing out my boots and fairing at Snetterton in 1961

Francorchamps brought its fair share of surprises and not all of them on the track. The first of them came in the paddock loo - there was only one - not long after we'd parked the van. I was in need of relief after those beers in town when this rather nice blonde walked into the same loo and started filling a can with water, just behind where I was standing. It didn't half put me off, I can tell you. The amazing thing is that you get used to it after a while; it's just a matter of losing that English reserve and preference for privacy. Having said that, having no doors on the sit-down loos at Daytona was disgusting.

Talking of privacy reminds me just how little we had in a place like Francorchamps, or in fact at many circuits on the Continent. Everyone lived right on top of everyone else in the paddocks. Frank Perris used to tell a story - you could say it was a 'Dan Shorey Story' - that happened at Francorchamps. Frank had arrived at the circuit in good time to make sure he could park his caravan on the only hard standing area of the paddock. Just over the hedge from him in the overflow field, in what must have been considered a fairly secluded spot, was a certain English privateer with a reputation for sartorial elegance under his racing leathers, he wore a collar and tie when racing. It was hot and humid that night, so Frank had all his caravan windows open. Just as he was dropping off to sleep, a voice filters from behind the hedge, entreating in an increasingly desperate way, 'Go on love, you let me last night.' 'No, no Dan', a girl kept crying; and on this went for much of the night. Poor Frank and Rita didn't get much sleep, despite being camped in the prime place.

My first visit to Francorchamps brought no such problems, in sleeping, that is. My problems were out on the track. Everything looked bright when a good 500cc practice saw me on the front row of the grid alongside Hocking, Hailwood, John Hartle, Paddy Driver, and Ron Langston. There was no 350cc round in the meeting, so my other interest centred on the 125 race. Unfortunately the EMC went sick, forcing me to retire, and a similar thing happened in the 500. I'd been going quite well in the early stages and was in the hunt for points when the Norton's engine began to rattle ominously on the twelfth of the fifteen laps. It wasn't worth risking a blown engine, so I coasted to a standstill at the fast Stavelot right-hander and watched the great Gary Hocking and his MV roar on to another championship victory.

Naturally enough, Francorchamps left me feeling a bit detuned; but by the time we had driven back to England, to the relief of Ann's parents, I was beginning to put things into perspective. I couldn't really have expected much more from my Grand Prix debut unless I had more money or a factory bike, but it was good experience for my next Continental Circus season.

England was cooler and brought a return to short-circuit racing and success. Indeed, things went well enough for me to end up the season with the ACU 350cc Star championship, a good start to my professional career. It was about this time, with the season drawing to a close, that Steve Lancefield approached me with the suggestion that I use one of his 500cc engines at Snetterton and Brands Hatch. I didn't have to give the matter much thought. Among the racing fraternity Steve was already a legend - the man who tuned the first Manx Norton engine to lap the Isle of Man TT circuit at more than 100mph.

Much more than a tuning genius, Lancefield was a development engineer, an honorary member of the Society of Automotive Engineers, and to belong to that you have to know your business. Steve actually built his bikes from scratch - in the back room of his own home in South Norwood - ordering the parts from the factory and then assembling some of the most competitive Nortons you've ever seen. I jumped at the chance of a Lancefield engine for my 500 and the immediate result was a second at Snetterton and a win at Brands.

Chatting to genial Jawa factory rider Franta Stastny

That win at Brands was just as pleasing for Steve, for the man I beat to the line was Derek Minter, then known as the King of Brands. He had started the year riding Lancefield Nortons, but apparently around the time of the TT things had turned sour between them, and Minter moved on. I was to ride Steve's machines a couple of years later, in 1963, and I found him wonderful to work with. He was pernickety, but when you could do to a bike what he did to his Nortons, you had a right to be. During one of my visits he told me we couldn't race that weekend because the rear drive chain sprockets were ten thou (0.25mm) out of line! I still sometimes think it was criminal that his great engineering experience, resources, energy and love of racing were never put to better use in the blinkered British motorcycle industry. The trouble was, I suppose, that he never beat about the bush. He called a spade a spade. No wonder we got on so well.

Before the 1961 season was through, I managed to slip out of England once again, but this time only as far as Northern Ireland, for the Ulster Grand Prix at Dundrod. Even though I had missed the East German round, I was still sitting well up on the 350 table, and another world championship round not so far from home was tempting. I knew I would never get to the Italian and Swedish rounds. In the event I had to settle for fourth in Ulster, just missing out on a top three placing yet again. This time Stastny blasted past me when I was holding third position. The winner, yet again, was Hocking and that unbeatable MV, on his way to a 350-500 World Championship double. At the time I was third on the table, but Gustav Havel on the other works Jawa pushed me down to fourth by the end of the season.

With the season over in England and the Continent, the problem now was how to fill the winter months. I could have found a job, although I shuddered at the thought, and then the answer came; an invitation from Jim Redman and Paddy Driver to winter on the South African circuits. Apparently other British riders were invited, but for one reason or another, none of them showed any interest. I was delighted. I was young, I was free, and it seemed a marvellous opportunity, a great adventure. Besides, it was a chance to race, and racing is racing anywhere in the world.

Carving through the 350cc field at Northern Ireland's North West 200 in 1961, ahead of Tommy Robb and Derek Minter, although Bob McIntyre won, I broke the 350cc lap record on my Norton at 101.78mph.

On the Arter Matchless, October 1961

Initially there was a bit of a problem regarding bikes, because it was obvious that I would need spare engines for my Nortons because of the hectic schedule of races and travel and I just didn't have the cash to buy them. Luckily, Tom Arter, from Canterbury, came to the rescue, offering the loan of a 7R AJS and a G50 Matchless, complete with engines and spares. It was a really generous offer, and without it I could never have made the trip. The organisers were paying no expenses, and all I was guaranteed was £100 start money per race, plus prize money. Not that the voyage itself was very expensive at £200 return for the van and myself. It was good value, too, and the journey out on the *HMS Edinburgh Castle* passed a pleasant fortnight. I enjoyed myself sightseeing at the various ports of call. As was traditional I was dumped, fully clothed, in the pool when I crossed the Equator for the first time, and had I not been such a shy young man I might have enjoyed myself even more. The opportunities were certainly there aboard that ship.

Only halfway through the voyage did it really hit me what I had let myself in for. Thousands of miles away from home, on my own, I was going to race at nine meetings in twelve weeks, I would have to drive some 12,000 miles, many of them on dirt roads, most of them alone, in a van. I told myself I must be mad. Once we sailed into Cape Town, however, all misgivings quickly disappeared.

The sight of the sun rising over Table Mountain was worth the boat fare alone, and the friendliness with which I was welcomed was beyond all expectation. In fact, this new environment was so overwhelming that it would have been easy for me to let the racing take second place to the social life. My only problem was getting the van and the bikes through customs. Filling in forms and documents by the dozen was all new to me; my mother, and latterly Ann, had usually looked after the racing paper work.

With my old school friend John Gutteridge outside the coachhouse workshop at Mother's old Luton farm, just before I left for South Africa at the end of 1961

57
828

How did we manage with two bikes and all our gear with these little vans?

It took a couple of days to complete the formalities, during which time I stayed with Ray Flack, an injured South African racer I had met on the ship. Then I was off to Johannesburg via a call to meet a young lady I had also met on the ship, Miss Rita Bond. She was to start a new job as a receptionist at the fantastic Hamanus Hotel a 100 miles up the Garden route from Cape Town. We didn't really get it together as I wanted, so after a few days I set off on my journey North. My Bedford Dormobile belted along really well, a factory tuning session and a cylinder-head conversion had increased the top speed to 85mph - quite a bone-shaker on dirt roads. On my way I stayed with a friend's family at Grahamstown over Christmas and my 22nd birthday on 1 January. Then I was off to Johannesburg to find Paddy and Janet Driver's homestead. I made the Drivers' place in pretty good time. I'd have been there even earlier had I not been flagged down by a motorist just a few miles short of my destination. For a moment I thought I'd been stopped by a plain-clothes policeman, but it was just a homesick Englishman wanting a chat after he'd seen the GB plates on the back of the Bedford. Eventually, some time later reluctantly he let me carry on. I could see that I would be anything but shy by the time this trip was over.

Just as in Cape Town, so the social life in Jo'burg was fantastic. I just couldn't believe that I was so welcome, and accepted, wherever I went. Me, a struggling motorcycle racer from Luton. A week at home with the Drivers simply flew by, but it did give me the opportunity to get acclimatised to the heat and the altitude before Saturday's racing.

The circuit was a new one, and the atmosphere in the paddock was easy-going and friendly. Both my bikes went well, and I finished the day with a victory in the 500 and a second to Gary Hocking on an unbeatable 7R AJS in the 350 race. Actually, Gary took this whole series very seriously, obviously out to show his peers - he had grown up in Rhodesia - that he was a worthy world champion. He and his friend Bruce Beale had put in a lot of work to get the Ajay to run on methanol fuel, legal in African racing, and it was nearly as fast as my 500cc G50 Matchless, which I had also converted to run on methanol. I would have given anything to know what jetting they were using, but there was no way. They made sure there was no snooping around.

Anyway, even if I had known, there was no time to work on either of my bikes because I now had to get to Bulawayo, and the way I was going, Southern Rhodesia (now Zimbabwe) was a long way off. First I had to go in the opposite direction, down to Grahamstown, near East London, to pick up a helper I'd met on the ship from Southampton. He was interested in bikes and had offered to be my mechanic at Rhodesian events.

Having opted to take the Garden route, I let myself in for a long drive. I suppose we should have stopped somewhere, but once on the road I like to get to where I'm going even if it is hundreds of miles away and even if it means driving through the night. Part of the trouble was the heat. I don't function well in it, and even with the doors slid open it was unbelievably oppressive and dusty. I kept the vital canvas water bag hanging outside the van to quench my thirst many times during these long journeys.

The radio station we were listening to shut down, and then the only sounds were the van and the bush on either side. I just kept going, hearing strange, unfamiliar noises. I remembered all the natives I'd seen earlier in the evening, standing at the roadside with their staring eyes. I tell you, I wasn't going to stop for anything. I didn't smoke much in those days, but I went through a few packets that night. Not surprising, really, that I was in such a mess when I arrived in Grahamstown in the early morning light. I'd driven 500 miles non-stop, my throat was parched and sore, and my hands were shaking. Nothing in town was open at that hour, so I spent the next few hours wandering about, looking in shop windows, trying to stay awake.

As soon as the shops opened, I went straight to a gunsmith to buy a revolver. I had already seen what I wanted, a small .32 automatic, but I was told I'd have to get a licence first. A mere formality I was told. It was, too. The policeman asked what I wanted the gun for; I said I was driving long distances on my own to race meetings and I felt I may need a bit of protection. I told him the type I wanted to buy, and he gave me the licence. Back at the shop I paid my money, selected a shoulder holster to go with the gun, and walked out into the sun feeling a good deal safer. Gun-slinger Phil Read was ready to hit the trail again - after a shower, some breakfast, and a few hours sleep.

Rhodesia was several days' drive away, but with someone else to share the driving, and some sightseeing thrown in along the way, the journey passed pleasantly.

Visiting Salisbury (now Harare) also provided a contact with home through my cousin Vivienne who, though ill in bed at the time, made sure that I was well looked after during my stay.

The only fly in the ointment was that 7R of Gary Hocking, there seemed no answer to it. While in Grahamstown I had phoned Tom Arter, asking him to fly out two special high-compression pistons for the 7R and G50, cylinder head and valve springs, plus a big carburettor to run the bike on methanol. Setting the bike up to run on dope, however, was not so straightforward. Only by testing against a comparable machine, as Hocking did with Beale, could I find what jet size gave the best performance. There was no chance of learning anything from the Hocking camp. Nor was there time for experimenting; we were on the road too much for that.

Years later I would learn the explanation for the incredible extra speed of Gary's 7R: I was told he used to add about five per cent nitromethane to his fuel.

From Rhodesia it was another cross-country trip to Durban; and some sea air. I won the 500 and finished in the top three in the 350, which meant I could choose either machine for the handicap race. Originally I was going to ride the 350, a decision that was noted by my rivals, but it occurred to me I might be better off with the more powerful Matchless which was faster than Hocking's 7R on dope. I slipped back into the paddock, and drew a few surprised looks when I wheeled the 500cc G50 on to the grid. By then it was too late for the others to change machines, and I must say I was feeling pretty pleased with myself as I set myself up to charge past Jim Redman's 350; so much so that as I passed him I looked across and, rubbing my thumb and fingers together, indicated that the cash was already in my hand. I spoke too soon. At the next corner, a very fast right-hander, the con rod broke as I was peeling off. The bike and I went sliding down the road, and the next thing I knew I was in hospital with the side of my face worse for wear from contact with the road.

Tom Mortimer on the Kirby bikes

While I was working as an R&D technician at AMC in 1961, Geoff Monty first told me about Phil Read's notable pace and riding ability. So I was pleased that by the end of the '61 season, Phil had some support from AMC who supplied him with special components for the '62 GP season. The opening event was in South Africa, where the rules allowed higher octane fuels. Factory assistance made a big difference in situations like this.

On the 1 December 1961 Monty Sayer the race department manager handed out the work to be completed for the season opener, mine being the machining, mensuration and the weighing of two 7R pistons. The pistons had to withstand a new higher compression ratio of 15:1 and still had to keep in balance with the standard 7R motor internals and this was achieved with a measured .330 inch crown thickness and a piston weight of 363 grammes.

At the end of the AMC era 1963-64 I joined the Kirby racing team and it was here that I worked closely alongside South African Paddy Driver. Sometimes I worked on Phil's bikes along with other AMC veterans Eric Goodfellow (frame builder) and Burt White (toolmaker). The Kirby team had salvaged factory G50s and 7Rs for the ensuing GP season to be contested by Phil and Paddy, where under the Kirby banner they finished 3rd and 4th in the championship. After a good championship finish Phil would always be in high spirits and he often recognised our support by way of a bonus. Not many riders did that!

I left Kirby's at the end of 1964 to open up my own company, where our paths would cross again...

Kirby G50, prepared for Phil to ride in the 1964 American GP

Worse was to follow. One of my first visitors was Jim Redman, trying hard to hide the grin that broke out when he saw me lying there. I asked him who won, and the bastard raised his right hand slightly and rubbed his thumb and fingers together, just as I had done when I passed him. Even though it hurt to do so, I couldn't help but laugh with him.

Still, I was really annoyed at being in hospital, for it meant missing all the fun. Durban was really swinging that weekend, for as well as the motorcycle brigade, the motor racing crowd was in town for the Formula 1 South African Grand Prix. We had shared the same Westmead circuit (now disappeared), giving the fans a load of thrills, and the invitations to parties and barbecues simply flooded in.

One thing I'll remember of that meeting was the Grand Prix commentator. Stirling Moss was the big favourite. He hadn't even bothered to practise, and the commentator concentrated solely on him as he worked his way easily through the field. Up front was a young Scot, very quiet, who was just setting out on the road to fame, Jim Clark. And you should have heard the shock in that commentator's voice when it became apparent that not only was Moss not going to catch Clark, but that Clark was actually drawing away from the great Moss. He just couldn't believe it!

I spent two days in hospital, with a spot of concussion and my face badly grazed. In fact, my face was quite a mess, even when it was partly healed, with a great scab where the skin was scraped off. It was no consolation to be told that my bike was in an even worse state!

An unexpected visitor to the hospital was Jim Redman's wife, Marlene, someone I had not really had a lot of time for. It came as a pleasant surprise, then, to be invited to stay up at the Redman ranch in the hills when I was discharged from hospital. Having begun to revise my opinion of the lady, I was in for a shock when I arrived at the Redman's, complete with suitcase in hand.

'Well, here I am', I said cheerfully, when Marlene came to greet me.

'What for?' she asked.

'I've come to stay, like you said.'

She looked astounded.

'But there's nothing wrong with you. You're all right now. I meant you could stay if you were still hurt.'

Thank you, Duchess! I knew when I wasn't wanted.

Ironically, I was helped out by Marlene's first husband who lived nearby. He and I got on really well together, enjoying the Durban night life and working hard on the bikes during the day. I also managed to sneak a look at Hocking's 'magic' carburettor, which he had carelessly left lying on a bench in Jim's workshop when taking a phone call. The temptation to see what main jet he was using was too great for a weak-willed boy like me. I stripped it down, inspected the jet and had just finished putting it together when Hocking returned, blissfully unaware of what had happened. He would have remained that way, too, if Redman hadn't gone and told him. Did Gary go mad? He ranted and raved, leaving me in no doubt as to the slimy creature he thought I was. I was unmoved. In my opinion he shouldn't have been so careless. Eventually we patched things up, and later in the year Gary and his helper Nobby Clark would stay with me in Luton. But our relationship was never quite the same. Perhaps we were two of a kind, each a serious competitor, determined to win, over-anxious for success.

My Arter Matchless G50 running on methanol fuel with a 16:1 compression ratio at East London in South Africa, wow!

It was inevitable that our racing aspirations should bring us into conflict, and even on that South African trip, where most of the riders were relaxed and easygoing, Gary and I seemed to be the only ones so consistently intent on winning.

The final race of the tour was at East London, a scenic venue beside the ocean. It was so close to the sea that spray from the surf got on our goggles along the back straight. In the Grand Prix event I beat Paddy Driver home in a last-lap dash, setting the fastest lap in doing so. It was a good way to end what, on the whole, had been a happy and exciting 'holiday'. I had some money in my pocket, a good sun tan, and I'd made a lot of friends. Now I wanted to get back home to marry Ann and have another crack at those European World Championship circuits.

The 1962 season was to be a strange one: full of disappointments and yet ending with a third place in the 500cc world championship, despite finishing only at Assen and Monza. Talk about crazy! Looking back, there seems no reason why things should have been worse than 1961. I had two new Nortons, and had found a wizard, if eccentric, tuner called Jim Smith. There seemed to be many Smiths in the motorcycle world but this one lived out in the wilds, near Barton-le-Clay, Bedfordshire, working on engines in a dusty converted railway carriage lit by paraffin lamps. He knew a thing or two about Nortons, and my aim was to have the fastest engines out there.

The TT was an anticlimax after the previous year; seventh in the Junior and a depressing retirement in the Senior after lapping at 100.39mph when lying second and chasing Hocking's MV. Even more upsetting was the news after the Junior that Tom Phillis, the Australian, had been killed when his 285cc Honda four crashed at Laurel Bank. For the first time I became aware that accidents, fatal accidents, could happen to anyone, even the most experienced riders. It was a sobering thought, intensified later that year by the death of Bob McIntyre after a crash at Oulton Park in August when I was following him in torrential rain. Then came the loss of Gary Hocking, who crashed a Lotus 24 Formula 1 car in practice for the Natal Grand Prix in December. It has been alleged that Stan Hailwood bought Gary the car to encourage him to leave MV Agusta, so leaving the door open for Mike. MV did take Mike to ride their 350cc and 500cc fours but, it is said, only after Stan offered to order 10,000 MV road bikes for his dealerships. 'Stan the wallet' was such a dynamic force that such stories were bound to circulate, but whether they were all true we shall probably never know.

The Mallory Park Post TT meeting followed the same disappointing pattern as the Island, but at Brands the next day my luck changed at last. In the 350 race, Hailwood overdid things and took a tumble off his MV while in an apparently unbeatable lead, leaving me to beat off the rest and win. I also managed to fight off the pack to follow Mike home in the 500cc event.

At Mallory Park, 1962

Leading Alastair King and Peter Middleton in a Mallory Park 350cc race, 1962

That was more like it, but I needed money as well as success. Now that I was married I had the future to think of, as well as the present. We were having a house built in Luton which had to be paid for, so, instead of searching for competition against the top-liners, I looked around for some easy pickings to boost my bank account. The Southern 100 races held on the Billown circuit near Castletown on the Isle of Man fitted the bill perfectly, and with a clean sweep and record laps thrown in, the trip was both successful and financially worthwhile. I was not all that popular in some quarters, though, being accused of doing an 'Al Capone', on the lesser riders by stealing their prize money. But when you are racing for a living, a race is a race. After all, there was no restriction on entries to the Southern 100 as anyone was at liberty to enter.

Nonetheless, it was soon back to the hard stuff, with another crack at Assen. I finished sixth in the 350 just behind Derek Minter, but I was convinced I had the better of him in the 500 when the two of us were dicing for second place behind Hailwood. Then a brief excursion onto the grass put paid to that, and I had to settle for third. The Belgian GP was a complete disaster, yet again, and so it was back to England for the rest of the season; or so I thought at the time. Instead, much to my surprise, I was given the chance of riding in the Italian Grand Prix at Monza.

With the possibility of improving my position on the world championship table I went, to discover that my racing education was far from complete.

Arriving rather late in Monza, I was looking for a hotel when I came across a group of riders, including Jim Redman and Paddy Driver. Thinking I might get a free drink if nothing else, I wandered across - to be met by an attitude that really surprised me. In England, and at the Isle of Man, the Continental circus riders had always been as friendly as could be, but now there was a tangible reserve and aloofness. It seemed that my arrival, further afield than the usual British scratcher's trip to Holland and Belgium, was a possible threat to their own existing or hoped-for works rides. I could see that it was a case of every man for himself.

Racing careers are short as a rule, with big chances coming few and far between, and I realised that I could not expect help from my fellow riders if I was to achieve my ultimate ambition of winning a world title. So, I was even more determined to do well on race day, and although I was forced to retire from the 350, I was more than happy with my fourth in the 500, behind the MVs of Hailwood and Venturi and Grassetti on a factory Bianchi.

Nevertheless, that Monza episode taught me a valuable lesson. I never treated a newcomer to the Grand Prix circuits as an outsider. Rather, I tried to help as much as possible, because I knew from experience that it's a long road ahead and the wheel always comes full circle.

That winter there was no South African jaunt. Instead, my days - and nights - were spent decorating, finishing off the house so that Ann and I could move from my mother's place to our own home, just five hundred yards or so down the road. In fact, our back garden led directly to the garage where I had my coachhouse workshop with the original solid wood benches. It couldn't have been better.

We spent a lot of time planning for the racing season ahead, taking stock of everything; machines, mechanics, tuners, transport, and organisation. My nature is such that, when things go wrong, I adopt a definite, aggressive policy, and I had a good ally in Ann. She had a quiet knack of getting things done efficiently, so that I was able to devote all my time to the bikes while she looked after the business side of racing - a side that has never appealed to me, although I'm ready to cope with it if necessary. I found a new tuner, too, Allen Dudley-Ward. By the

Winning the Senior race at the 1961 Isle of Man Southern 100, the 350cc race was a dead heat between me and Alan Shepherd.

Norton 650ss Wins at Thruxton 1962

At the 1962 Silverstone 1000km Production race, Syd Lawton's Norton Domiracer 650SS just kept running and with no crashes, I took the win with co-rider Brian Setchell.

Read (650cc Norton) and Minter (250cc Honda), Thruxton 1962

New Year we were looking like a good outfit, ready to give the rest a run for their money. It's funny, though, how things didn't turn out quite as you've planned, and so it was in 1963. No sooner had I congratulated myself on getting everything sorted out than Southampton dealer and ex-racer Syd Lawton came along with a proposal that was to affect my entire racing future. How would I feel if he approached Steve Lancefield with a view to my riding Lancefield's own machines? Steve would supply all the machinery and look after it. All I had to do was ride.

What an opportunity! Lancefield, I knew, had been in hospital for part of 1962, but there had been no indication that he was thinking of returning to racing. I asked Syd whether he thought Lancefield would be interested. 'Oh yes,' came the reply, 'he is interested!' In fact, admitted Syd, they had spoken about the possibility the previous weekend. What it needed now was for us to get together, and before Syd left that afternoon I had arranged to go to Lancefield's home in South Norwood, near Crystal Palace.

The other reason for Syd's visit was to check that I was still interested in riding his production 650cc Nortons in long-distance races. I had raced these for him in 1962, with my old mate Brian Setchell as co-pilot, and we'd met with a fair bit of success, winning the Thruxton 500-mile race, the 1000km race at Silverstone, and picking up a second at Oulton Park even after Brian had crashed. Actually, we'd been lucky at Silverstone, because I'd crashed in practice in the wet, messing up the bike so much Brian wasn't able to go out before the race itself.

And at Oulton Park I'd had to put in a lot of work to pull through to second after Brian had lost the bike at Druids in the wet. He half-pushed, half-rode it back to the pits, and by the time we'd straightened everything out we were down in sixth place. Still, those endurance races were great fun, and I was looking forward to renewed success with Brian. In the event, though, circumstances dictated otherwise, and our only victory together in 1963 was a repeat performance at the Thruxton 500 miler.

With Syd Lawton and Brian Setchell

News that Steve Lancefield and Phil Read were joining forces caused a ripple of interest in the motorcycle press, but that was nothing compared with the coverage being given to the racing comeback of the great Gilera marque, under the management of the legendary Geoff Duke. Enthusiasts from all over the world were excited at the prospect, and it says much for Duke's reputation that the factory was prepared to lend him the four-cylinder 'fire engines' that had carried him and Bob McIntyre to numerous victories in the 1950s. The machines had been out of action since Gilera withdrew from GP racing at the end of 1957 after winning six 500cc titles.

Originally, Bob Mac was lined up to lead the Scuderia Duke team but those plans fell apart after Bob's sad death at Oulton. Now Derek Minter and John Hartle had been signed. Hartle hadn't raced since September 1961, but he looked good on the Gilera, having an advantage over Minter in that he had raced MV fours back in 1958 and 1959.

Mallory Park 1963, slipping under Joe Dunphy (12)
to take my first win on Steve Lancefield's 500cc Manx Norton

Brands Hatch, Easter 1963, with Derek Minter

My first racing clash with the Gilera duo in 1963 came at Silverstone. As Steve Lancefield was still preparing his Nortons, I was on my own Dudley-Ward tuned bikes and they didn't let me down. I was able to stay with race leader Minter, and later with Hartle, before the Gilera's superior power took them out of my reach. Even Hailwood's current-model MV had been unable to withstand the Gileras at an earlier international meeting at Imola in Italy, so it was obviously going to be an interesting season.

Easter brought the first of the Lancefield bikes, the 500, gaining me a second and a third at Brands on Good Friday and a third at Oulton on Easter Monday. There was no doubt that bike was a good one, beautifully prepared and competitive. The 350, when it arrived, was just the same, superb. Steve's bikes would rev to 500rpm more than a standard Manx. More than once I felt it was such a waste that no oil company was ready to back him in a European effort. Still, European trips or not, we made a happy team: Ann looking after the paperwork, Steve preparing the bikes, Eddie Carter travelling with us at weekends as mechanic and me doing the racing. It was marvellous being able to arrive at a circuit, knowing the bikes would be there, jetted and geared to suit that particular circuit. And if something felt a bit off with the bike I was able to tell Steve what I thought was wrong, a change for him from the 'it won't go when I open the throttle' complaints he'd had from some other riders. Having run my own bikes for so long, I had a 'feel' for bikes and I had learned early on the advantages of adjusting jet settings, float levels and gear ratios to get the best from an engine.

Mind you, we had our moments. I remember one occasion at Oulton Park when I came in from practice in a really foul mood, throwing the 350 against the van and saying in no uncertain terms that it couldn't blow itself out of a paper bag. Poor Steve was staggered, but he fixed it after my faithful helper Eddie Carter had persuaded him to check, just in case. All it needed was a bit of adjustment to the float level and jetting for that same bike to show a clean pair of heels to the best riders on the British short-circuit scene, so much so that people thought it must be a 500. There was no denying it, Lancefield knew his stuff: he just needed coaxing sometimes.

He knew how to handle riders, too, and passed on a number of useful tips that I was glad to use. Mind you, if he had told me to do this or that, he would have been wasting his time; and he knew it. Instead, he would quietly mention some particular point and then it was up to me. And he was fair, splitting the start and prize money 50-50 instead of taking the larger share as I knew some entrants liked to. More than once in my early days I turned down offers of bikes simply because the terms were anything but favourable.

Before April was out I had won my first race for Steve, a 500cc event at Mallory Park. Then there was a slight break until early May at Brands Hatch, where fate played a large hand in my immediate future. In an unfortunate accident at Stirling's Bend, Dave Downer was killed and Derek Minter broke his left shoulder blade, fractured a couple of vertebrae, and suffered bad cuts and bruises after the two collided. The rumour was that Derek could be out for three to four months. So talented on short circuits, he had developed a reputation as being something of a 'hard case'; to such an extent that many people at the time were not surprised he'd had a bad crash. I didn't actually see what happened, being too busy fighting for my second place at the time, but I recall Bob McIntyre, rather a quiet and unflappable type, assuring me that the next time Derek Minter dived inside him at a corner he would knock him off into the nearest ditch.

The upshot of Derek's injuries was an invitation from Duke for me to join his team, riding number two to Hartle. Nor was the offer only a stop-gap measure until Minter was fit: Duke intended to race a three-man team. Steve Lancefield, not the kind of man to stand in a rider's way, sportingly agreed to release me from my contract with some compensation from Castrol, though I continued to race his Nortons in national meetings for much of the season, notching up a series of doubles and emerging as 350cc British champion.

My first outing on the Gilera was to be the West German GP at Hockenheim, on a 350, as there was no 500cc race. I was tingling with excitement as I set off with Duke and Hartle to drive there. Geoff made sure there were plenty of thrills en route, too, taking a detour to put his Vauxhall estate through its paces round the Nürburgring, hurling the big car around with much skill while Hartle and I bounced about, trying to hold down the luggage in the car. I wondered what I had let myself in for!

The Gilera, however, was nothing like as exhilarating, even though I did manage third in the 350cc event, one lap behind Jim Redman's Honda and Remo Venturi's Bianchi. Both my engine and Hartle's refused to rev properly in practice and we couldn't even keep up with 305cc Honda twins.

In the race John retired with serious vibration problems and I was lucky to finish, losing compression after valves touched the pistons. Maybe I over-revved it, but the most likely cause was that the old valve springs had lost their strength during the last race at Monza in 1957 and five years in storage.

From Germany we made a mad rush back to England, driving straight up to Liverpool and crossing over to the Isle of Man for TT practice. There was a shock waiting for us at our hotel, though, a telegram from Commendatore Gilera forbidding us to use the 350cc engines. It was my first experience of the strange workings of the Italian mind, but Duke had been through it all before and knew how to handle the situation. Even so, he seemed to be on the phone an awfully long time before getting that decision reversed.

The background politics did nothing to improve my confidence in the bike and there were times on the Island when I needed as much confidence as I could get. For one thing I was handicapped by a 'dying' 350cc engine and wasn't surprised when it finally blew up during the Junior race. That one engine had been used for practice and racing at Hockenheim, and again for practice on the Island.

My other problem was the 500's handling on the Mountain Course. It was now seven years since Gilera's heyday, and the machines just hadn't kept pace with racing developments. The more I tried to wrestle with the bike, the more it seemed to shake its head, and for me that year's TT was one of the most frightening I've experienced. Down the straights the bike behaved itself, but on the flat-out curves it seemed to be doing everything in its power to fling me off. I returned to the paddock a very relieved man, I can tell you.

For all that, though, there was no denying the 500cc Gilera's power, and in the Senior TT Hartle had a great scrap with Mike Hailwood on the works MV, with the verdict ultimately going to Mike. Yet the result might so easily have gone the other way. I returned to the paddock, having taken third place, to find John complaining that he had been losing revs and that this had cost him the race. In the end he and Geoff stripped down a carburettor to discover that the bike had been deliberately over-jetted by an Italian mechanic to ensure it finished, irrespective of performance loss. Hartle and Duke were furious, but what could they do? Motorcycle racing history is full of examples of an Italian factory 'knowing best', despite the knowledge and experience of those on the spot; something I was to discover later in my career.

Riding the 500cc Gilera four to my only win on it, at Scarborough's demanding Oliver's Mount circuit in 1963

With John Hartle at the 1963 Dutch TT

Thank goodness we had some time off before the Dutch TT at Assen. With the bikes not coming up to expectations, nerves were beginning to fray, and I was glad to get away on my own for a time. I was even able to give my morale a boost with a couple of good rides on the Lancefield Nortons at Mallory, winning a 500 race and retiring from the 350 after winning heats for both races. Then it was back to Scuderia Duke.

The bikes had been rebuilt for the Dutch, and the team reassembled in a more relaxed frame of mind. This didn't prevent fuel starvation keeping me out of the 350 event, but a Hartle-Read one-two in the 500, after Hailwood's MV holed a piston, put us in high spirits. Actually, I felt I could have won the 500, because John was having trouble with his wrist for most of the race.

But team orders are orders - or they were in that case!

The following weekend at Francorchamps brought another second in the 500cc round, this time behind Hailwood after John was forced to retire. And then, much sooner than anyone had thought possible, Derek Minter returned to the scene, so it was a three-man team that set sail for the next world championship round at Ulster. There, my luck really ran out when my footrest dug into the road and pitched me off. I fractured my back so badly that I was still lying in hospital when the others set off for the East German Grand Prix. I missed the Finnish round at Imatra, too, although nothing of note happened to Gilera fortunes during my absence. Nor did they improve when I returned to the team at Monza for the Italian Grand Prix. John Hartle crashed in the last practice session, putting himself out of the race, while I retired when my gearbox leaked oil onto the rear tyre causing me some scary moments. Hailwood won with slower times than Derek had achieved when he was first testing the machines before the start of the season, but Mike did not need to hurry. It was a disappointing finish to a year that had begun with so much promise.

Senior TT, 1963

Another 1963 Senior TT shot, looking down at the machine on the Mountain, a frightening race on the difficult-to-ride Gilera

At the end of the racing season Geoff and John were testing Earles leading link forks on a Gilera in an attempt to improve stability. One of the former engineers from the closed-down Gilera race shop arrived to talk with Geoff. He said that to improve tyre wear when using the full 'dustbin' fairing (banned after 1957) the engines had been moved back in the frame. We were using dolphin-type fairings, which did not produce a high down-force. It proved that my complaints to our leader had not been imaginary: the chassis were dangerously out of balance.

My own hopes for success on the iconic Gileras had been dashed, and there were times when my confidence took an awful battering. It required a lot of convincing that it was not just my fault, and that I really was as good as I thought. Fortunately, there were the Lancefield bikes to prove my capabilities. Still, I did manage to finish off my Gilera days with a win at Scarborough, and my fourth place in the 500cc world championship was some consolation for my frustrations. John Hartle finished third, behind Hailwood and Alan Shepherd, who rode a G50 Matchless single!

One of the biggest problems facing Scuderia Duke that year was the failure of Geoff Duke and the Gilera factory people to realise how much the MVs and racing technology had improved since they last raced in 1957. At the end of the year, Geoff said he thought the bikes had never lived up to their potential and that if the factory had worked hard during the winter, they could have been competitive.

Somehow I just don't see that it would have made much difference without using the many new and improved components and fuels available.

Fuel stop in the 1963 Senior TT, with pit officials getting in the way, as usual!

Brands 1963, on the grid, Bill Ivy, 49, on the right

On a personal level, my own disagreements with Duke never helped. Right from the start he thought I was not riding the Gilera properly, and there was quite a post mortem after the Hockenheim, West German race, where my times were ten to twelve seconds down. Apparently I wasn't changing gear correctly. Hartle, he said, was quick-shifting, so I was told to use less clutch and barely close the throttle. However, no mention to be made of the fact that Tommy Robb, on a 305cc Honda twin production racer, had blown me off down the straight on what was then a very fast circuit.

Duke didn't like the way I cornered either. In fact, in the Isle of Man, he didn't like the way many people cornered. What he seemed to forget was that times, and tyres, had changed. His cornering technique was to pick a braking point and to use it on every lap. Similarly, his peeling-off place was consistent, the aim being to use the full width of the road for cornering, bringing on the power gradually as he accelerated round the bend, with his chin firmly planted on the petrol tank. It was a joy to watch, of course, and his skill couldn't be denied, he had six world championships to show for it. But if you had tried to race like that in 1963 or since, you would have found ten riders scratching past you on the inside. It was all very well for him to criticise riders for cornering with their knee out and a bit offline, but they were probably going through that bend ten miles an hour faster than Geoff had ever done. I used to get so uptight when he came up to me with a remark like, 'You're taking the wrong line', as he did about Stavelot at Spa, for example. He'd never tell me what I should be doing instead. Nor was he interested in the fact that I thought the Gilera's forks were the worst I had ever encountered and that the new fairing was like something *Steptoe and Son* might have thrown together. No, it didn't do to question Geoff Duke. What he seemed to expect was 'Yes sir, no sir, three bags full, sir', and I think I did pretty well to bite my tongue and hold back what I often wanted to say. Many times I came close to telling him to put on his leathers and show me how it should be done.

Nonetheless it was an interesting experience and my first taste of team life, even if organisation was often a bit haywire and machine preparation second-rate. I never felt I belonged, though. I always felt like the new boy, and I didn't fit into the off-track social life that Duke and Hartle made so light of with the local ladies. Team orders meant that Ann wasn't allowed to attend race meetings, so I went home whenever possible.

When I was away, all I wanted to do was race and if possible, to win. Certainly I always gave it my all. Nor were my efforts being ignored elsewhere, for unknown to me certain people had their eyes on me. Fortunately they were satisfied with what they saw; satisfied enough to send me an invitation to fly to Japan in October and race in the 250cc event at the Japanese Grand Prix at Suzuka on 10 November. I'll never forget the day that telegram came, 13 October. It was waiting for us when we returned to Luton after a 350-500 double on the Nortons at Brands Hatch. Suddenly, Geoff Duke and Gilera were forgotten. I just stared at the telegram, unable to believe it, to believe that it was the final step towards every rider's dream, a real works contract. I've never been one to show my emotions in a big way, but that night I danced for joy around the kitchen saying over and over again,

'Yamaha want me to race for them and I'm going to Japan!'

4

John Hartle and myself with Geoff Duke and Gileras at Jurby Airfield on the IoM for testing, thanks to Castrol Oil, the team would have new fairings fitted in place of these scruffy ones for the races.

3 World champion!

One of the problems of success is that the more you have, the more you want.

And the more you achieve the more the pressure's to do more. In the end, you wonder what happened to that person who set out looking for his first success, in my case a world title. I suppose it was inevitable. Once I got one I'd want another, but I never thought of it like that. I planned one year at a time. In motorcycling, making plans for future years is simply pushing your luck. But in any case, I could never have prepared myself for the pressures that came with fame and success.

Suddenly things are expected of you. People note and record your words and feel they have the right to criticise you. Some feel they have a right to your time... and your money. The person you were no longer exists. You become public property.

I often wonder if my life would have been different if when I set off for Japan in 1963 I'd known what I know now. But that kind of reflection is futile. I left Luton full of hope that I would be good enough to clinch a team ride, and hope that eventually this would lead to a world title. Fame, riches and the trappings of success never entered my mind. I was happy with my lot, a new home, a Jaguar 3.8 Mk 2 in the garage. I had even been able to take flying lessons in an Auster at good old Luton Airport, where my father flew before I was born. Yamaha brought the promise of bikes on which I could race and beat the world's best.

I loved this factory RD05A;
250cc, four cylinders, 153mph.

A longer wheelbase would have improved the RD05A's handling.

I knew very little about the company when I flew out to Japan. I was aware that they were at the 1961 TT, but I'd had enough to worry about without paying much attention to their bikes. I knew their early 125cc and 250cc two-strokes lacked speed and the reliability needed on the TT's long and demanding course. Their development men had something to think about. Staying away from grands prix in 1962, Yamaha reappeared in 1963 with something very special, an impressive 250cc seven-speed, air-cooled, twin-cylinder, disc valve two-stroke. In the 250cc TT, their number one rider Fumio Ito was only narrowly beaten into second place by Redman after my old mate Tony Godfrey crashed when leading, following a sizzling 95mph first lap. The new Yamahas were fast; there was no doubt about it. But like most two-strokes of that time they were notoriously prone to engine seizures, the cause of Tony's crash.

After the TT the Yamaha team did the Dutch and Belgian rounds, Ito finishing second and first respectively. Then they packed up and went home for more development work, which was when I entered the Yamaha story. Flying into Tokyo airport via the long and tedious southern route with many stops, I got my first real indication of how seriously the Japanese took motorcycle racing. The guy who checked my passport actually knew who I was! Maybe it was a one in a thousand chance that I should get a race fan, I don't know. But I was impressed, and I couldn't help feeling just a little bit important as I strode out to meet the Yamaha reception committee.

Those first few days in Japan were like nothing I had experienced before. So much was new, so many different sensations, their food, which I loved, sleeping Japanese-style on mats with a bean pillow, friendly and subservient girls, and very nice inexpensive tailor-made suits. My head spun with excitement and exhaustion. I arrived by train at the Suzuka circuit, venue of the season's last GP event. It had taken my interpreter and me 10 hours from Tokyo. The 200mph express rail hadn't been built yet. Exhausted and ready to die in bed at the Station Hotel I looked out of the window after my shower and saw there was a nightclub below. Well sleep had to wait. I walked in, asking for an English-speaking lady to join me. A vision of beauty duly arrived, we had a drink or two, danced to a slow number, and then after some arrangements we walked to a small nearby hotel, where we removed our shoes before entering, as is this civilised Japanese custom. The bath was run and I experienced the pleasure of being washed from head to toe in the most sensual way. Her skin was like porcelain, she never said 'no' and nor did I to the things she was doing. Until official practice began we spent beautiful nights together, during which time I must have become the fittest rider at Suzuka.

Meanwhile, at the circuit, I had to keep alert, following conversations through a translator and learning to use my hands to explain to engineers what I thought might be done to the machines.

I later got to know Japan better. I travelled on the 200mph Shin Tokaido railway and visited the massive Yamaha factory in the industrial centre at Hamamatsu. I came to admire the nation's efficiency and technology, and the way the people went about their work. The stories we heard in Britain, that Japanese workers were paid a bowl of rice a day and made to work like slaves were quite false. Yes, they did work hard, but because they wanted to. They had company housing, their own hospital and sports centre; and what most impressed me was that workers didn't clock off until they had finished the job they were doing. Also, they were all proud of the Yamaha name.

After the chaos and inaction of Scuderia Duke, the Yamaha race department was like paradise. I also liked the feeling that I had been invited to help them up the learning curve and hopefully win some races for them. It gave me enough confidence in myself to begin to impart knowledge and information in pidgin English-cum-Japanese. It was an intense learning process and we were out to challenge the world's best. What a great opportunity!

Where I really saw eye-to-eye with the Japanese technicians was on the question of power.

'What do you want?' they would ask. 'How is the handling?' 'How is the power range?' My answer was always the same: 'Don't worry about the range, just give me more power.' There would later be times when I wished I'd never opened my mouth.

Another thing I admired at Yamaha was the way they made full use of their resources. For instance, staff from the long-established musical instrument side of the company helped improve the speed of the bikes. An important factor in making two-strokes faster is to control the resonance of pressure waves in a carefully shaped exhaust pipe. How well this effect is working can be judged by the pitch of the exhaust note, which needs to be tuned to get optimum power. Instead of puzzling over sound theory themselves, the motorcycle engineers simply passed the problem over to the music people, who understood about sonic engineering and were able to design an exhaust system perfectly tuned to the engine. The result was that Yamaha stole a march on their rivals. Would the same thing have happened inside a British company at that time? It would probably have caused a strike.

Racing two-strokes were unbelievably noisy in those days, but that never bothered me when I was on the move.

Getting to know the machine was quite an experience, although I had tried my hand on one of Tony Godfrey's bikes earlier in the year. Putting a machine through its paces around the Suzuka circuit was another story, however. At first I was at a loss to know what to do with so many gears. Hadn't I had enough trouble switching from the four-geared Norton to the five-geared Gilera; how was I to cope with the Yamaha's seven? Still, that's what practising is for, and it was surprising how quickly I managed to find the right permutations. It did take me a while to get used to the Yamaha's aggressive acceleration and for a while I was doing a good line in wheelies!

With team manager Hasegawa, later to become President of Yamaha Motor Company, at the Suzuka circuit in Japan, he is credited with designing Yamaha's revolutionary 250 and 125 racing engines of the period.

Leading the Brands Hatch pack on Tom Kirby's AJS 7R during 1964, Tom allowed me to race his 7R and Matchless G50 bikes at Continental GPs, provided I took care of maintenance.

Kirby Matchless, Silverstone

It turned out that Steve had been banking on my riding his bikes in British races during 1964, and it's true we had discussed this late in the previous season. But that was before the momentous Yamaha telegram arrived. We had not been in touch since my return from Japan, so I was surprised to see Steve's views published in the *London Evening News* early in 1964.

'I take an extremely poor view of Phil's switch (to Tom Kirby's bikes) at this late stage, particularly as I had taken the trouble to change oil agreements to suit his commitments with Yamaha lightweight racing.'

Happily we were able to sort out the confusion and remain good friends. I owed him a great deal, and we both knew it. At least I've thanked him and that's more than Geoff Duke ever did when Steve released me to ride the Gileras and so disrupt his racing plans in 1963.

Kirby G50, East Germany

An advantage of being in at the start of a new racing team is the interdependence built up between the rider and the factory. Certainly this was the case in my early years with Yamaha. I became an integral part of the organisation. From the outset, they asked my advice on things like jetting and particular problems relating to various circuits. They even asked me to suggest a possible number two rider, and as a result the up-and-coming Canadian, Mike Duff, joined us. My suggestion that the team use my Luton workshop as the main base was to our mutual advantage. For the mechanics, Seki and Tanaka, it meant plenty of space in which to work and it meant that I could be home more. My son, Michael, was born during that first Yamaha year, so Ann did not travel much.

Our first outing was Daytona, where an FIM grand prix was being held for the first time. It was my first race in America and the opening round of my bid for the 250cc crown. Luck looked to be sitting on my shoulder when Jim Redman refused to ride after an argument with the organisers over expenses (I wasn't the only one who did that sort of thing!) but plug troubles struck again. Things were better in the 500cc event, with the big Matchless pulling me through into second place behind Mike Hailwood on the MV four and just ahead of John Hartle's Norton. Ultimately I was to end up third on the 500cc table with Hailwood the champion, of course.

From the States I moved on to another first-time circuit: Montjuich Park, Barcelona. Twisty and testing, it was not the ideal circuit for getting to grips with a new bike. Whoops! Did I say new bike? I thought I would be racing a new bike. When the machines were unloaded I discovered they had sent me the old orange bikes. Yamaha may have given in to my plan to race the whole season, but it became obvious they were not releasing their latest bikes until they were ready at the Isle of Man TT. Abrasive telegrams didn't make the slightest difference. Whoever coined that cliché about the Japanese being inscrutable surely knew what he was talking about.

There were many works machines on the 250cc Spanish GP grid, among them the Suzuki 'square fours' and Jim Redman's Honda, yet the winner was that incredible Italian character, Tarquinio Provini, on a Benelli four. His was a really popular victory, and he was waving back to the fans long before he had the race in the bag. But then, that's the sort of person he was: extrovert, explosive, full of life and out to get the most from it. Even on a circuit like Montjuich Park, he seemed to go as fast around the bends as he did on the straights, and that's the way he lived. The Italians and Spanish idolised him, chanting his name and waving enormous banners wherever he appeared.

Start of the 1964 250cc Spanish GP at Montjuich Park, Barcelona; I'm number 24, riding my first race in Europe for Yamaha to finish third behind Provini (11) and Redman (22).

What I liked about Provini was his independence. How many other Italians would have dared disobey team orders from Count Agusta in their very first season with MV? Provini had done just that in 1958, actually snatching the world title from MV team leader, Carlo Ubbiali. I can just imagine him standing there, shrugging his shoulders and making an expansive gesture with his hands, asking how they honestly expected him to lose on purpose. I was to have a similar problem with Yamaha in later years, with Bill Ivy and team orders.

I had put Yamaha on the map. How could they expect me not to win? Had I not given them my life for their first four world titles?

The fantastic 250 race at the 1964 Dutch TT, with Jim Redman, Honda, he won by 6 inches.

I finished third at the Spanish, with Redman picking up the six points for second, and I was more or less happy, considering I hadn't been happy in practice. The problem was that the machine oiled plugs if you let the revs dip below 8,000, and as the top of the power band was 10,500rpm, this didn't leave much to play with on a very twisty circuit. Anyway, I told myself afterwards, I'd have a new bike for the Isle of Man, and then we'd really see what Jim Redman and Honda were made of.

There were people at the time who grumbled about Jim, saying that he was unspectacular and that he treated racing solely as work and not as entertainment. But then a lot of professional riders felt that way but they were not all like Jim, who openly admitted that he rode at the slowest speed possible to win and took the minimum of risks. But no-one could deny that he was versatile, aiming at every title from 125cc to 500cc and draining the last ounce of power from every bike he raced. And I'll testify that he could be fast. In that 1964 season our duels gave the 250cc class a new dimension. The 250 used to be a supporting act to the 500 class, but now it was the race the fans wanted to see. The reason was Read and Redman. They were giving everything they had; intelligence, nerves, guts, everything but their lives, and who knows, there were times we laid them on the line, too.

Just how fast Jim Redman could ride I discovered first-hand at Clermont-Ferrand, venue of the French Grand Prix, round three of the 1964 world championships. My bike was a beauty, super-tuned and very quick, and we had solved some of the handling problems experienced in Spain simply by removing the hydraulic steering damper. Making the fastest lap in practice gave me pole position and a boost of confidence. I needed both.

It's an incredible feeling to find yourself alone and well away from the bunch; even more incredible when you're winding away from the field right from the start. Throughout 1964 this was happening to me, except that I was never completely alone. I always had company in the shape of Jim Redman and his Honda. So it was in France, where we hurtled off into the distance right from the word go, wheel-to-wheel, sometimes side-by-side. Never more than a bike's length appeared between us as we diced for the precious lead on the twisting mountainside Charade course. First I was in front, then Jim, riding like a demon and braking hard and late, swept ahead, the scream of the Yamaha and the Honda's high-pitched bellow sounding as one as we hurtled down the straight. Again I led, but now he was playing it canny, sitting there and letting me take the pressure. And when he did decide to move, he went, using the Honda's wide power band and going over maximum revs to pull away from me. At first I didn't know he was going, but gradually came the realisation that I couldn't hold him any longer. I was beaten. I had reached my limit.

This was my first grand prix win for Yamaha, in the 1964 250cc French GP at Clermont-Ferrand. Here I'm chased by Jim Redman, who stopped after over-revving his Honda's four-cylinder engine.

buried her somewhere in the garden before he went off. I don't know how they hope to find anything in there now,' she added. 'It's all overgrown. Have you seen it lately?'

By the time I'd driven home, I'd more or less forgotten our conversation, but it came back to me a few days later when I read in the paper that police with tracker dogs had located the body of a woman in a garden in West Hill Road, Luton, and that the woman's husband was helping police with their enquiries. I remembered that summer night in the mid-1960s. Could it have been the same person? I'll never know, but you can't help having your suspicions, can you?

Still, that's taken us away from the Isle of Man and the chase for the 1964 250cc championship. And if ever there's a TT I should have won, that year's 250 Lightweight was it. For one thing the new bikes, the first of the red, white and olive green ones, were much better with incredible maximum power, although the Honda was better lower in the range. The Yamaha's handling wasn't fantastic, but it was reasonable and it was an amazing feeling, even in practice, to scream into the pits and have everyone there attendant on you, all intent on making sure your machine was perfect. Often in the past I'd looked enviously at the MV, Honda and Suzuki riders as they sat on their bikes surrounded by eager mechanics.

Now I was a factory rider and it was great. I felt I belonged - that I wasn't a loner anymore.

May 1964 Brands

But practice is one thing, racing is something else! There's always something that can happen; call it luck, call it bad luck. You might feel a hundred per cent, and the bike can let you down. The bike might be perfect, but you might not be on song. It's one of those things, frustrating, but nonetheless beyond anything you can do. At the Isle of Man that year I was on top of the world; my Yamaha wasn't. At the end of the first lap I had to change both plugs, losing a valuable minute at least. Out I went again, blasting up and down hills, twisting through the bends, furiously looking for Jim Redman. I hurtled round on my third lap in a breathtaking 99.42mph, just 0.16mph outside Mike Hailwood's lap record. That lost minute was gradually being hauled back. And then the plugs oiled again. Another pit stop, another minute wasted. It seemed an eternity, but what can you do? No use screaming and shouting; you just wait, blood boiling, getting more and more worked up. They've finished and you're off again, out down the road with the engine screaming under you. But it was all for nothing. At Quarterbridge on the fifth lap the engine seized and that was it. Nothing left to do but watch Redman win with an oil leak at a sedate 97.45mph, and go on top of the championship table.

Big Jim won the 350cc Junior, too, on a Honda four. But there was some consolation for me. I finished second, behind him on the Kirby AJS single. That was something for Uncle Tom (Kirby) to enjoy and I must say he was a great sponsor: several of us rode for him and he didn't mind if you crashed.

We learned from our misfortunes with the Yamaha that year. For reasons perhaps peculiar to that year's engine, carburettor jetting was really critical. Some parts of the Mountain Course are down at sea level, where the air is denser and a richer mixture is needed, while up on the hills less fuel is needed for the optimum mixture. Because of this, trying to keep the revs constantly in the power band resulted in the plugs oiling up. Trying to solve problems like that appeals to me, and whenever I could I'd give it a fair bit of thought. In the end I suggested a handle-bar control to adjust the mixture according to the altitude variations of the Mountain Circuit. The idea was taken up, showing how we all worked as a team in those early years.

Flying Tom Kirby's AJS 7R over Ballaugh Bridge in the 1964 Junior TT, I finished second to Jim Redman's 4-cylinder Honda.

The two Japanese mechanics thought it was a great joke at first when I started jumping about, pushing my fingers down my throat to make myself vomit. They soon panicked when they saw something serious was up. Sure enough, there was a wasp down there, and I grabbed a length of flexible tubing to put down my throat just in case it did start to swell. It didn't, thank goodness, but when I think how close that wasp came to ending my season - phew!

After that, the race itself was less traumatic, and for once everything went as planned. I sat tucked in behind Jim until there was a lap to go, at which stage I simply wound on the power and gave him a taste of his own medicine. My Yamaha just pulled away, lopping eleven seconds off the circuit's outright lap record set by Bill Lomas back in 1956 on a 500cc Moto Guzzi V8. It was some last lap, I can tell you, and Jim Redman knew it too. There were some thoughtful faces in the Honda pits that evening. Down our way, everything was rosy! A win like that was just what the Yamaha chiefs wanted to send them home in good spirits.

One final reflection on that Solitude GP. Early in the 250cc race, Jim and I encountered some character on one of those super-fast single-cylinder Morinis trying to get a piece of the action. We managed to shake him off after a lap or so, but the way he rode created quite an impression. I made a point later of finding out the name of the Morini rider in the red, green and white crash helmet, just in case he cropped up again. Oh yes, I was told, he's some Italian called Agostini. 'Looks good,' I said, smiling at some girl who was hanging around, and wandered off. This same Agostini was to turn up a while later in the Italian Grand Prix, where he added to his growing list of admirers, among them the Godfather, Count Domenico Agusta, multi-millionaire boss of MV. The Count's great ambition was to see an Italian rider win the 500cc title on an MV. Giacomo Agostini - Mino to his friends - was the chosen one.

The full team commitment ended after the West German GP, and so for the last two Continental meetings and Ulster it was back to my Citroen Estate for the bikes, Seki, Tanaka, and myself. Back to the long hours of non-stop driving, snatching sleep in a lay-by with me on the front seat and the mechanics nestled in the back, one under the bikes and one on top. Does it sound crazy? Believe you me it was crazy. You'd never have thought we were out for a world title.

East Germany was an experience, being the first time I had travelled behind the Iron Curtain. I can't say I was particularly impressed with all I saw, like the tough customs controls, armed police and machine-gun towers along the exit roads. Autobahns in the Eastern Bloc had not been improved since before the last war and due to the lack of traffic they only used one side of these dual carriage-ways with self-pumping fuel stations every 100km. But the enthusiasm of the spectators was absolutely amazing. On race day there were a quarter of a million people lining the circuit, all of them keyed up more than usual because the great Mike Hailwood was going to ride an East German MZ in the 250cc Grand Prix. Alan Shepherd, the usual pilot, had crashed in practice.

1965 Ulster

Mike's presence in the race was something I hadn't bargained for, but I stuck to my earlier policy of letting Jim take the early lead. Mike quickly tucked in behind him, which wasn't quite my idea, so I had to be content with third as we zipped and zoomed around this road circuit. Up till then I'd taken little notice of the MZ, but with Hailwood on board it was a different machine. I was getting worried as the better Mike got to know the bike, the faster he rode, and proof of that was an 100mph-plus lap. How that massive crowd roared him on.

Then, without warning, our little duel was over. Going into a tricky section through the town of Hohenstein-Ernsthal, Mike lost the bike totally accelerating out of an uphill second-gear corner and was high-sided off. Wowee! Now I knew just how Jim Redman had felt that day at Francorchamps. It's really incredible

In my pit during the 1964 Lightweight TT after making the first 100mph lap of the Mountain Course on a 250, from a standing start

how fast your brain can work, how your reactions make you do all the right things in the quickest possible time. You don't even have time to think what you're doing; it's a natural reaction.

How I missed hitting Mike that day, I'll never know. One moment he was just in front of me powering up the hill, then he was all over the road in front of me. The next moment I'd swept past unscathed; a bit shaken, it's true, but not enough to stop me chasing after Redman. Again I sat ten feet behind for a while until the final lap down the fastest downhill run to the last corner, intending to out-brake him on the inside of this corner. With some demon late braking I pushed past, rubbing knees with Jim. Then it was all over as soon as I asked the bike to power out to the chequered flag. It was an incredible sensation, a feeling of perfection to win this way, knowing that everything has clicked just as you planned. No wonder it took hours before the adrenalin stopped pumping through my veins. That combination of speed and power was a like a drug, always leaving you wanting more.

From East Germany, it was the long drive home. But it was a happy one, even for my mechanics resting behind. We knew we had it over the Honda and I felt confident that I'd mastered Jim Redman. All we needed were two more victories and that title was ours. Ours! Yamaha could keep their manufacturers' title - it was the riders' crown I was after.

How the time dragged before that Ulster Grand Prix at Dundrod; I just couldn't wait to get out there and add another maximum eight points to my championship tally. Before that, though, there were jobs to be done: bikes to be stripped and refitted in my workshop. Usually I was happiest working alongside the mechanics, but now I was jittery and getting on people's nerves, getting on my own nerves. I just couldn't sit still for a moment.

When race day finally came at the Ulster, what a relief for us all, I think. But what a day. I was going to say it rained, but it did more than just rain, it absolutely bucketed down. I could have cried for joy. I could not have asked for more. It was like being drawn at home in the FA Cup. Rain was my kind of weather on a road circuit. Perhaps I took a few risks that day, but I like to think they were all calculated ones. Jim, on the other hand, preferred to play it safe, and I won by more than a minute. I even picked up a double, by just beating Dick Creith and Jack Ahearn in the 500cc race on a Norton, loaned by the famous sponsor Reg Dearden. I only just managed to beat local hero Creith, mind you, as a loosened bolt allowed the gearbox to start moving about, which lost me speed.

Redman told me that Honda's chief engineer came to him after the race and enquired, 'Machine trouble Jim-san'? 'No,' Jim had replied, 'rider trouble!' I was pleased that race was over when I remembered the year before and being rushed to hospital with a fractured back after crashing the 500cc Duke Gilera.

Now we had only the Monza GP to go, with Suzuka in the background if it came down to a last-round duel. The odds were in my favour, a win in Italy would secure a first world title for both me and Yamaha, but my mechanics had now returned to Japan. I now only had my faithful British mechanic, Eddie Carter, to help me at Monza. My number one mechanic, Seki-san, had given him the carburettor settings for the factory engine.

It was unbelievable that the factory didn't appreciate how important this race was for them, with their first world championship at stake. But, remember, for the 1964 season they had only planned to compete in five GPs, and it was Rebel Read who had tried to change the racing plans of the great Yamaha Motor Company. I begged them to send Seki-san to me in Italy and they eventually agreed. Thank God they did, for it transpired at Monza that the goal posts had moved, in favour of Honda.

I knew Redman had to win at both Monza and Suzuka to keep his crown. What I hadn't allowed for were those inscrutable Japanese. They were always up to something, but you were never sure quite what. My first indication that there was something afoot came not long after our arrival at the Italian circuit. Word was out that there was a six-cylinder Honda being kept under cover in the Redman camp.

Stories like that circulate around Grand Prix paddocks all the time, and most of them are just stories, more than likely spread around to upset a rival. I thought this was the case with this Honda tale, but when you've not been sleeping too well at night and you've just driven a long way from the UK, rumours can upset you. I must admit I was feeling a bit worried. But what was I to do? If I had walked over to Redman's transporter, trying to look all innocent, they would have known straight away that they had me worried. There'd probably be a sentry out and as soon as he said 'here comes Read' they'd all act nonchalantly, drinking Coke and playing cards as if there was nothing better to do. You'd go away no better off, but Redman would know he'd got you worried. So, in the end, you stay away, and he's still got you worried, only he might not know it. It's a war of nerves.

The minute Jim took that new bike out on to the track, I knew the stories were true. For a start the noise was like something from out of this world, enough to send everyone running to the trackside to see what it was. And sure enough, they could count the exhaust megaphones: one, two, three, four, five, and six - a six-cylinder Honda. Blue number plates, indicating that the bike was a 350, didn't fool me. Honda had already clinched the 350cc championship; there was no need for them to bring out a new bike in that class at Monza. Oh no, I knew that this was for my benefit. That machine was a 250, specially produced to give Redman the power to run away from my Yamaha and hold on to his world title. They must have worked like mad to finish it, but that's how it is with the Japanese. They'd even flown Jim out to Japan to test it. Not only that, they'd managed to keep the whole thing secret. You had to hand it to them. Honda had flown the bike in on a passenger jet from Tokyo to Milan Linate airport near Monza the day before official practice. You had to hand it to them, but Yamaha and I had caused them a great additional expense.

The problem was what to do now. My mind was working overtime, but that sinking feeling in my stomach was growing. Just when I thought I had the title in my hand! Championships aren't won by sitting around, but by action and positive thinking. We talked over our tactics, revising the plans that had already proved so effective. A quick start, then slipstream the Honda six and wait there, hoping for a getaway if the Honda slows or Redman makes a mistake. There seemed no other way, other than gearing up my machine with a tooth less on the rear to stay in Jim's slipstream if the new bike was so much faster than his old four.

Race day came, and with it the attendant thousands upon thousands, milling everywhere, noisy and vibrant. For the Italians, all eyes were on the new boy, Agostini. I only had eyes for Jim Redman as we lined up on the grid for the 250cc race. Ten seconds, now everything was concentrated on push-starting my faithful Yamaha as fast as possible; a deep breath and... Go!

All I remember from that start was the noise; the incredible scream from the six as it blasted from the grid like a jet fighter on action alert. The spectators and the pit crews were momentarily deafened. Those of us left in the Honda's wake were simply shattered by the speed at which Redman jumped away from us. I thought I'd made a good start, and Agostini must have started well, for he was up there beside me on the Morini. But within a minute, neither of us was in the hunt. The Honda was some hundred yards ahead, Redman powering on the pressure with every passing lap.

There are times when you feel there's no use in trying any more; something occurs and you feel you've been kicked in the stomach. I used to feel that way in

exams at school. You look at the exam paper, and you panic. You want to stand up and walk out of the room. But you don't. You sit there, read the questions again, and try to answer them as best you can. So it was that day at Monza. My first feeling was one of panic and depression. 'I can't stay with that sort of power' was my thought as Redman hurtled away in front of us. But the feeling lasts less than a minute. You don't quit. You know that there are more than twenty laps to race, seventy-six miles. A lot can happen.

A lot did happen too. I spent the first few laps shaking off Ago, leaving him to dice with my team-mate Mike Duff while I tried to whittle down the gap between Redman and myself. By lap five the position seemed as hopeless as ever, but by the seventh I was getting encouraging pit signals. I was closing up on him. Next time round I was even closer. It could mean only one thing, Redman was slowing. I knew I wasn't going much faster.

Now my entire approach changed. It's amazing how quickly you can be down, and then up. For six laps I had simply been chasing. Now I was the hunter, my eye on my quarry, narrowing that gap on every lap. By halfway we were level, dicing for the lead, and I knew the Honda gamble had failed. For it had been a gamble. With so little time for testing, it was perhaps only natural to expect teething troubles. When I think back, they must have been uncertain as to the machine's reliability, because in practice they were doing no more than two laps at a time. Obviously they hoped to frighten me into doing something foolish, like coming off, or blowing up trying to go too fast after Jim. Happily, I wasn't prepared to push my bike beyond its limits, and my patience was rewarded.

I learned later that the Honda's engine was overheating - it was a very hot day, too - and whenever Jim opened the throttle beyond the three quarter mark the bike began misfiring badly. This they would rectify by the next season by adding more air ducting and fitting oil coolers in the fairing, but that would be too late to keep the 1964 championship from Yamaha.

At the time, I couldn't care less about the Honda's problems. I was reeling off laps in record-breaking style, cracking up a 113.91mph race average and winning my first crown the way a world champion should. But it had been close; if the Honda hadn't overheated it would have been a different story. Still, now the race was over there was nothing to worry about. Even Mike Duff had been able to pick off the ailing Honda on the line for a Yamaha factory one-two. There was going to be plenty to celebrate that night.

People always ask how it felt, winning that first world title. To be honest, I don't remember any particular feeling at all, apart from the exhilaration of winning the race.

Even when I was standing up on the winner's rostrum with garlands around my neck, silver trophies in my hands, and pretty girls at my feet, I was still in a daze. It was only days later, when the parties were all over, the sore heads were cleared, and the lionising diminished, that I had time to contemplate what it all meant, the people behind me, from my mother in the earliest days right through to the Yamaha works team who had made it all possible.

The future now opened wide before me, with expectations of a better works contract, better start money, improved sponsorship contracts. I would be able to... what wouldn't I be able to do? My mind whirled, and with good reason. I had paid my money, bought my ticket and - with luck - was riding the roundabout to fame and glory.

The Yamaha people were really thrilled at my success. As well as my winning the riders' 250cc title, the factory won the manufacturers' world championship. Both were Yamaha's first world titles, and, most significantly for the future of the sport, it was the first time the 250cc championship had been won by a two-stroke.

I was their hero, and when I next visited Japan they couldn't do enough for me. At the factory, it seemed that everyone wanted to congratulate me. In the stores, in my hotel, I was given the full Japanese preferential treatment. It was like being a king - or visiting royalty at least. Mind you, I had to work for my keep. There was another season coming up; new bikes would have to be prepared and tested; plans made on a bigger scale than in 1964 because the 1965 season would see the Yamaha works team at full strength all season, and by then the Honda six would be perfected, which meant I would have to ride harder or get the factory to make a faster machine.

I was given a pay rise as well, which proved that the Japanese were grateful for my efforts. As well as excellent bonuses for winning, I was offered a contract for the 1965 season and enough to buy a five-bedroomed house with an acre of garden. That was a lot of money in those days, and I had no hesitation in accepting, even though it was chicken feed compared with MotoGP riders' contract fees today.

What I needed at that point in my career was a manager who might have negotiated for a small royalty on every Yamaha motorcycle sold, or a company shares-option. Something like that would have been a really valuable asset for my family's future.

June 1965, with mechanic Takehiko

YAMAHA
26
26

I check the rear tyre of the new RD05A four, still under wraps, at Monza in 1965, while Mike Duff adjusts his front brake.

At Assen, everything went perfectly. I was unbeatable that day. But there was no living with Redman and the Honda six at Spa-Francorchamps or Sachsenring, although second places at both kept the points rolling in and me at the top of the table. The Czech round at Brno proved the turning point. In the previous two rounds, Mike Duff and I had concentrated on finishing, knowing we couldn't hold the Honda on ultra-fast circuits. But in Czecho we really revved the Yamahas as hard as they'd go and they showed they could take that sort of treatment. Mike stuck on Redman's tail, worrying him, while I cruised along in third until it was time to take them both. This time it was Redman who couldn't stand the pace, and Mike followed me home to keep Jim back in third place.

One more to win, and Ulster was next on the programme. Again race day dawned with the weather on my side, wind, rain, and occasional bursts of sunshine. Not only that, it seemed that the 'little people' liked me that day. After crashing in the 350cc race Redman was a non-starter in the 250cc contest in which Mike Duff and I took the race fairly quietly and the title was mine for the second year running.

This time celebrations were kept to a minimum. The factory people were already looking forward to a hat-trick in 1966, and now that the title was in the bag they wanted to try out their latest invention at Monza. The new 250cc machine was a water-cooled, disc valve, V-four, built to beat Honda's six. Basically two of the proven 125cc engines bolted together with a seven-speed gearbox, it could really hum. At a circuit like Spa, given the right gearing, a top speed of 160mph was not out of the question. For a 250cc engine, that was really fantastic.

We'd had the fours in England for testing since June or July, but trying to keep the thing secret in England was too much to hope for... as we discovered when we took them to Snetterton. We thought we'd cleared the place before taking the test bike out, but no sooner had I returned home than Mick Woollett of *Motor Cycle* was on the phone. Word was out that we'd been testing a four-cylinder 250 two-stroke.

'Bullshit', I said. 'Someone's been having you on.'

Exit Mick Woollett, fairly satisfied. The phone rings again.

Motor Cycle News this time.

'We heard you were testing a four-cylinder 250 Yamaha at Snetterton this afternoon.'

'Rubbish', I said.

'Oh no', they said. 'We've got the pictures to prove it, and the guy who took them swears it sounded like a two-stroke four. Any comment, Phil?'

Unprintable!

Sure enough, out comes *Motor Cycle News* and there are the pictures of Read and Duff, with the works mechanics and the new bike. So there's no secret any more. But the story didn't end there. The weekend after the photos appeared in *MCN* was the East German Grand Prix at Sachsenring. I was sitting chatting to Malcolm Edgar in the Castrol transporter when Mick Woollett comes storming up, calling me all the blue names under the sun for not giving him the story, making him look a fool, letting him be scooped by *Motor Cycle News*. I tried to stop him, but a fully charged Mick Woollett with a good head of steam takes a bit of getting under control. In the end I lost my temper, just like that. Wham! I was on my feet, ready to have a go at him... and would have if Malcolm hadn't stepped in to keep us apart. Sorry Mick!

That 1965 season was memorable for another clash between a rider and a member of the motorcycle press; only this time things really got going. It was at Monza, where the new 250 made its debut, and the combatants in question were *Motor Cycle News* man Charlie Rous and diminutive Ralph Bryans, a Honda team rider. Just what was said remains a mystery, but Charlie, a jovial sort of fellow, tended to get a bit 'bolshie' after a few glasses of wine, and he sure upset Ralph. Charlie was twice Ralph's size, but once Ralph's Irish temper was roused there was no stopping him. Before anyone could intervene, Ralph landed one on Charlie's jaw and down he went. I must say the little Ulsterman went up a few notches in my book after that. There have been many times I'd wished I'd done something similar although to be fair to Charlie he was the wrong man to hit. I could think of many less likeable characters in the press world than him.

Our new four created a storm of interest at Monza, the Italian factories in particular taking a very active interest. Too active for my liking, in fact, for all sorts of special parts went walkabout from our workshop; cylinder heads, barrels, pistons. Heaven knows where they went, though it's a well-accepted fact in the motorcycle world that it's the Italians, rather than the Japanese, who think nothing of stealing ideas and improvements. The number of requests we had that weekend to study and photograph our new engines was quite extraordinary. I think every industrial spy in Italy must have been at Monza.

For all that, it was the ideal place to test the bike, for it needed a high-speed circuit to show up any deficiencies. Air flow to the carburettors was the first problem we encountered. It just wasn't possible to keep the machine running at high-speed for the full distance. Another thing was that it lacked an instant delivery of power. Still, that's what we tested for, to find the faults before the races that really mattered. Now it was up to the factory to sort out the problems, and as usual there was no messing about. By the time I flew out to Japan for the Japanese Grand Prix, a race-ready four was waiting for me.

There was no doubting the bike's potential. It was as quick as any 350 I'd ridden. I wasn't too happy with the handling, though, and felt that Yamaha might have been making the same mistake Honda had made with their six, aiming too much for engine performance and neglecting the handling. Jim Redman had found the six quite a brute in 1965, and when at the end of the year Mike Hailwood joined Honda after his dispute with MV, he described it as 'bloody awful'. Mind you, he could still ride it well!

My main concern during testing was wet weather. If the bike was difficult on a dry surface, what would it be like in the wet? I voiced my doubts at one of our round-the-drawing-board conferences. The Japanese looked back at me as if I had just demanded the impossible.

'How can we test it in the wet,' they said. 'It does not rain.' You can't argue with logic like that.

But it did rain one night and the track was still wet when we went to test. I was right in thinking it would be a bit of a handful in the wet, and was busy trying to work out where and how adjustments could be made when trouble came from an unexpected quarter. She seized - at near maximum speed. I could tell she was going to, too, but even though I grabbed the clutch as fast as possible, I wasn't quick enough. The rear wheel locked and I was high-sided off and thrown high into the air. Fortunately the bike slid away from me, but nonetheless I came down with a thump, sliding down the wet track on my back at very high speed and coming to a stop on the grass run-off. I lay there, my eyes closed, in perfect peace. I'm alive, was all I could think. I came off at 140mph and I'm still alive and okay, I think. Shit! That was close!

4

Ivy and me - team orders

Bill Ivy died on Saturday 12 July 1969, when his two-stroke Jawa 350 V-four crashed during practice for the East German Grand Prix. He was 26. A hero to many, he would become a legend, the James Dean of motorcycle racing. His hair was long, cut at an exclusive London salon; he dressed in the latest fashion and his cars, Ferraris and Maseratis, were fast and expensive. Into his 26 years Bill had packed everything that life could offer, some of it beyond his means, and he gave great entertainment to millions. Crowds everywhere loved the man from Maidstone, Kent, for they recognised, as we all did, that his diminutive 5ft 3in body possessed a hundred per cent aggression, skill, and courage.

Bill was my friend, yet I became his enemy. Even today, so many years after his death, people still make nasty remarks about when we raced together.

Some come from guys, most are from girls, a lot of them too young to have even seen Bill race. They have read biased stories and soaked up myths along with the legend. The Ivy-Read feud seems to live on, not allowed to die.

Yet even if I had known what would happen in the years ahead, I would still have phoned Bill from Japan on that October day in 1965, asking him to join me in the Yamaha team. He was one of the world's great riders, and they are rare. We were many times a world-beating combination on the tracks. His tally of successes would have been even greater but for the presence in 1966 and 1967 of one Mike Hailwood, racing the 250cc Honda six. The Honda factory was able to turn its formidable six into a much more successful bike; with Mike's brilliance added to the Honda factory's technical skills it became an almost unbeatable machine. He won nine of the twelve World Championship rounds in 1966, and that was the end of my hat-trick hopes. I had to settle for being 250cc runner-up both years, and in the 125cc class I ended the season in fourth place. Bill, whose principal interest was the 125 title, finished second behind Swiss rider Luigi Taveri on the novel five-cylinder Honda. That incredible

On the Yamaha four, leading Hailwood's Honda six in the 250cc 1966 Czech GP, where bends were flanked by stone walls and metal barriers;Hailwood won and went on to take the 250cc title, I'd held for two years.

machine based on Honda's 50cc grand prix twin was, like the six, developed in response to the ever-improving Yamahas. Bill had good reason to feel satisfied with his first World Championship season, especially as his 125cc victories included his first-ever TT win at the Isle of Man. I was second behind him there with Mike Duff, back with us for the TT, taking fourth spot behind former world champion Hugh Anderson on the Suzuki twin.

But the five wasn't invincible and one of its defeats was in the Finnish GP at Imatra, where Luigi and I crossed the line side-by-side. It took the organisers an hour to decide the result in my favour, which was all wrong. They should have announced a clear result straight away and as far as I was concerned it could have been a dead heat, with Luigi and me sharing the podium.

That 1966 season was Hugh Anderson's last, just as 1967 would be Suzuki's last for a while. A lot of people were sad to say goodbye to the New Zealander in the red helmet with a white Kiwi emblazoned on the front. In his few years at the top with Suzuki he gave two-stroke riding a new dimension; and apparently he was quite a hell-raiser in his time. By the time I got to know him he'd cooled down a bit, probably as a result of marrying Jannie, a Dutch nurse he'd met in hospital after a bad crash at Assen. In fact, to see him sitting outside his caravan, reading Churchill's memoirs or some novel, you'd wonder where he got his raunchy reputation.

A Suzuki mechanic who once visited the Yamaha camp said what a terrible man Anderson-san was and how he'd never travel with him again. At least, that's what I gathered with my little knowledge of Japanese. I had to ask my mechanics for the full story. It seemed that Hugh, Jannie, and the mechanic had been driving late at night. Feeling tired, they pulled into a lay-by. The mechs slept in the van while Hugh and Jannie retired to the caravan hooked up behind. It was late so nobody bothered to put the caravan jacks down. Five, ten minutes go by. It's quiet. The mechs snuggled down on the front seat of the van, almost asleep, and suddenly the van starts going up and down. He looks out. The caravan's rocking rhythmically up and down, too, taking the van with it. And apparently the poor little mechanics didn't get much sleep that night! I never doubted the Hugh Anderson stories after that.

Hugh was lucky to have Jannie travel around with him. From 1966 I was spending more and more time on my own. Not that this was anyone's fault; it was just the way things worked out. That year, mainly for tax reasons, Ann and I sold our home in Luton and moved to Guernsey, buying the Island's former French Consulate. The Reads were moving up in the world.

I set up a marine business in Guernsey as an importer for Yamaha boats and main agent for Mercury and Mercruiser.

Heading for a win on the 250cc four in the 1967 Spanish GP

With Ann and Mike at the TT

Naturally enough Ann wanted to spend more time in her new home, especially now that Michael was growing older and we had Graham on the way. But it meant we saw less and less of each other, and being in different places inevitably meant we developed different lives. So, over the next few years we drifted apart. My world was the circus of motorcycle racing, Ann's was the world of home and children. I'd come home after a weekend's racing and find people in our house I didn't know, and who didn't want to know my world. In 1967, I opened a marine engine business on the island, selling Yamaha boats and Mercury and Mercruiser motors, and there were times when I found it easier speeding across the water to Herm or Sark than sitting at home wondering what had gone wrong. For me, marriage should be a togetherness thing. I needed someone right there alongside me to share the ups and the downs, to haul me through the bad times and get me going again. Those years of 1966 and 1967 had too many downs and too many uncertainties, and I needed someone to pull me through. That someone wasn't always there.

However, my marriage to Ann wasn't all bad. We had two wonderful sons, and I'm very proud of them. Mike joined the RAF and became a great Tornado pilot, surviving the Iraq War. He now flies Boeing 777s as a senior officer for Cathay Pacific. Graham is Dunlop's racing consultant working for GP2 and GP3 teams around the world. Mike has three daughters and finally he and his second wife Toni, produced my first grandson three years ago.

Yet, paradoxically, I was becoming more confident socially, despite my problems on the track and then later at home. Maybe it was because of them, I don't know. But certainly I realised in 1967, that I, too, could be one of the crowd, one of the swingers, one of the jet-set. I could mix it with the best of them at the post-race parties. Now, instead of looking on, shy and envious, I found myself joining in. It helped take my mind off Hailwood and the wretched Honda six, and there were always plenty of people around willing to help you forget.

Bill, of course, was in his element, but then it's essential to remember that this was the height of the swinging sixties. Being British and long-haired was the next best thing to being a Beatle, and if you rode super-fast racing bikes, drove a Ferrari and were mates with Mike Hailwood, you couldn't go wrong. They used to say that Bill had more birds than an aviary at feeding time!

Not that it affected his riding, far from it. In 1967 Bill was really on song, winning the 125cc world title with me backing him up in the runner-up spot. In the 250cc title chase he did a fine back-up job, finishing third in the championship behind Hailwood and me, with wins at the French and Belgian rounds. The trouble was that I finished second in the championship behind Hailwood, yet again.

Mind you, it was close. So close that we went to Japan for the last race of the series equal on best-results points, with 50 each, though I had an over-all total of 56 to Mike's 54. We had everything to race for but in the event neither of us finished. So who had won? The FIM officials huffed and puffed, looked up their little books and declared Phil Read 250cc world champion. Then they huffed and puffed again and next day gave the title to Mike, by virtue of his having one more GP win than me. It was a sickening way to end the season, as all I'd needed to do was finish that last race in the points and things were made worse by the uncertainty of the FIM officials' decision.

I have never doubted that I could have won that title. After so much trouble the previous season, everything was starting to come right again, especially the bikes. The Honda six was now in its third year and Mike reckoned it gave away 10mph to our Yamaha fours. Certainly our bikes were handling much better, and they were lighter than in 1966. Indeed, in that first year on the fours, Bill and I were finishing races with blistered hands, often having to grip an iced handkerchief to reduce the pain once we'd taken our gloves off.

Really, it was a patch of oil on the road at Dundrod's Hairpin that secured the title for Mike at the Ulster GP. I'd caught and passed him on the second lap when my back wheel stepped out on the oil and down I went. I was soon on my feet again, but damage to the throttle grip meant I couldn't re-start. Mike, who had taken avoiding action, romped off to a win.

Still, for all the disappointment at losing the title again, 1967 had its lighter moments, none more so than right at the end, in Japan. About a dozen of us from the European contingent, plus American rider Gary Nixon, were staying at a hotel quite near the Fuji circuit. That meant we didn't have to go far to the paddock but we were some distance away from the more interesting night life, ten miles away, in fact. Sitting around a hotel bar can get pretty dull, so one night a group of us, including a cheery little American journalist whose name I forget, set off to Tokyo for a piece of the action. We didn't have to look far, Tokyo's that kind of town. It wasn't long before we were in a pleasant little bar with some charming company. Later in the evening (or was it early the next morning?) you'd have found us all back at the hotel, trying to get things going there. The only trouble was that there weren't enough young ladies for all the riders still propping up the bar. I don't know what the others did, but rather than prolong the agony of my fellow riders I decided to remove my lady companion to my room where, thanks to my knowledge of her language, we were able to discuss a few topics relevant to the time and age we lived in.

There goes my 250cc world title! This fall at Dundrod lost me the first or second place I needed.

However, our intimate conversation was interrupted by the sound of someone trying to open the door. I wasn't worried. It was locked. But I forgot that hotels have pass keys. The next minute the door burst open and in rushed Gary Nixon, Polaroid at the ready, with many others behind. Trouble was, the flash failed to go off and Gary hot-footed it down the corridor before he had time to try for another shot. Anyway, I don't know why he bothered. The young lady and I were still perfectly respectable. If it had happened ten minutes later, though, who knows? Whatever my chances, they were ruined by all that noise and commotion.

We were already unpopular with the hotel management after John Cooper's performance the previous night. 'Mooneyes' had stripped off and walked into what he understood to be the communal pool. But when some women arrived on to the scene they took one look at John, screamed (who wouldn't!), and ran out. Enter the manager to inform the now blushing Cooper that he was in the ladies' bath house. The gentlemen's was next door. Exit John.

Battling with Hailwood at Brands Hatch, racing anti-clockwise in the 1967 Hutchinson 100

Dangerous days, leading Stuart Graham (Suzuki) over the railway bridge approaching Hohenstein-Ernst in the 1967 125cc East German GP, where a few straw bales offered the only protection for riders and spectators.

Hohenstein-Ernst.
Bez. Karl-Marx-Stadt

Chasing 125cc winner Bill Ivy in the 1968 Ulster GP, both on 125cc fours

The Japanese really loved Bill that year, especially when he iced his world title cake with victory in the 125cc race at Fuji. Suddenly it seemed that everyone wanted to know him. He was the bright new star. I kidded myself that he was popular because the Japanese didn't need to look up to him when they talked, but I knew the true reason. I'd come only second in my class. Bill had won his, and in the hard world of motorcycle racing, just as in so many other walks of life, winning is the only virtue. As Charlie Brown once said in the *Peanuts* comic strip, 'Winning may not be everything, but losing's nothing'. How right he was.

Nonetheless, there would be 1968, I thought, and it looked as if we would be in for an easier season. Honda, like Suzuki, were pulling out of racing, so the chances of winning back my 250cc title were first-rate. True, there'd be the occasional challenge from up-and-coming riders on ex-works bikes and production machines - people like Rod Gould, the Banbury Flier - and MZ, those temperamental two-strokes from East Germany, would still be around. But as I spent Christmas in Guernsey, I looked ahead to 1968 in eager anticipation.

I was in for a shock. There was to be a change of plans. For the coming season, without any discussion with Yamaha, I was told by Mitsui, the UK importer, of new team orders for the coming season: Bill would go for the 250 title, I could have the 125. As in the previous seasons, we would back up each other's attempts. To say I was stunned would be putting it mildly. After all the assistance I'd given the factory... after I had given Bill the chance of a works ride... after giving Yamaha their first world titles, this was my reward, the 125. I felt I'd been kicked up the backside.

I was disappointed in Bill, too, I realised his personality had changed with success but I hadn't expected him to go behind my back to the factory chiefs and woo away the prize I most coveted. I should have known better. The super-ego doesn't stand for second best, and while I was number one jockey on the Yamaha fours, Bill had had to remain second best. Now it was different. Whatever the reassurances from Yamaha, it looked as if Bill had taken over as number one. And I'd be the first to admit that, in 1967 especially, he did ride like one of the greats. But he didn't have a shaky marriage, two young sons and a marine business to worry about. I did.

By the time we set out on the 1968 championship trail at the Nürburgring, something else was bugging me. Things seemed ominously quiet on the development front at Hamamatsu. Previously, pre-season, I'd been whisked off to Japan to test and help develop the bikes Yamaha would be racing in twelve months time. The fours were in their third full season, with nothing coming up to replace them. Okay, there was no opposition from their main competitors, but it seemed unlikely the Japanese would rest on their laurels, that was a British habit. To my mind, already wary of Japanese machinations, it only meant one thing. Yamaha intended to follow Honda and Suzuki out of racing as a works team, probably at the end of this 1968 season. That would mean goodbye to my works contract and possibly my racing future.

Funnily, though, you can think all sorts of things prior to the opening of the season, but once you're on the line in search of those precious championship points, all you think about is the racing. So it was at Nürburgring. I had already resolved to concentrate on my racing, with maybe a few dalliances on the side, just to keep fit of course. I would win the 125 title. I would also help Bill win the 250. Then I would ask the factory to let me go for the 250 in 1969... if there was a works team. Of Yamaha's plans, nothing was confirmed or denied. My Japanese friends were at their inscrutable best.

The 125cc dice with Ivy at the 1968 Czech GP, he crashed and I won.

Yamaha TT Isle of Man 1968

Nürburgring got off with a bang, literally, when Bill Ivy knuckled a German pit marshal's nose. Bill should have had a pass, but didn't. The official was having no nonsense from a stroppy long-haired Britisher who couldn't obey the rules. The argument didn't last long, little Bill punched his way past... and ended up being frog-marched off to the nearest *polizeiwache*.

'Now I win both world titles,' I quipped to the Yamaha team boss. He was inscrutably not amused and hurried off to secure Bill's release.

If nothing else, that incident really fired Bill into action out on the track. In the 125 race he set off as if the whole West German police force was after him and slashed the lap record before a broken crankshaft put him out. It's interesting to reflect on what would have happened to team orders that day, because the way he was going I don't think I could have caught him up without him making it very obvious... and, riding to team orders was against FIM rules. Oh yes. Team orders only ever exist by word of mouth. There was nothing in my written contract to say that I would concentrate on the 125cc title and allow Bill to win the 250. According to the FIM, every rider should be out there trying his utmost to win the race, though of course unofficially it was acknowledged that some form of riding to orders was sometimes used to secure a world title.

125cc TT, 1968

Anyway, Bill's crankshaft ended any problems in the 125 event, which I duly won with ease, then a leaking radiator ended my interest in the 250cc race, which Bill won comfortably.

Team orders went out the window in Spain, but only because the bikes let us down. At least, mine did in the 125. In the 250 I hummed along nicely and, with Bill retiring, I took the chequered flag for what proved to be a very valuable eight points.

The Isle of Man TT, however, went according to plan, although I heard later that Bill made it pretty obvious that he could have won both TTs had he not been such a good boy and obeyed the riding instructions. I think I'd have preferred it if he had won both. Let's face it, the way he rode the new four-cylinder bike in the 125cc race he deserved to, shattering the record books with the first-ever ton-up lap by a 125 machine... a blistering 100.32mph of memorable magic not surpassed by a 125cc machine until 1989, when the circuit had become smoother, with several corners eased and hugely improved tyre technology. Try as I might I couldn't get my lap times above that magical ton - being heavier than Bill made a difference - but I still won at a record average speed of 99.12mph. Famously Bill, out ahead of me, actually stopped near Creg-ny-Baa to ask the crowd who was leading. The implication was obvious. 'Well, I've got to let him win, you know. Now you all know that I could've won if I'd wanted to. I'm just that much better than Read!'

Still, Bill did win the 250 TT and it was a classic victory. From the standing start he lapped the mountain at a record 105.51mph and then continued to hammer away from the rest of the field, building up such a comfortable lead. I could have caught him but my engine was slowed by a punctured expansion chamber.

It was a brave ride, too. Cranking over at Milntown, Ivy struck his foot on the roadside bank, and at the end of the race he was so exhausted from his effort and from fighting the pain that he allowed himself to be dramatically lifted from the bike.

My race was nowhere near as eventful. I finally went out with a flat tyre - that old TT luck again, even though like many others before me I had been to the Fairy Bridge and said 'Hello' to the little people, which was meant to ward off misfortune. Dunlop must have had a guilty conscience about my puncture, they gave me a set of their golf clubs.

By now there were some suspicions that we were riding to order and the press

Leading Ivy in the 1968 250cc Dutch TT, he won this one.

was starting to make a big issue of our rivalry. With every win, Bill's ego was boosted. Had we won our respective races and said, 'a good day's work', I think I might have been able to live with the situation. But I always felt that Bill had to show he was better than me. Whenever he was interviewed - and that was pretty often - he made a point of saying he would win the 250 title on merit and that he could beat me whenever he wished. Deep down I burned, and the longer the thing went on, the harder I found it. At Assen, I was sure I could have had him in the 250. We were wheel to wheel all the way in a high-speed dice that left third-place rider Renzo Pasolini on the Benelli four more than two minutes in arrears. On the line I let Bill go through, as I had to, but it hurt.

I think it was about that time that I telexed Japan to ask Yamaha for definite confirmation that they would be racing a team in 1969. Perhaps the seeds of rebellion were already planted, perhaps I was just worried about my future. Who knows? But my performances in the next two grands prix - Belgium and East Germany - and Yamaha's failure to reply to my question, paved the inevitable course to my decision in Czechoslovakia.

Certainly the Belgian GP reaffirmed the stupidity of trying to decide racing orders at the beginning of the season. It had always seemed to me much better to wait until several rounds had been run, by which time some sort of pattern should have emerged, before deciding who would back up whom. At Francorchamps, Bill went straight out into the lead while I spent the first lap spluttering round on oiling plugs. When Bill was opening it out down the Masta straight on lap two, I was pulling into the pits for a set of new plugs. The trouble with a four-cylinder bike was that it took twice as long to change the plugs as it did on a twin, and by the time I was ready to rejoin the fray everyone was ahead of me.

Not for long. One by one I began picking them off, impatient to get within dicing distance of Bill. Bill? There was no Bill. The pit signal said he was out. I was on my own, on an unhappy bike, yet I knew I could win if I could work my way through. This time I wouldn't have to hold back. What a race! There were times I thought I'd never make it. One moment she'd be firing on two or three cylinders, the next moment there'd be a sudden surge and she'd be back on song again. There was only one person ahead of me as I flashed past the pits for the last time - Heinz Rosner on the works MZ. I'll have him, I thought, as my mind registered the time on the signal board... and I did, picking him up on the long straight and leading him home by seven seconds. I coasted into the pits feeling very pleased with myself. I'd shown them how a 250 Yamaha should be ridden.

Sachsenring was something of a farce. Not that the racing wasn't serious. It was deadly so, especially as I was still riding high after that marvellous win in Belgium and out to show Bill that I was still the master of the 250. In fact, I almost overdid it, opening up a twelve-second lead that I wasn't sure how to lose in order to let Bill catch up. In the end I decided on a pit stop, telling my mechanic, Roy Robinson, to splash a bit of water around the radiator to make it look as if I had stopped for a genuine top-up. It didn't fool anyone, least of all the press, but it did give Bill the chance to pull ahead. Out I went again, overtook him just for the devil of it, shot him an 'I guess I'd better let you win' glance, and eased off so that he could take the flag; by a tenth of a second.

On the rostrum with Ivy and Rosner

Earlier I'd won the 125 race, so all I needed was another first in the Czech GP at Brno and that title was mine. A week later I had it in the bag, although I almost made a mess of it, coming close to crashing. It had been raining, and parts of the circuit were still wet. I went into a glorious slide at one corner, but although I managed to control it, Bill, who was tucked in behind me, reacted much more slowly. He must have seen my rear wheel break away, yet he waited just a moment too long. Down he went into the muddy ditch.

FÜR DEN GANZEN TAG
verhaltet Euch
IFA
MZ
IFA
MZ
101
106

Riding to orders at Sachsenring, East Germany

Winning the 1968 250cc Czech GP on the four, why am I holding the clutch lever in?

Well, I thought, what now? There was still no answer to my repeated enquiry to Yamaha about 1969. I'd had a gutful of reading that Bill Ivy could beat me any time he chose, although as yet I hadn't told anyone of my intention to rebel against team orders. True to form, I had let everything bottle up inside me until it was ready to burst. I had been doing the same with my problems at home. No one knew how mixed up and unhappy I was. It wasn't my style to go around telling people that sort of thing.

Now, however, it looked as if Bill might not race in the 250, in which case I had no need to rebel. But if Bill did decide to ride, I was going to look a right swine if I went out there, with him still shaken up, and told him he was going to have to race for his title.

Bill, was at the first-aid centre, so I wandered down to see how bad he was. In the end he helped me make my mind up, ironic though it seems. His leg was bruised, requiring some support strapping; that was all. There was nothing wrong with his confidence. He was as cocky as ever, bright and chirpy. It was nothing to worry about, he said. So I didn't. I walked back to my caravan, my decision was made.

I've said before what the tension is like on the grid before a grand prix race. This time, waiting beside my bike, the engine revving impatiently, I felt as I'd never felt before. I was about to throw down the gauntlet; to issue a challenge to someone who had once been a friend, someone I'd shared bikes and laughs with. I knew that I had to beat him to make the whole thing worthwhile. As usual we were alongside each other. Silence. I looked across at Bill. This is it, I thought.

'You're going to have to race for this one, Bill,' I said. His mouth opened and shut. He swallowed. 'Wha... what d'you mean?' he asked. 'Just that,' I said. 'You're going to have to race me for this one.'

Seconds later we were on the countdown to the start. What was going on in Bill's mind I don't know. Mine was perfectly clear. Although one hundred per cent tuned to go with the green light, I felt beautifully relaxed for the first time in months. Now that I had made the decision it seemed that a great weight had been lifted. I was my own man again, racing to win.

Leading Heinz Rosner's MZ, 1968 250cc Czech GP

The green light came up and I was gone. Behind me Bill fought out an early duel with Rosner on the MZ, which gave me the chance to open up a good lead. With the roads drying I was able to improve my advantage over Bill to ten seconds... at which stage the Yamaha pit crew decided things were getting a little out of hand. 'Slow down' came the pit sign. In my mind I gave them two fingers and kept my hand steady on the throttle. I was enjoying myself. Behind me Bill was just holding on to second place, and that was how we finished; me first, Bill second. Rosner was third.

To say the atmosphere in the Yamaha pits was muted would be an understatement. They were all bloody well dumbstruck... until Bill came in and gave vent to his feelings in no uncertain manner. The press heard it all. If there were ever any doubts that we had been racing to order they were now dispelled. As I walked away to the victory rostrum I could almost see the headlines.

'Read Rebels'; 'Rebel Read wins Bill Ivy's Race'; 'Read-Ivy Feud out in the Open'.

Well, they say every dog has his day. The press were going to have theirs for the rest of the season.

As far as the 250cc world championship was concerned, the title fight was perfectly poised for a terrific finish. With seven of the ten rounds gone, Bill had thirty-eight points, I had thirty-six. My biggest worry now was the reaction from the Yamaha people in Japan. They could easily take my bikes away, and yet somehow I had this feeling that they wouldn't. Czechoslovakia was Yamaha's last fully-supported world championship meeting. Bill and I had known they didn't intend to race for the whole year and were well aware that from then on we would have to pay all our own expenses, including mechanics. A fine arrangement, I don't think. The factory would, however, continue to provide the equipment. All in all, I would say that the last three rounds - in Finland, Ulster and Italy - cost Bill and I something like £1,000 each, quite a sum 42 years ago. They were very emotional affairs. Our disagreement in Brno caused us to split into two teams in the race paddocks of the remaining three GPs. My helper and driver was the great Roy Robinson, while Bill had his friend Ron Eldridge. Our two mechanic helpers were great friends and travelled together in our two transporters, but this created embarrassing situations for them at circuits and prizegivings. I must give them great credit, they worked well and were discreet.

I was banking on Yamaha's racing philosophy. I hoped that they wouldn't really mind which rider won, as long as he was riding a Yamaha. Moreover, they already had three world titles en route to Hamamatsu: the 125cc, the 250cc manufacturers' and the 125cc riders'. Obviously Bill or I was going to win the 250 crown, so there could be a fourth title for Yamaha. Moreover, it didn't need a particularly astute mind to see how much media publicity would and could be generated from the feud between its two riders on Yamaha machines, even if such a scrap was below Japanese so-called dignity. And - a big 'and' - in my decision to go against team orders, the factory wouldn't give a hoot about bad blood between their riders if they weren't going to be racing as a factory team next year.

I went off to telex the Czech GP results to Japan, fairly sure that the bikes would be mine to continue racing for the remaining GPs. I kept my fingers, and legs, crossed awaiting their reply.

Remember in 2010 how the Yamaha riders, Rossi and Lorenzo, caused great excitement with their pulsating and angry scraps? It infuriated Lorenzo so much he complained to Yamaha boss, Masao Furusawa, who gave Vale a dressing down, even though Lorenzo had the championship 'sewn up' after Rossi's earlier misfortunes and Dani Pedrosa's serious accident. Lorenzo only needed to finish in the points, whatever, to win the title. I guess Jorge wanted the post-race acclaim which Rossi seemed always to monopolise, regardless.

Along with the results I put in another request for Yamaha to confirm their plans for 1969. Back came a telegram instructing me to follow team orders and keep good relations with Bill Ivy. No mention of 1969. Another telex from me pressed the point. No reply. Now I knew the answer, my suspicions were confirmed. There would be no Yamaha team next year. And if there was no Yamaha team in 1969, why should I let Bill Ivy win the 250cc title in 1968? You may be in the wrong, I told myself, but you must go for it.

Now that the rivalry between Bill and me was out in the open, thanks to him shouting the odds to all at Brno and exposing the Yamaha team plan, my outlook on life brightened considerably. Anyone with a sense of humour could see the funny side of the situation. For example, with the Japanese personnel gone, the Yamaha 'team' became a split camp. Yet our two English mechanics thought the whole thing was a load of nonsense and stayed the best of friends, although they made sure to keep their bikes safe and secure, just in case. As far as they were concerned a bit of rivalry was a good thing, as long as it remained friendly. Unhappily Bill and I went to the other extreme, and I don't think we spoke to each other again after the Czech Grand Prix.

I remember those two mechanics giving me a nasty shock one day, though. As I've said, I didn't think Yamaha would take their bikes away from me, but I was never entirely sure throughout the rest of the season. I felt my suspicions confirmed when I flew into Rome airport for the Vallelunga races held just outside the city. There to greet me were Roy Robinson and Ron Eldridge, Bill's mechanic. Ron came over to meet me, looking rather embarrassed and uncertain.

'Er, ah, Phil, er, look, sorry, but there's this Japanese gentleman over here waiting for you.' He motioned over to where Roy was standing, apparently in conversation with a smartly-dressed oriental gentleman. My heart sank. They'd come for the bikes.

'The bikes?' I asked.

'Don't know,' said Ron. 'He's not saying anything. Just wants to talk to you.'

Well, I thought, I've bluffed it through so far; I might as well try to bluff it through further. I strode over to where Roy and the Japanese guy were standing. When Roy saw me coming, he moved away, looking serious. He wished me luck as I passed him. The Japanese gentleman smiled pleasantly as I came up. 'Well then, what's the problem?' I said, getting my attack in first.

He stared at me, his face blank, uncomprehending.

'What you want? No take bikes,' was the sense of what I said in jumbled Japanese.

His face beamed. I spoke Japanese. He was off, a torrent of words that I couldn't understand. What the hell was going on? I looked around for the mechanics and there they were, killing themselves laughing. The penny dropped. This poor guy had nothing to do with Yamaha. He was just some innocent traveller they had button-holed to play their little joke on me. I could have throttled them. However, I soon saw the funny side which showed just how much more relaxed I'd become since the bust-up.

Another example came in Finland, and again the story had a funny ending. Unfortunately, it began with a robbery of sorts - kidnapping might be a better word - and ended up with me being too close to prison for comfort.

A lot of us were staying in the same hotel, one of the big, castle-like places in Imatra, and just lazing around the bar, talking, when in walked Rod Gould with this absolute knock-out girl, a real dream. Beautiful long blond hair, one of those perfect tanned Finnish bodies and pert bra-less boobs. This, I thought, was very unfair. Rod's days as Yamaha wonder-boy were still to come, while here was I on the way to my fourth world title. They sat down at a table, so I strolled over, as casually as possible, to ask Rod if he and his friend would like to join us for a drink. It was a good ploy. Get Rod involved with a group of riders and I knew he'd be unable to stop talking about racing. That way I'd get my chance to talk to the young lady. She made life very easy by speaking good English. Would she like to go downstairs? There was a disco and we could dance while Rod was talking. She smiled, we told Rod and went downstairs. Was she going to the race I asked, thinking Rod would be taking her along. But no, she wasn't. I was very surprised. Would she like to go? Oh yes, very much, she replied. Well, I'll take you, I said. From the look on her face I knew that I'd said just the right thing. Sorry, Rodney.

If I was going to take her to the racing, of course I'd have to know where she lived so that I could call for her. Perhaps I could give her a ride home... if she wasn't waiting for Rod, that is. But she wasn't, and she'd love a ride home, especially as she lived several miles away from the hotel. I was glad I'd driven my Mercedes up and not bothered to fly. We nipped upstairs, said goodbye to the guys, and waltzed off.

Finland's a funny place at that time of year. It doesn't stay dark for very long. By the time we got to the young lady's home it was still dark. We'd had a nice, lingering kiss and cuddle and things were just starting to get interesting when it started to get light. It was probably about two o'clock, no later. I looked out of the car window, and over to one side, not too far away, I could just make out this large, forbidding building through the gloom. 'Oh that,' she said when I asked what it was. 'That's the prison. My father's chief warder there!'

Well, you've never seen such a gorgeous creature put inside her front door so quickly, or so chastely. And before she could even ask me in for a drink, the new 125cc world champion was hot-footing it back to Imatra.

She did come to watch the racing at the Imatra circuit and we spent the following days sight-seeing with her friends and then we said our fond farewells before I drove three days back to England then flew to Guernsey. But I still don't know if Rod's ever forgiven me. Mind you, if every time he thinks of me he remembers her hair and her lovely figure, I don't blame him!

If my lovely lady did get to the Grand Prix, she'd have seen me in fine form, notching up a 125 and 250 double. The 250cc race was hair-raising, though, thanks mainly to a sudden heavy shower between events. Instead of blasting away right from the start, as I had in Brno, I decided to change my tactics, as I had against Redman, letting Bill take the lead while I slipstreamed him and let him wonder what I was up to. The way Bill rode, though, it wasn't easy. While Redman rode to percentages, Bill took it to the limit and often beyond. My heart was in my mouth more than once, especially when we diced for the lead, but once in front I felt I had control of the race.

But Bill wasn't letting up, determined to get the better of me. In the end he overdid it. One minute he was there on my back wheel, the next time I saw him he was on his back on a stretcher. Without him there to push me, I eased off a little to make sure of finishing, but I later discovered I'd had to break the old lap record to keep ahead of Bill during our dice. It was a good win, one that I felt proud of and one that gave me the same number of wins as Bill in the title chase. However, I had two seconds to his one, so for the first time that season I was sitting at the top of the table. Two to go and the championship still open, to win - or to lose!

By the Finnish meeting, my rebellious behaviour was having wider-reaching repercussions than I had anticipated. At Imatra the FIM stepped in, in the person of its president, Henry Burik. It had already been discreetly pointed out to me that the FIM recognised that some form of riding to order was acceptable - in an unofficial sense. What was not acceptable was making loud noises to the press that I was no longer racing to orders. That, they said, was tantamount to admitting that we had raced to orders all along.

Mr Burik's message was less complicated; and more to the point. If, during the remaining rounds, it was evident and could be proved that I had deliberately slowed to let Bill win, the FIM would bring proceedings against me. Against us both, in fact. On the surface it looked as if I was cornered. On one hand Yamaha were still saying, 'Race to order or else... ' and on the other the FIM were saying, 'Race to order and you're out.' In reality, though, the FIM's stricture was just what I needed. I was virtually under orders from them to race to win. I assured Mr Burik that was exactly what I intended to do.

Between meetings Bill was doing everything possible to salvage what he saw as his title. Yamaha sent him some special exhaust systems, and he even experimented with Norton forks to try to improve the handling. In my corner, Roy worked away magnificently, using parts we had had all season, often toiling through the night to bring the machines to perfect pitch for race day. He was great and I couldn't have asked for a better person to have around. I don't know if he agreed with my stance, but he stood by me throughout and I was really grateful.

I was also grateful to the dear old Dundrod weather when it started raining before the 250cc race of the Ulster GP. It was said that Bill didn't like rain, and after the way he had beaten me in the 125 race earlier I knew I might need some help. Man, that 125 was some race, with both of us blazing round that fast circuit over the ton. The lap record had stood to Bill at 99.53mph but by the time we were through I had upped it to 102.44mph in a last-lap attempt to catch him, to no avail, as it turned out: I over braked and shot down the slip road at hairpin on the last lap.

Whoever said Bill Ivy didn't like racing in the rain had to think again after the 250 race. I decided to make him chase me from the start, thinking he'd hold back in the wet, but not Bill. He tucked in behind, slipstreaming me all the way. Every time I glanced behind there he was. His brave riding was rewarded too. When the rain stopped, the bloody track began drying fast, but before I had time to take advantage of it, Bill swept past into the lead and I chased him hard. Those 90,000 spectators had every pennyworth of their money from that one race alone. But I paid the price for dicing so close to him. His back wheel threw up a stone and it smashed a hole in my radiator. That was the death knell for my engine as the precious water trickled away and I was forced to stop. Bill picked up a maximum eight points and I had none. His total was forty-six from five wins and a second. I had forty-four from four wins and two seconds.

Relaxing with Bill at the 1968 Belgian GP, I won the 250; there was no 125cc race that year.

So now, it was all down to Monza. I had to win there or everything had been in vain. Yet I nearly didn't make it to the grid for the 250cc event in Italy. You'd think, with so much depending on that one race, that I'd have taken things easy in the 125, especially as the title was already decided and there was rain about. Oh no! Bill Ivy was in that race. It shows how deep our feud was that I was prepared to fight him all the way. My determination cost me one hell of a pearler and it could have cost me much more. Bill and I, wheel-to-wheel as usual, had swept among some tail-enders in the final stages. Bill picked them off like Clint Eastwood in a western movie but I was held up. Once through, I tore after Bill, caught him, and then tried to get round him at the Lesmo One curve. Wrong! I overdid it running off the dry line and down I went. I must admit I got to my feet very gingerly, praying that nothing was broken. Nothing was. The bike was in a mess, but nothing that a few good kicks and a tug here and there couldn't fix. The engine was only firing on one cylinder, but that was enough to get me home, more than six minutes behind Bill. However, because we had both lapped the rest of the field, I still took second place crossing the line at no more than 20mph. They'd even started the presentations by the time I arrived, and Kawasaki rider Dave Simmonds, who thought he'd taken third place, had to stand down to make room for me on the podium. It goes to show that there's no sense in quitting.

In some ways, after all the brouhaha and the wheel-to-wheel dicing that had lit up the season, the 250 race at Monza was something of an anticlimax. It started well. For the first three laps we were at it hammer and tongs, with my fastest lap a heart stopping 113.15mph on a damp track. But once again Bill did one of his disappearing acts, tripping along the grass verge after trying to take me at Parabolica, the last corner. Apparently he had to fight desperately for control to avoid coming off, and the effort took a lot out of him, both in physical effort and time. That's it, I thought, the title's mine. All I have to do is finish. It didn't matter if Bill was second, for I knew how the FIM would determine the Championship in the event of a tie. After the fiasco with Mike Hailwood the previous year I wasn't taking any more chances. The FIM would add up the times where Bill and I had finished first and second to each other. The rider with the most time difference would be champion. Well, we had both finished in only three races to date at Assen, Sachsenring and Brno - and it was my super-fast ride in Czecho that would decide it. Taking those three races into account I was 2 minutes and 5.3 seconds up on Bill.

Our feud made racing more exciting for the public. 'Keep your head when all about you are losing theirs.' (Rudyard Kipling)

But in motorcycle racing you can take nothing for granted. I should have known better than to think that the title was mine. One moment everything was lovely, the next second the bike was misfiring. And as if that wasn't enough, it began slipping out of gear. This is it, retribution. All the gods in Japan had been called out to wreak vengeance on me for disobeying my masters. I slowed down, I let it settle, I coaxed it. There were times when I felt like kicking it right between the cylinders but I didn't. And it came good again, getting me home safely. Bill, back in second place and almost two minutes behind me, was having trouble with a cylinder, too, but like me he nursed it through. Don't think we were hanging about, though. My winning average was 110.737mph compared with Agostini's 110.759mph on an MV in the 500cc race. The track must have been quite damp and tricky as my winning speed on the slower Yamaha twin in 1964 was 113.90mph.

So that was it, celebration time. But it was hard to feel elated and impossible to recapture the feeling I'd had when I beat Jim Redman in 1964. That had been factory against factory, rider against rider. With Bill and me it had been more like civil war, rider versus rider in the same factory team. And, as in a civil war, there had been too much bitterness. Too many words had been spoken in anger and frustration; too many words had been written, mostly biased against me. The victory felt hollow.

There was too much that couldn't be forgotten in such a short time. I had won my title, but what had I proved? In the final analysis we had each won five races, we had each been placed second twice.

According to the record books I was 2 minutes 5.3 seconds better than him in the four races where we'd both finished. But what about the races when only one of us finished? What about Bill's magnificent TT rides? What about my fightback to victory at Francorchamps? If the statistics proved anything at all, they merely proved that we were two great, brave and possibly stupid riders and Yamaha didn't know how to handle that. But it did make for some very exciting races, kept the fans very emotional and gave the Press much to report when watching our 'no holds barred' racing on the limit - and sometimes over it.

I was champion, but in all honesty I couldn't say I was better than Bill, I could say only that he wasn't better than me. If I hadn't ridden to team orders in those earlier races it might have been different... probably would have been, because I'm sure I'd have beaten Bill at Assen and Sachsenring. On the other hand, if Bill hadn't stuck to team orders, would I have won the 125 title? His being small and light did give him extra speed and acceleration. The little man was superb on the 125s; much happier on them than I was. The four-cylinder 250 was my bike. I'd helped develop it and I'd tamed it. I didn't want the 125 title: I wanted the 250. I thought I'd earned it, and if Yamaha knew they were pulling out of racing I thought they should let me have a final crack at it on a full works machine. I didn't want Bill to ride as my number two. All I wanted was a fair chance to go for bust. The factory wasn't prepared to give me that chance - so I took it and I don't regret that.

I do feel sad that I lost a good friend on that day in July 1969, and I never had the chance to explain myself to him.

5

Back on top - as a privateer

New Year's Day, 1969 was my 30th birthday. I could look back on a rich past of four world titles, of world travel, of success, excitement, and satisfaction. But if I looked to the future there was nothing. In November, my race machines, engines, and spares had been returned to Mitsui, Yamaha's UK importer and for the first time in seventeen years I was without a bike of any kind. Family life was virtually non-existent; my marriage, shaky for so long now, was finished. At the age of thirty I was stepping into the world afresh.

What I lacked was direction. For a while I had entertained vague thoughts of retiring.

I had a young family to support and the marine business in Guernsey seemed to not be progressing. I badly needed someone to confide in, yet I couldn't bring myself to talk even to my mother about my problems, personal or business. To all outward appearances I seemed to be relaxed, sociable, easygoing. Deep down I was tense, confused and unhappy. There was only one person who understood what I was going through, but she was in America.

I had met Madeleine in October at Brands Hatch, at one of those end-of-season meetings on a cold, rain-swept day. I wasn't racing myself but was there as a guest. Madeleine was with a girl-friend, helping to entertain a friend's son. She'd never been to a race meeting before and in fact knew nothing about motorcycle racing. But she did know something about powerboat racing, and, possibly through this connection, thought I looked familiar. She and her friend had taken refuge in the clubhouse.

'Who's that?' she asked her friend.

'Surely you must know him,' her friend said. 'That's Phil Read. He's world champion in the 125 and 250 classes. Would you like to meet him?'

1968 Boat Show

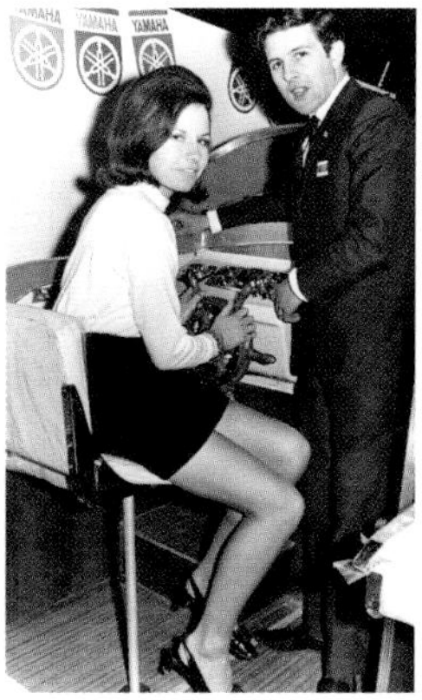

They came across and I found Madeleine Carroll attractive, amusing, and positive. Most of all, I found we communicated well together. Such a change from the here-today gone-tomorrow dolly birds who'd filled the past eight months or so. *Go Away Little Girl* was a pop song that had a lot of air-time in the 1960s and if any lyric was applicable to my life at the time, that was it.

With Madeleine it was different; very different. She wasn't impressed by what I was. She'd met famous people before. Dublin-born and just a few years younger than me, she'd come to London after dropping out of university - and that was in the days before dropping out was the fashionable thing to do. Much of her year at university had been spent working as an extra for five pounds a day on the Kim Novak film, *Of Human Bondage*. It's typical of her generosity that the day's wages were always shared with her friends. Now she was personal assistant to the managing director at the head office of the successful transfer lettering company Letraset, and had already worked in the United States and various parts of Europe. I was pleased that her interest in me was as a person, not as a world champion in a dangerous sport.

At the time we met she was working and living in London, but we'd hardly known each other long before she was offered, and accepted a job marketing a Letraset product in the States. So I was on my own. Not for long, though. Happily for me, though not perhaps for the company, the American venture failed to take off and Madeleine returned to London. We both realised how much we'd missed and needed each other. It was only a matter of time before she moved into my flat on Streatham Common. It was a far cry from my ex-Consulate home on Guernsey, but I was happy at the prospect of us building a new future together.

With Madeleine's enthusiastic encouragement, the twin problems of the Guernsey business and my racing future were resolved, if not immediately settled. She and my mother travelled together to Guernsey, where they went through the business accounts and came to the conclusion that the best thing I could do was to sack my manager who had been trying to take control of it and sell the company. As far as racing was concerned, I would ride as a privateer. It seemed that I'd gone full circle. I was starting again, this time with the support of Madeleine.

With Madeleine after my 1974 500cc Belgian GP win

By now the 1969 racing season had already started and I needed to move fast to get things organised. My initial problem was money: it was scarce, very scarce and I needed enough to buy two bikes plus spares and a van. I still had the Mercedes, but I was reluctant to sell such a good car, for there was always the hope that I would one day be getting something from the sale of the business. Good old Castrol Oil topped the list of trade sponsors, coming up with a useful sum, and without them I don't know if anything would have been possible that year. Chris Lowe of Motor Circuit Developments, the company that owned many of the British tracks, was a big help too, offering me good start money to race what were, after all, just production machines, not works bikes. Still, I was a double world champion, and he knew I'd be concentrating my efforts on British short-circuit events.

My two bikes were both over-the-counter Yamahas, a 250cc TD2 and a 350cc TR2, air-cooled piston port twins developed from the factory world beaters I'd ridden in 1964 and 1965. I got what I thought was a reasonable deal for the two machines, plus spares, direct from Yamaha in Japan - until I learnt that they'd sent Bill Ivy a new 350 absolutely free of charge. A subtle rap over the knuckles for me, perhaps!

As I had expected, Yamaha had decided to withdraw from world championship racing. What was completely unexpected was the beautiful miniature golden pagoda from Yamaha's President that had arrived just before Christmas 1968. With it was a framed letter of appreciation, which said:

Mr Phil Read,

This is to appreciate your past excellent achievements you have made in the series of the World GP races on YAMAHA machine, and also this is to express our sincere gratitude for your ungrudging efforts which have contributed to elevation of YAMAHA reputation throughout the world. We thereby present you with a souvenir in honour of your entire cooperation offered to YAMAHA.

(Signed) Genichi Kawakami
President of **YAMAHA MOTOR CO., LTD.**

There didn't seem to be any bitterness there!

All in all 1969 was a decent year, with victories over Agostini at Cadwell Park and Brands Hatch to boost my morale. Money was often a problem and things like having all my tools stolen didn't help. I even knew I'd have to give the TT a miss as the ACU didn't pay appearance money, then. That's how low finances were at one time, but then Benelli offered me a ride on one of their works bikes. It was only a one-off affair, I understood that, but with times as they were, any competitive machine was welcome.

I'd already ridden for Benelli once, racing their 350cc four at the previous year's Vallelunga meeting near Rome. I had been on my way there, remember, when those two mischievous mechanics played that trick on me at Rome airport. Benelli's four-cylinder bike was impressive, and I'd got close to beating Agostini on the MV, pressing him so hard that he took four seconds off the lap record. Bike for bike, the Benelli was not as fast as the MV, but with enough development, especially a move to four valves per cylinder, I felt it could be just as good. There were handling problems and brake fade, too, but these were things that could be remedied.

Benelli seemed to be as impressed with me as I'd been with their machine; so much so that race chief Innocenzo Nardi-Dei had offered me a contract for 1969. But at that time, with so much uncertainty surrounding Yamaha's future - and my own role in the company's plans - I delayed making a final decision. This didn't please the Italians. They like you to be at their beck and call, jumping when they snap their fingers! Consequently I was surprised at the offer of a bike for the Isle of Man 250cc race and even more surprised when told I'd be riding to win ahead of their works rider, Kel Carruthers. Perhaps I should have been suspicious. As it turned out, the bike they prepared for me never looked like finishing, let alone winning, and as soon as I began dropping back during the race, the pit gave Kel the signal to go ahead.

My machine eventually stopped, while Kel went on to win and eventually take the 250cc championship. As I said, I'd never thought of racing my own bikes at the TT that year, but someone obviously felt it would be 'good insurance' to know exactly what I was up to. As for Kel, I like to think I played a part in setting him on the road to a great career after Benelli. He and his family came to stay with us before he set off back to Australia and I suggested he go via America and see Don Vesco. The Californian Yamaha tuner had invited me over, but because of my family commitments I didn't want to go. Kel went to see him and they worked together, especially on exhaust development to get great results from a 350cc Yamaha in 750cc racing. That led to Kel moving permanently to the US, becoming heavily involved with Yamaha International and being mentor to Kenny Roberts in his entry to grand prix racing in Europe.

TT 1969; a frustrating time with a second-rate Benelli

On the 250cc Benelli four at the TT before it stopped

TT practice on the Benelli

A problem with that 1969 season had been finding a mechanic, as all the good ones seemed to be working for other riders. The person I decided I wanted was Dutchman Ferry Brouwer, famous in recent years for running his Yamaha Classic Racing Team after selling his Arai helmet distribution business..

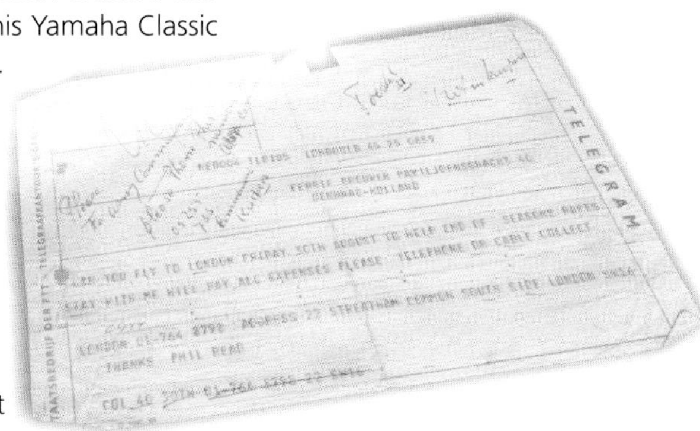
TELEGRAM
FERRIE BROUWER PAVILJOENSGRACHT 40
DENHAAG-HOLLAND
CAN YOU FLY TO LONDON FRIDAY 30TH AUGUST TO HELP END OF SEASONS RACES
STAY WITH ME WILL PAY ALL EXPENSES PLEASE TELEPHONE OR CABLE COLLECT
LONDON 01-764 8798 ADDRESS 22 STREATHAM COMMON SOUTH SIDE LONDON SW16
THANKS PHIL READ

Young Ferry had trained as a mechanic, had a burning passion for bike racing, and spoke English. He suddenly appeared as a helper with the Yamaha team during the 1968 season and at first I didn't take much notice of him. But in time I realised that he was one of those valuable mechanics who listened to what changes you asked for and then carried them out. But there was a snag, he was doing his compulsory military service. Fortunately he had friends on the Dutch racing scene who had pulled some strings to get him time off and when I sent him a telegram asking if he would join us for the end-of-season meetings he agreed to help at the Italian GP, held at Imola that year.

Benelli approached me again at Imola, but only when I'd made the fastest time in 250cc practice on my own Yamaha! This time the deal was that I should finish behind Kel who was now seriously chasing the 250cc title. That would give him a comfortable ride and, of course, remove me from the opposition - a clever scheme. For all this, I would receive absolutely nothing from the factory, just the honour of riding their superior bike. Well, I may get fooled once, but never twice. As politely as possible I turned down their offer.

I was sufficiently annoyed at Benelli's game to play a little joke on them. I said I didn't want a ride their machine as one of the four-cylinder Yamahas was being flown in especially for the meeting. And when the Benelli people arrived at the circuit the next day to see four pipes sticking out from under a blanketed Yamaha with green 250cc plates, they wanted to talk terms all of a sudden. Nothing doing, I said. After all, I was going to win on the four-cylinder, wasn't I? Except that there was no four, of course, just my TD2 with a couple of extra pipes rigged on to it. And as this was the first time I'd raced either of my production machines in such top-class company I was actually far from confident of winning.

All-out on the Benelli down Bray Hill, where were the spectators?

10
Benelli
10

Yet when it came to the day that mattered, those bikes were superb. Ago's absence from the 350 race gave the rest of us a chance without the all-conquering MV. Silvio Grassetti, on an MZ, and I gave the Sunday crowd their money's worth. For a time, I thought I was actually going to walk away with the race. I was out in front and no one looked like touching me. But then I couldn't understand why Ferry held out my signal board telling me: 'Stop. Exhaust'. Why should I stop, I thought. I'm doing fine. It took a spectator to put me right when powering out of the hairpin, I noticed this guy pointing furiously at the bike. I looked down. Hell! The exhaust bracket had broken and the pipe was trailing on the ground. (A working pipe, by the way, we only put the false pipes on the 250.) No wonder Ferry wanted me to stop. I passed the pits, signalling that I'd come in next time round, and hoped they'd be ready for me. They were. Ferry had snipped some wire from a nearby fence. He was a great lad for on-the-spot improvisations. A few twists of the wire with pliers secured the pipe, but by now Grassetti had taken the lead. With only two laps remaining I was still six seconds down, and there seemed no way I could narrow the gap. But Silvio is Silvio, and on the last lap he took every available opportunity to give the crowd a victory salute. He did it once too often, losing concentration and took a short trip over the grass when rounding a corner. That was all I needed. Riding like mad, I caught him... and then passed him. The crowd were in hysterics. Silvio was furious. But was he himself to blame for his defeat? Oh no. That's not the Italian way. The steering was no good, the brakes were no good, a hundred and one other things were no good.

Mind you, if anyone had any reason to find excuses I could have provided plenty myself. Thanks to a paddock mishap on the day before the race, I nearly didn't have a bike. Ron Herring, who'd been helping Ferry most of the season, was thrown off my 350 while warming it up for practice. He had accelerated down the warm up area, then - just like some club racer - squeezed the brake too hard, locking the front wheel. Next thing he was on the ground. His arm was grazed down to the bone, a footrest on the bike was damaged, the screen shattered, the fairing split, and the exhaust dented. It was only due to an all-night session by Ferry and Ron that I took my place on the grid. Still, I wasn't complaining. You don't after that lucky win, do you?

The 250cc race was even better; especially as I got off to a bad start. For the first three laps, Carruthers, Gilberto Parlotti on another Benelli, Dieter Braun on the MZ, Kent Andersson on a production Yamaha, and Börje Jansson on a Yamaha-Kawasaki were locked in combat. Then, just as I was closing on the leading bunch, Kel made a break. I'd already clipped 1.4seconds off Mike Hailwood's lap record making up lost ground and my Yamaha was going like a dream. Threading through the early pacemakers I eased into second, and now had my sights set on Kel. Two laps later I was with him and the duel was on. Although the Benelli was faster, my Yamaha had better acceleration, especially uphill, and we had a rare old tussle, out-braking each other at every corner. Into the last lap I edged ahead. Crafty Kel sat in the slipstream, waiting to pounce in a final effort but I drained every ounce of power out of the bike and it was just enough to keep ahead to the finish-line. There was just one-fifth of a second in it. Fantastic! Third place man Andersson was fifty seconds behind us.

Travelling back to England later that night I was given another example of mechanics' on-the-spot improvisations. The four of us, Madeleine, Ferry, Ron, and myself, were in my Jaguar Mk 2, while the bikes were on a four-wheeled trailer I'd had specially built at Brown & Greens, where I had served my engineering apprenticeship in 1962. Somewhere near Varese I felt the trailer pulling to the left and, looking in the mirror, saw a cloud of smoke billowing up. One of the tyres had punctured. There was no spare, so we took the wheel off and continued with three wheels at a slower speed until Varese where we hoped there might be something open. Some hope! The whole place was sound asleep. We were cruising slowly around the town when Ferry suddenly shouted: 'There's a Mini! Stop the car.'

Sure enough, there in a car park, all alone, was a Mini. Our trailer had Mini wheels. Out jumped Ferry, raced over to the car, quickly looked about him, opened the boot, and came racing back with the 'borrowed' spare wheel under his arm. 'Now go like hell,' he said, tumbling into the car after the wheel.

I needed no second bidding. We were off to fit the new wheel in a quiet back street, then drove to the border in fear that someone had seen us, taken my Jag's number, and that we'd be arrested at the border.

With the Guernsey business still not sold, money was a continual problem, so an invitation to race in South Africa that winter was most welcome. The trip was organised by Frank Perris, who was then looking after Mike Hailwood's house-building business in South Africa. It promised to be a good series, for he'd booked Ago as well. Looking back on my first visit to South Africa nearly ten years before, this one was quite a contrast. As well as having my own bikes, the Yamahas, I had Madeleine and Ron Herring with me.

The South African heat was the same as ever, though, and we almost melted when we stepped out of an air-conditioned car at Pietermaritzburg, venue of the first meeting. Ron immediately foresaw tuning problems, but we reckoned that if the locals could cope with conditions like these, we could too. Nonetheless, I must admit I was pretty apprehensive when we had to jet down my Yamahas' carburettors to an almost unbelievably small size. I was sure they'd seize. They didn't. They went really well, carrying me to a hat-trick of victories including the South African Grand Prix. Ironically, the man giving away the prizes that day was my old rival, Mike Hailwood - retired from motorcycling since 1967 and then living nearby. I think he got a bit browned off as I kept coming up for the trophies. 'Not you again!' he said with a smile.

At the Kyalami circuit near Johannesburg, which is over 1000 feet above sea level, we jetted the carbs down even further. In fact, by the time we'd finished playing about, we were a hundred sizes down on the jetting normally used in Europe. I kept my clutch trigger finger at the ready every time I went out, yet there were no hair-raising moments or unexpected thrills for the fans. We really turned it on with some close racing in Jo'burg, after agreeing that the last lap would count, showing the mainly car-minded fans that close dices between bike riders could bring them to their feet. I think they all agreed afterwards that racing motorcyclists were not such a second-class breed as they'd thought.

It was at this time, on my return from South Africa, that I bought a new home, Thatched House in Oxshott, Surrey. Madeleine and I had already looked at some houses late in 1969, among them this one. With its beautiful thatched roof and big garden, it had enormous potential. Back from South Africa we found it was still available. By now the sale of the house and business in Guernsey was going through, so there was the possibility of sufficient capital to buy the house and its big double garage... as well as setting up for the 1970 season, of course.

Ferry had been able to spend Christmas with us and we badly wanted him to do a full season with us in 1970. But his military commitments seemed insurmountable.

Then Madeleine sat down and wrote several letters, including one to the Dutch Minister of Defence and even one to Queen Juliana of The Netherlands. I must admit I was sceptical about whether that would work. But the phone rang one afternoon. It was Ferry. His superiors had decided that he could be released from his service several months early, allowing him to join us for a full season. He didn't have to do his military service immediately. I looked at Madeleine in amazement. With a woman like that around me, I thought, how could I fail?

Ferry would spend a lot of time at our home and really became part of the Read family - he even used to call me Dad and Madeleine Mum!

There was another pre-season problem however, money. I needed a large amount to secure our new home: bear in mind that it can be a problem for a racing motorcyclist to obtain a mortgage. Still, I had until April to find the extra cash, and there were the three early-season Italian meetings in March, for which I managed to negotiate excellent start money. Moreover, the news from Guernsey was good, so we set off for Rimini in good heart for my first race.

Our spirits sank, however, when we reached the Adriatic resort. Rain was lashing down, and except for one solitary, bedraggled figure, the promenade was deserted. I stopped the car and leant out, asking in halting Italian where the paddock was.

'Just down the road, mate.'

I looked more closely. It was none other than the late John Brown, racing reporter for *Motor Cycle News*. No journalist could have been more welcome that cheerless night. He climbed in, and we came to a gentleman's agreement that we'd provide him with food and drink in return for him showing us to the race paddock, 'And to help us unhitch the caravan and fix the awning,' added Madeleine.

'Where did you find this woman,' John groaned.

Still, I was glad of his help... and he certainly earned his keep. The caravan was new, the awning a test of skill and ingenuity, and it was an hour's rain-soaked work before we could relax.

Overnight the rain cleared, giving us better weather for practice, but Sunday was yet again wet and cold. So cold, that when I came in after winning the 250cc race I had to thaw my hands out in a bowl of warm water. Madeleine came up with a good suggestion: wear a pair of her tights under my race leathers. She had another good idea, too,

'Crepes Suzettes when you've won this one.'

'Fantastic,' I said, my mouth watering already as I went out for the 350cc race. But we never did get around to eating them that day.

I jumped into the lead right from the start, leaving Agostini and Pasolini trailing in my spray. In those conditions, once you were out in front there was a good chance you'd stay there provided you kept going, and I think Ago must have realised his chances of winning this one were slight. Perhaps there was something wrong with his bike, I don't know, anyway, he pulled out... and did that Italian crowd give him the bird, along with rude signs!

They soon had reason to cheer, though, because Paso took up the challenge, giving me quite a tussle and actually taking the lead. I didn't mind too much if Renzo did win - the difference in prize money wasn't so great - but I wanted to put on a good show to improve my bargaining power for better start money in future Italian races. The next thing I knew I was in hospital. My pelvis and wrist were broken; my back was agony.

It seems that I had actually re-passed Renzo. The only trouble was that I did it without the bike, sliding down the wet road on my back fast enough to overtake the Benelli. I had tried to out-brake him, but due to the heavy rain I couldn't see white lines on which I braked and the front tyre lost grip and down I went.

For two days I hovered in a state of semi-consciousness, and when I did come round I was greeted by the news that I would have to stay where I was, flat on my back, for at least five weeks. Five weeks! They must have been out of their tiny Italian minds. Thanks to some very good Italian friends, especially Vittorio

Fabbri, I was moved to the hotel Cavellino Bianco at Riccione, where Madeleine and I stayed, free of charge for four weeks. That's the warm and generous side of the Italian nature. The hotel proprietor Eugenio and his family couldn't do enough for me.

Vittorio drove me to Bologna for regular, even daily, visits to the Institute where I was treated by the legendary racing man's medic Dr Costa, son of the Imola organiser. And all this time my body and left arm were encased in plaster. I thought sometimes I'd itch to death. During my convalescence in plaster, I am sure Ferry had a good time living in my caravan by the beach, not having to spend all his time fixing my broken machine.

However, hospital treatment was expensive, and with high fees to be paid I was determined to race at Milano Marittima. It was agreed by the club president to pay me extra to cover 'medical expenses', which would enable me to race at their event. All that remained was getting rid of the plaster. The doctors weren't keen on the idea. In fact, they were so upset when I tried cutting it off myself with a pair of metal cutters that they inserted a metal rod to stop me having another go. I wasn't to be beaten, though, and in the end I persuaded a reluctant Ferry to hack the plaster off with a pair of chicken secateurs. His hands were blistered from hacking through the metal rod.

I still had to ride the bike and just starting it was hard with a weak leg, not to mention the difficulty of pulling in the clutch lever. The best Ferry and I could do was cut off my reduced wrist plaster and tape on a strip of aluminium. My race start was slow as I struggled on the grid before the machine chimed in, by which time the rest of the field were half a lap ahead of me. Hell I was mad; bloody mad and frustrated. I ignored the pain as best I could and set out to chase the backmarkers. I gradually worked my way through the field, and once I had the leader in my sights I thought a second place would not be so bad, but he made the mistake of waving back at his fans. He crashed. I screamed past to take the lead and the chequered flag. Every muscle, every nerve was protesting. But, I thought as I limped off to the organisers' office for my money, it was worth it.

Imagine my surprise and anger, then, when the organising club failed to pay over the extra fee, agreed on earlier in the week by their President. Madeleine and I shouted at them; but they shouted back. To have seen Madeleine that afternoon you'd have thought King Kong was about to take her on a tour of New York. She really went to town on them. But to no avail, apparently the President had disappeared with most of the club's cash. Finally, they locked us in the room and refused to let us go until we agreed to their terms. What could we do? We had to give in, I needed whatever cash we could get to drive home and to pay Ferry.

That unhappy experience taught Madeleine and I never to trust an Italian organiser again. No matter what they promised, we had to get it in writing. At least we had learned what was to prove a valuable, if expensive, lesson. In later years I learned to demand that my appearance fees are transferred to my bank account before I leave home.

There were further shocks in store when we returned to England and started moving into the Oxshott house (which, I notice came on the market at a cool £1.75m in recent years). At last, it seemed, the boat business had been sold, so there was money to pay for the house. Yet on the very day that we moved in, before we'd finished unpacking, the estate agent told us we would have to get out. There'd been a last-minute hold-up and the money from Guernsey hadn't come through. And when the estate agent said 'out', he meant 'out'; there and then. He was a typical petty official with a jumped-up sense of power, out to make the most of the situation.

A friendly bank manager is probably now a thing of the past, but back then we were lucky in having one. When I explained my predicament he was more than sympathetic; he was extremely helpful. Not so long before, Barclays Bank had invited me to their Sportsmen's Luncheon, which I'd attended with the manager of my Streatham branch. He'd introduced me to some of the directors, who showed quite an interest in motorcycle racing, and I must have made a good impression because they agreed to give me the needed loan for six months. We had somewhere to live, but it also meant I had to make quite a bit of money racing in 1970, just in case something went wrong and the sale of the business didn't go through. It was quite a pressure, I can tell you, racing in the knowledge that every start, every finish, every bonus was essential. Happily the money did eventually come through and I was able to repay the bank loan. But for a time it was very unpleasant indeed. Racing creates enough pressures of its own without other complications.

As in 1969, I concentrated most of my efforts for 1970 at home, still racing the 250 and 350 Yamahas, both of which we'd improved radically by fitting my own-designed Phil Read frames. A total batch of 20 were made for me by Eric Cheney, famous for fabricating off-road chassis.

For economic reasons, I had to give the Isle of Man a miss, but I did manage a trip to Assen for the Dutch TT and, later in the season, to Monza for the Italian. I had intended to do the Belgian as well, but start money of a mere £100 was ludicrous. It wouldn't even have paid expenses, so I refused to race. Not that my gesture made any difference. Other riders accepted the miserable pittance offered them, and one leading rider told me at the time that he was going to race in East Germany for just £60 start money - and that was for two classes! It just shows how little the organisers valued the riders and how they took advantage of those who didn't stick together for their own future benefit.

Instead of racing at Francorchamps I went to Switzerland for a hill-climb event. That was my first taste of this predominantly Continental sport, and I thoroughly enjoyed myself, actually taking my first trip up the seven-feet wide track on the local butcher's Kawasaki. I did well, finishing second to European champion Walter Rungg. The prize money was quite reasonable, but the start money was fantastic; ten times better than I'd have received in Belgium. Moreover, the organisers were not out to make a fortune, as they were at Spa-Francorchamps. Nor was it just about money. The Swiss couldn't have done more to make us welcome, treating us like royalty.

The Dutch TT, 1970 on my private 250 Yamaha lifting the front wheel and wearing the first ever coloured leathers.

I loved the challenge of becoming a privateer racer with little sponsorship.

With Kel Carruthers on 250s at Mallory Park, September 1970

There were money problems at Monza. Even before practice started, the Grand Prix Riders' Association (GPRA) tried to force the organisers to pay acceptable money to its thirty or so members. It had been agreed that Kel Carruthers and Rod Gould, both GPRA members, would ride because of the crucial state of the 250cc World Championship, but the rest of us agreed to boycott the event. In the end, like so often before, the boycott failed simply because the organisers could always find enough able Italian and other European riders to replace us. The meeting would go ahead without us and we'd be the losers. So we were virtually forced to race. Any protest would be meaningless.

As I saw it at the time, the only hope we had of improving our lot was for each national federation to draw up a grading list and set start money for each individual rider. Otherwise, the problem would keep recurring, and riders would always be the losers financially. I felt, too, that it was time for an association to concern itself with more than money. Safety was becoming a major issue, with bikes going so much faster and organisers failing to provide safety measures to counter the escalating risks.

Ironically, after my decision at Imola the previous year, I decided at Monza to help Kel Carruthers in his bid to retain his world 250cc crown after hearing that Rod Gould, his main challenger, was planning to enlist the help of New Zealander Ginger Molloy if the title chase went to the deciding round in Spain. As it happened, Rod decided the title with a great win there at Monza, holding Kel and me off all the way. Consequently there was little I could do but hold third spot, an interested spectator to their hard battle for the victory.

That third place brought my championship year to a close, but already I was looking ahead to 1971 with a view to a serious bid for my fourth 250cc world title.

One of the things that had spurred me into action was an approach from MZ earlier in the year to ride for them in that 1970 season. However, it was only a one-year contract and the total payout offered was insufficient for us. But I was intrigued as to why they wanted me for a year only. I made some enquiries, and gradually the story came out. Silvio Grassetti had agreed to ride for them in 1971 and had guaranteed them the world title. Italian promises again!

The feeling was that Phil Read was over the hill as far as a world title bid was concerned. Over the hill, my foot! I'd show them. It was just what was needed to get me going.

That streak of obstinate determination began to shine through again.

At the Race of the Year at Mallory Park, I renewed my acquaintance with that phantom photographer of Fuji, Gary Nixon. He and French-Canadian Yvon du Hamel were making their first visits to Britain. Though they had some trouble getting used to the shoving and pushing on corners, they soon found their feet, racing well enough to give us the first inkling of the major force that Stateside riders would become. Come to think of it, Gary and Yvon were really up against it that day because they had to use the unfamiliar push-start method, since the British authorities were still reluctant to employ the US-style clutch starts.

On a personal note, that Race of the Year meeting was memorable for another Phil Read innovation. It was the first time I raced with the protection of a Bell Star full-face helmet, although I later changed to a more comfortable and lighter Premier helmet.

The old 'Rebel Read' tag re-appeared in 1970. The occasion was an international meeting at Cadwell Park, Lincolnshire, where I'd entered for the up-to-1000cc race as well as for the 250cc and 350cc events. The trouble originally

On my 350 in the 1970 Snetterton International

came about because the gearbox in my 350 broke in practice, so I decided that rather than withdraw, I'd ride the 250 in the open category race. The problem was that there'd already been a practice for this class, and I badly needed another practice session to sort out the 250 Yamaha against the bigger bikes. Well, I thought, I'll take the 250 out in practice against the bigger capacity bikes when they're practising for their own class. At least that's what I thought. When it came to going out on the track with the bigger bikes, with whom I'd be racing, the officials wouldn't let me onto the circuit. I argued my case, which escalated into a row with Chas Wilkinson, the Cadwell circuit owner. It was made very clear to me that if I didn't like it, I could go home. So I did, loading up and setting off back to Oxshott as the fans were still pouring into the circuit.

Apparently this wasn't what Mr Wilkinson meant when he said I could go home if I didn't like the way he ran things. The next thing I knew, the organising Louth Club had sent an official complaint to the ACU, who in turn called a court of inquiry. However, when I explained my actions, the members of the court said that, in the circumstances, they had a great deal of sympathy for me. My own sympathies lay with the fans who had paid to watch me race. But I do have my principles and I hope my fans understood my reasons for leaving Cadwell that day.

The winter of 1970-71 was spent at home; renovating and decorating our new home, and planning my campaign with Ferry and Madeleine to try to win the 250cc world championship, hopefully my fourth. I had already made up my mind. I was going to be the first privateer to win that title. But the opposition was strong, for as well as Grassetti's MZ bid, Yamaha, through its Amsterdam-based racing department, was forming a team headed by reigning 250cc champion Gould and Sweden's Kent Andersson. For a horrible moment I thought this new Yamaha venture would seriously obstruct my hopes. In retrospect, during that season, I can't speak too highly of the help and encouragement I received from Mr Naito of the Yamaha factory. He had been my team manager during those stormy days with them, but if I had ever made life difficult for him, he certainly didn't carry any grudges. During that 1971 season, nothing was too much trouble for him to help me.

Malcolm Edgar of Castrol was generous. Everything was looking good, even before the season was under way. I treated myself to a Rolls-Royce Silver Cloud II, which, at that time, was not expensive. With the amount of travelling I had to do, I figured it would be a good investment; comfortable, reliable, morale-boosting and, it has to be said, ideal for pulling a caravan. If I was trying to be the best in the world again, the least I could do was show a little class. Besides, Madeleine was expecting our first child in April, which meant we would be travelling around Europe with a very young child. There was never any question of her not travelling; she was an essential part of our team. So it seemed a good idea to have a car that was fast, powerful, and comfortable. It also seemed a good idea, having divorced Ann in 1969, to get married, which we did in February 1971. We hoped it would prove a good omen for the season ahead.

Snowballing the photographer, myself and Madeleine with Paul and Maggie Smart, Christmas 1970

Leading Ducati team-mate Gilberto Parlotti at Ospaedaletti, if the Bologna 500cc V-twin had been shorter, lower and lighter it would have challenged MV Agusta.

'Experience: that is the most brutal of teachers. But you learn, my God do you learn'. CS Lewis.

I enjoyed a few flirtations, too, in Italy - with factories, I hasten to add and not with the ladies. Benelli were first to woo me. Now without Renzo Pasolini, who had moved to the Aermacchi factory owned by Harley-Davidson in those days. (The former Aermacchi plant by Lake Varese is the production base of the present day MV Agusta marque). Benelli asked John Cooper and me over to Pesaro to test their latest bikes, which we did. We were both enthusiastic, and the factory people talked of the possibility of our racing production machines during the season. But talk is cheap in Italy. The delivery of the finished article is another story. So it was with the Benelli venture, as they were only lukewarm about future prospects the next time we met. When the promised production machine failed to appear only two days before the Imola meeting, I knew it was time to part company.

Ducati were my other suitor, offering me a new 500cc V-twin engine fitted in a British-designed Seeley chassis to race in all the grands prix, as part of their plan to extend their racing activities. I spent three days at their Bologna factory, but while I was quite keen, I wasn't going to count my chickens on their proposal, either.

I eventually tested the Ducati at Brands Hatch in the summer of 1971, but had a big-end failure when holding third place at the Silverstone International. I only rode the V-twin in one GP at Monza, where I took fourth and I got a second place at the end-of-season international at San Remo in Italy. In that race, I realised the Ducati lacked the necessary level of performance because Ago just kept pulling away from me on his MV. Also, I found the chassis designed in England by Colin Seeley about four inches too long and too high. Yet I think that if Ducati had been prepared to spend more money that 500 could have been an MV-beater. As it was, they chose to concentrate on bigger V-twin desmo engines.

I had spent most of the season racing only my two faithful Yamahas. Still, when you're a privateer you look at any good bikes going, and Benelli and Ducati were just two factories who had approached me.

At different times my name had been linked with Kawasaki, BSA (who were racing 750cc triples) and Jawa, just as in 1969 I'd been involved with the Spanish Ossa factory and the ill-fated Read-Weslake engine venture.

I'd first become involved with Weslake through journalist Charlie Rous, who'd been down to their factory in Rye, Sussex, to see a new engine they were working on, a 500cc dohc twin based on Dan Gurney's Eagle Formula 1 power unit. With their fine reputation for engines in the car racing world, Weslake seemed to have the technical knowledge to make a competitive motorcycle engine, and reports of strong horsepower figures from the 500cc twin during development raised hopes for the all-British project.

I felt confident enough to outlay a lump of money when Ray Creek, of the Read of Leytonstone dealership, offered me his company's share in the venture, suggesting that I was the best person to help develop the idea. At the time, it looked a worthwhile investment, both from a racing and commercial point of view and I enlisted the help of racer, tuner and chassis builder Dave Degens. On the racing scene, there was only Agostini and the MV to beat in the 500cc class, and on the business front the big Japanese two-strokes had yet to dominate the category. There was a definite market opening for a competitive British machine. However, all this was speculation, for we still had to see how the bike performed. Judgment day came at Lydden Hill circuit after several months spent sorting out the frame and components. The test was disappointing - the machine was slow! The compression ratio was so high it took two men to push the engine into life, and when I closed the throttle there was so much drag from engine braking that the rear wheel almost locked up solid.

Hockenheim 1971, I had passed Ago's MV, but was robbed of a win by a broken gear selector spring.

The bike went back to Rye for modifications while I continued racing my two Yamahas. Weslake and I came together again in Ulster for 1969's early-season North West 200, where the engine seized in practice and I realised that this particular project would never be competitive. To be frank, it was absolute crap. As a result, I decided to withdraw my interest. Over a period of six months I'd spent a lot of time and money on the project, and I was most grateful when Harry Weslake considerately returned the money I'd originally paid in. It was money I could ill afford at the time. It was all so frustrating. I'd entered the project with a feeling of optimism that here could be the answer to Britain's decline in the motorcycle racing industry. Instead it was just another disillusioning blow for me.

Back to the 1971 250cc world championship. The first round was a new event on the calendar: the Austrian GP at Salzburgring. A specially-made circuit in picturesque surroundings, the Salzburgring was never very lucky for me, and that season's opener set the pattern. I was an early retirement from the 250 race with piston seizure, while in the 350 I was sidelined by a broken gear-lever. My only consolation was that Rod Gould also failed to finish in the 250. The only rider to give any sort of challenge to Grassetti and East Germany's Günter Bartusch on their flying MZs was 20-year-old Barry Sheene on a factory Derbi twin. The brat who'd been a cheeky nuisance at the TT in 1961, when I'd raced his dad Frank's 125 Bultaco, had come a long way and was obviously going further. Watching the cockney boy's confident chasing off the MZ team-mates that day, I realised I had better watch out for him in the near future.

After the disappointment in Austria I picked up maximum points in the next three rounds to top the 250cc championship leader board. Yet at one time it looked as if the hat-trick would never happen.

Hockenheim, venue of the West German GP, provided all the drama we needed. First of all the 250 Yamaha packed up after just two practice laps. Piston seizure again! I was ready to pack up, but Ferry said he'd work all night on the engines if I stayed. But when I went out for another practice I crashed heavily at the newly constructed chicane, concussing myself and badly gashing my elbow. That put paid to Friday's practice.

Saturday morning's practices were run on a wet track, so considering the conditions and my physical state, my qualifying times for both the 250 and 350 events were pretty good. I wish I could have said the same for my arm. The morning's exertions had started it bleeding again and it was obvious that I needed stitches. Helmut Fath took me to a local hospital, where seven stitches were inserted in my elbow. At the same time, Ferry took the bikes to Fath's workshop at Ursenbach to be fettled for the race.

On my return to the circuit I noticed that the track had dried out. That's good, I thought, but I was in for one almighty shock. The organisers had decided to hold an extra practice session during my absence and, as a result, my morning's times were no longer fast enough to qualify. Not only that but they refused to heed my arguments. If they wanted to alter the regulations they could, and there was nothing I could do about it. You can see why I felt so strongly about the need for a united and powerful riders' association.

Happily the ACU came to my rescue, through Cliff King, their steward at the meeting. He supported my case and, very reluctantly, they agreed to let me start. But only from the back of the grid! And to complete my tale of woe, someone broke into our caravan and stole all my money. I was beginning to wish I'd never heard of Hockenheim.

However, Sunday's racing more than made up for the frustrations, and even though gearbox trouble yet again put me out of the 350 event when leading, I had given Ago a hard time while still involved in the race. But the 250 was a different story. Lady Luck smiled favourably on me - and on my spare, three-year-old engine. Ginger Molloy and Rod Gould weren't so lucky. After hotly contesting the early laps with me, both fell by the wayside with engine trouble, leaving me an easy winner by some twenty seconds from runner-up Klaus Huber.

Luck stayed with me in the Isle of Man too. Well, in the 250 TT race at least. MZ had recruited Peter Williams to ride the Mountain Circuit, so I knew I'd be in for a tussle. But I also knew there was a question mark over the East German two-stroke's reliability, especially on such a demanding circuit. Obviously the tactic was to try to break the MZ by setting a fast pace from the start in hope that Peter's bike, when trying to stay with me, would blow up. Off I went at a terrific rate, lapping at more than 100mph from a standing start, and incidentally recording the only ton-topping lap of the race. My tactic worked like a dream. As I pulled in for fuel at the end of the first lap, Peter rolled into view shaking his head disconsolately. When Chas Mortimer's Yamaha went sick too, it looked to be just a matter of finishing to pick up another fifteen points. However, Rod Gould was still out there, climbing through the field, and by the end of the third lap he was up in second place. But a pit stop at the end of the fourth and penultimate lap relegated him to fourth. This lost him vital world championship points, as events would prove.

It was my fifth TT victory, yet strangely enough my first on a 250cc machine. The feeling was still the same, though, even if it was my fifth win. No rider can ask for more than to ride to a world championship victory before his home crowd on the tough 37¾ mile circuit. The programmes and Union Jacks waved frantically as I went through Governor's Bridge for the last time, weaving round the two slow corners before accelerating down the final straight to the flag. The playing of *God Save The Queen* as I stood on the victory podium was fantastic! You can't beat that feeling of achievement.

On the long Mountain Circuit, our new extended fairing came into its own. The belly pan now stretched right back to the rear wheel and side panels were added below the seat. Improving aerodynamics is a really effective way to gain speed, since air drag increases as the square of speed and there's no getting over that.

At one time it looked as if I'd be in for a TT double that year, but the gremlins had taken a real dislike to the 350 Yamaha and I was forced to retire while leading. The frame broke and the chain jumped off! It was pretty galling, but my fault perhaps for not using the better and stronger Seeley chassis instead of my own. That Mountain Circuit, with its jumps, bumps and leaps, its climb up to 1,500ft beside Snaefell and sections over secondary roads, helps to develop great bikes as well as great riders. Let's face it. When the Mountain was first used in 1911, much of the course was just loosely-surfaced cart-tracks and the whole idea was to test the motorcycles of the time to the limit.

Starting the 1971 250cc TT alongside Peter Williams on a factory MZ, he retired and I won at 100mph on my Yamaha, transformed into a world championship-winning machine with a Cheney frame, Dunstall disc brakes, a Fath dry clutch, electronic ignition and fuller fairings. A wind deflector on the screen is a special Isle of Man fitment.

Still, I came even closer to that elusive double at Assen, when I enjoyed one almighty scrap with Ago and the MV before the gearbox started playing tricks again, and I felt I'd done well to limp across the line holding on to second place. It looked as if I was in for a hard time in the 250cc race, too. The opposition appeared to be bringing in all the big guns they could find, for as well as Rod and Kent, Yamaha Amsterdam had Chas Mortimer, Barry Sheene and Paul Smart on the grid. You can see why I was anxious to record best time in practice and secure the prime spot on the grid for a fast getaway. If I'd found myself stuck behind that mob I could've said goodbye to my chances.

Once out in front after a flying start, though, I found the sternest challenge coming from an unexpected quarter, a young Finn by the name of Jarno Saarinen. And I mean it when I say I felt very relieved when his Yamaha went sick, leaving me to canter to a relaxed twelve seconds win over Dutchman Theo Bult. For that meeting a second mechanic, American Steve Johnson, had joined our team.

My luck ran out at Francorchamps. Or did it, I wonder? Perhaps I ought to say I was very lucky. What happened was one of those small, inexplicably careless things that cause accidents. In this case one of the front brake's hydraulic hoses rubbed against the front wheel, wore away and leaked. How can such a thing happen, you might ask. And I'd answer, 'Very easily'. Because it was typically hot, we'd whipped off the front mudguard that morning to let more air around the engine, so reducing the chances of overheating. It was a last-minute decision, and in the rush we forgot to tape the hydraulic pipe back properly. So simple; so nearly a disaster. I'd almost completed the first lap and was approaching the La Source hairpin when I discovered I had no front brake. You have to be virtually down to running pace when you go through the La Source, so there was no way I could tackle it. My only option was the escape road, which also happens to be the main road leading up to Francorchamps village. Except that on race days they close off the circuit with a pair of enormous metal gates. And it was to these gates that I was travelling at high speed, using my back brake and gearbox to haul me down from 130mph to near standstill in one hundred and fifty yards: an impossible task. The trackside faces were just a blur, but I'll never forget the look of open-mouthed horror on the face of a track marshal at the gates. Nor my own inexpressible feelings, as now only at 20mph I skidded into the gates. I was so drained of all feeling, all emotion, that all I could do was just sit there, unable to move, my limbs quivering. I'd never been so frightened in all my life. Grassetti won the race, with Australian John Dodds second and Dieter Braun third.

Shaken up by my near-death experience, I was furious with Ferry. Whether he personally had attended to the brake line or not, I saw the condition of the bike as being ultimately his responsibility. He took umbrage because we hadn't invited him to dinner that night, came and handed his paddock jacket back the next morning and cleared off.

That episode caused a rift between us, to say the least, but I am happy to say that the chilly relationship between us thawed over the years. Ferry was a key member of our world championship team and he went on to be very successful, running Arai Helmets in Europe, but never lost his passion for bike racing as is proved by his fantastic Yamaha Classic Racing Team.

Meanwhile, the 1971 title race was hotting up, and a third place in the East German GP at Sachsenring wasn't enough to take the pressure off. Rod Gould pulled himself back into contention with a second place and Dieter Braun improved his chances with 15 points from his win. It was still a Communist country then and any contact with the West was strictly controlled. So, for fear of an anti-government demonstration by the very large crowd of more than 300,000, the West German winner's name was not announced. Eventually, by word of mouth, the expectant crowd discovered the result. The jubilant East Germans, who refused to acknowledge any difference between their countrymen, celebrated in protest, throwing beer bottles and wrecking the local town.

We were now halfway through the series with the championship points as follows; Read 55, Marsovszky 40, Braun 35, Grassetti 33, Dodds 26 and Gould 25.

Depressingly, we remained in Eastern Europe, travelling south to Brno for the Czech GP and its road circuit. I say depressing, for I found that Eastern European countries did depress me. I'm not being political, just making a personal observation. Driving through different countries, you see more than the major cities and industrial centres. I began to get a picture of what life must have been like for many ordinary people there. In the Eastern Europe of those days I found buying food, petrol and sometimes clothes, difficult and when you got them, they were second rate. Things had probably become more difficult since World War Two and I gave a big sigh of relief when we returned to the West.

The people, though, were a different story. The bike fans were fantastic. Just imagine at the Czech GP, there were close on 400,000, pouring in from all over Eastern Europe. It was impossible to have enough stickers and badges to give away, and you could spend weeks signing autographs and still they'd keep coming, sometimes begging for any old pair of jeans we had.

Before a purpose-built track opened in the 1980s, Brno was one of those road circuits where houses and telegraph poles added to the hazards of riding powerful bikes at high speed. The roads weren't always that good either, and you could bet your life something was going to work loose on your bike after a few circuits. With me, it was the front brake lever during practice on the 350. The thing just snapped off in my hand when I braked from high speed! There was nothing I could do about it, and down I went, heavily and badly, breaking my shoulder and suffering concussion.

Obviously, the Czech race was out, so my main interest was in knowing how soon I'd be able to ride again. Sweden was only two weeks away. But do you think I could get any sense out of the doctors treating me? Come to that, do you think I was getting very much treatment? Madeleine said that not one nurse came into the room during the four or five hours she sat watching me regain full consciousness. Little wonder, then, we decided there was no way I'd stay in that hospital any longer.

I told Madeleine to get American mechanic Steve to load up the van, ready to set off, and to come back later with my clothes and the Rolls. It was early evening when she returned. It was quiet; there were few people around. I pulled my clothes on, not easy when one arm is in a sling, while Madeleine kept a look-out. She was holding Pip, who was then four months old.

Once out in the corridor we walked along as naturally as possible, trying to look like visitors. It was like something out of a wartime escape film. Naturally we came up against an obstacle. The lift was closed, and we couldn't get anyone to operate it. More to the point, no one seemed interested in helping us. Madeleine held the key to getting out - Pip. She pinched him in a very tender place which, naturally, made him cry. Immediately some officials appeared, and showed us the way out! We were on our way home, with me driving one-handed across Europe.

That shoulder injury was a curse, taking ages to heal properly. As it was, it was almost two weeks before I could even use my arm to ride a bike, so Sweden was out of the question. That made it imperative that I ride in the Finnish Grand Prix at Imatra the weekend after Sweden. I took a series of pain-killing injections, finished tenth, and received a solitary point for my pains. It had cost hundreds of pounds to transport my bikes and ourselves to Finland, but you never know when a championship point might come in handy, and it did.

With wins in Sweden and Finland, Rod Gould looked to be coming good just at the right time, and only one point separated us when we arrived at Dundrod for the Ulster round. Consequently, neither of us was very amused when it was suggested that the race might not even count towards the title. It appeared that the organisers had cancelled the 50cc event after receiving only eight entries for that class, leaving the meeting with just four classes; one under the permitted minimum for an FIM classic event. Happily, after much deliberation, the FIM gave their blessing. We were racing in earnest... and, of course, in the rain. Once again the weather was in my favour, for Rod, though he had set fastest time in practice, was not a good rain racer.

I found a couple of others who were, though: local boy Ray McCullough on the Queen's University Belfast-tuned Yamsel and that flying Finn, Jarno Saarinen. What a battle it was. But when Jarno dropped back I pulled ahead of McCullough and held him at bay. Then, with one and a half laps to go, she seized. I couldn't do anything but sit there in the rain and listen to the crowd roar McCullough home eighty seconds ahead of Saarinen. Rod, who had just tootled around to make sure of finishing, picked up five points for sixth. I was sick.

As far as races go, the 1971 250cc Italian GP was a little classic. It was so close that only two-fifths of a second separated the first four in a blanket finish. My only complaint was that I wasn't involved, being pipped on the line for fifth by Saarinen. My only consolation was that Rod came out worst of the front-four finishers, leaving him only seven points ahead with a round to go. The winner was Swiss-domiciled Hungarian rider Gyula Marsovsky. Australian Johnny Dodds was second and Grassetti third.

The deciding round was the Spanish at the Jarama circuit near Madrid, a new one to me although it had been used for the 1969 Spanish GP. I spent a whole evening walking round it, looking for all the bumps and visualising how to ride the corners. My shoulder was still stiff and painful, parts of my body were still blue from bruising, and when I woke the next morning for the first practice rounds I was aching all over from the previous evening's exercise. I hoped it would be worth it.

With only the six best rounds counting towards the world championship, I knew that the title was mine provided I finished in the top five in this race and ahead of Rod. At this stage, my scores stood at 15, 15, 15, 10, 1 and 5, totalling 61. Rod's were 8, 5, 12, 15, 15, 5 and 8, making 68. If neither of us finished, the title was Rod's.

We were at it hammer and tongs right from the start, but this time it was Rod's turn to run out of luck. I was already beginning to show an edge when his Yamaha developed ignition failure, and as he slowed I pulled away. I know how he must have felt as he struggled on, desperately coaxing his machine along in the hope that I'd blow mine up. But I didn't, and when Jarno put in a challenge I was quite happy to let him take the lead rather than do anything that might prevent me finishing, like crashing. Second would do very nicely, thank you. And that was where I finished. Rod had been forced to stop altogether, when lying fifth. The world championship was mine by just a few points - what a traumatic yet glorious season Team Read had experienced.

If I was asked how I felt about winning my fifth world title, I think I'd say 'great satisfaction'. It had been a long hard slog, a lot of careful organisation and planning and great work by my faithful engineers, mechanics, helpers and my main sponsor, Castrol Oil. There was no factory to fall back on when times got rough and no big sponsor to write out cheques when something special was needed. Yamaha and Castrol, as I've said, were generous, but for all their help I estimate that winning the 250cc World Championship in 1971 still cost me a great deal. It was worth every penny of it, too, and if I sound proud of my achievement, I am. People found it easy to write me off after 1968 and that hurt. I knew I was still good enough to win again, and if it meant doing it on my own, with Madeleine and baby Pip, then that was all right by me.

Much of the credit was due to Helmut Fath's engineering genius, for the way he prepared my engines. On my 250 he re-engineered the crankcase and changed the crankshaft balance factor, while his dry clutch was worth its weight in gold. After the early season Italian events I wasn't at all happy with the bikes, so Helmut stripped them and rebuilt them as carefully as possible with help from Ferry. They weren't quite as good as the works bikes, of course, but there wasn't much in it.

We took Helmut to Madrid with us as part of the team for the final round. He wasn't needed to work on the bikes. We just thought he'd be a psychological weapon, making the opposition wonder what we were up to. I felt he'd be a good omen, too. And when that title was mine, he deserved to share in the celebrations.

Helmut and Ferry were part of my team, the first private team to win a world championship.

TT plug checks at Creg-ny-Baa with Helmut Fath and Ferry Brouwer, while Madeleine sits in the van with Phil Jnr

6 Goodbye Isle of Man

When the 1971 season was over and we tried to wind down, Madeleine and I realised that although it had been a marvellous year, we were completely exhausted, both mentally and physically. As long as there had been a goal in sight, be it the next Grand Prix or the ultimate aim of the world title, we had driven ourselves on regardless.

Long hauls back and forth across Europe with baby Pip, the racking agony of a half-healed injury that even pain-killing injections could never fully subdue, the sleepless nights going over and over in my mind how to improve the bikes, how to beat Gould, Grassetti or Saarinen, focusing on their weaknesses, had been my strengths. And if I did sleep, there was little peace for Madeleine, lying half awake in case Pip would cry and disturb us. It's not surprising we sometimes vowed 'never again'. But when we started saying, 'Wasn't that great? Remember the time...', we knew that 1972 would see us chasing round Europe with the rest of them.

What I couldn't decide, though, was the extent of my involvement in the world championship. Naturally I wanted to hold on to my title but as well as being Phil Read, motorcycle racer, I had by then established Phil Read International, a company dealing with Premier Helmets and motorcycle clothing. This time I was determined to be fully involved in running the business. I didn't want a repeat of the Guernsey affair, so it meant being more than a figurehead. That, however, means time, something a privateer on a world championship campaign has very little of.

My involvement with Premier Helmets had begun at the Ontario Speedway in California the previous October after being invited to race a Kawasaki that turned out to be hopeless. When I was there, I saw these mind-blowing helmets with brilliant designs and metalflake finish. I arranged with Premier's owner Chuck Tinch to distribute his products in the UK. He sent over 200 helmets in time for us to take them to the London Racing & Sporting Show in January. We priced them at around £40 and completely sold out. The garage at the house in Oxshott became our distribution centre and Premier stepped up their European marketing operation, opening a factory at Shannon in Ireland.

As it turned out, my racing plans were virtually taken out of my hands by the last person on earth I expected to hear from. It was early May and I was in France, relaxing after winning the 250cc French Grand Prix at Clermont-Ferrand. On that Monday as usual, I phoned Barbara, my secretary, to see if there had been any important calls.

'There's a telegram just arrived', she said, 'from a Mr Agooster' (She was from north of Watford).
That's no mister, I thought. That's a Count! Count Corrado Agusta! My legs were turning to jelly as I put the phone down. There was a silly grin spreading across my face.
'What's the matter with you?' Madeleine asked.
'Count Corrado wants me to call him,' I stammered. 'What do you think he wants?'

Stupid question. It was pretty obvious what he wanted and it was equally obvious why. Two days earlier I'd given Ago and the MV team a terrible fright by leading Italy's hero in the 500cc French Grand Prix - and that was on my 250, except that it had yellow plates and was designated a 354cc Yamaha. Mind you, I knew I couldn't actually finish the race, because I'd be disqualified as soon as it was discovered to be only a 250cc machine, well below the minimum capacity for the 500cc class. That would have meant I'd lose my start money. So it was convenient to discover an ignition fault and retire with a few laps to go. That not only saved my start money, but helped Ago save face a little. But I must admit I rubbed it in a bit when I walked past the MV pits and jokingly quipping to the team, 'Please ask Count Agusta if he wants me to help Ago this season.' Someone obviously took me at my word.

Seriously, though, MV did have problems at the beginning of that 1972 season, the biggest of them being Jarno Saarinen and his fast 350c Yamaha. I didn't go to Nürburgring for the first round of the World Championships, but by all accounts Jarno was in truly superb form when he beat Ago in the 350 and I saw his brilliance for myself when he gave Ago a second dose of the medicine at Clermont-Ferrand. It half-crossed my mind then that Ago could do with a team-mate to relieve some of the pressure, and now, it seemed, it could well be me. It was a dream come true, like a jockey nearing the end of his career being asked to ride the best racehorse of the day in the Derby or a racing driver being offered a Formula 1 Ferrari. I had hopes of reaching new horizons with a possible contract to race the equivalent of Ferrari of the motorcycle world, the elite team of MV Agusta and Agostini.

Chasing Saarinen in the 1971 250cc Spanish GP

Ariston

The Read family afloat at Riccione in 1972; left to right; Mike, Phil Jnr, Graham, Roki, Madeleine and a slim me

John Player Norton days

But there was no rushing in like some eager schoolboy. Not with Madeleine around. 'Just phone him and tell him you're busy this week,' she advised. 'Say you'll try and see him next week.'

Anyway, that coming weekend I was contracted to ride a 750cc machine for the newly formed John Player Norton team at Cadwell Park, so I had a good enough excuse. To tell the truth, I was a bit scared the Count might not want me if he thought I was stalling in order to improve my negotiating position.

But there was no difficulty. He said it was okay and that I should make an appointment through his secretary, for Tuesday of the following week after I'd returned from Cadwell.

I could still hardly believe it. We hitched up the caravan to the Rolls and set off immediately for Italy and MV's Reparto Corsa (racing department), Mad and I talking all the way of the best way to negotiate that possible contract with Agusta. This may have been the chance of a lifetime, but I'd been around too long to let my natural desire to ride for MV Agusta override financial considerations. By the time we arrived at a camp site by the shores of Lake Varese we thought we had it all worked out. All that remained was to meet the Count and be asked to test their bikes. And just to make sure we arrived in time the following Tuesday, we nipped off to check the route to the nearby Gallarate factory.

Back to England and the down-to-earth realities of the John Player Norton. My involvement with Norton had come about during the winter through Frank Perris, who was the team manager. I can't say I was over-enthusiastic about the bike, powered by an obsolete road engine, as a racing machine. So it must have been more a genuine feeling of patriotism than any belief in its race-winning potential that made me sign a contract. A contract? More like 200 John Player ciggies per week! But to be fair, I did also get a red leather team jacket.

My first race for the team was in the Daytona 200 in March, open to 750cc machines under rules that were being broadly adopted worldwide as Formula 750. The other rider was Peter Williams who, as a Norton employee, was heavily involved in machine development. We were up against Kawasaki and Suzuki's new three-cylinder 750cc two-strokes and some fast 350cc Yamahas. I was 22nd in qualifying and Williams was 23rd, which said all that needed to be said about the Norton's top speed. Even so, I managed to grab the lead midway through the race, only to run onto the grass when coming off the ultra-fast banked section of the track, thanks to only having a single front disc brake which caused the forks to twist, reducing the braking effect. Then I had a hopelessly slow fuel stop. The other teams had the latest quick-fillers enabling 10 second pit stops but we had to make the best of some crude cobbled-up equipment. It spilled petrol over me - not nice.

Despite losing a lot of places while refuellling, I managed to work my way back up to lead the field, but again overshot onto the grass under braking to finish fourth behind three 350cc Yamahas. Willy's bike didn't last the race and neither did any of the Japanese 750s, which destroyed rear tyres. I've never had a high opinion of Daytona. It's what we called a Mickey Mouse circuit without any interesting corners, where everything is down to maximum speed and fast pit stops. I always had too much going on in Europe to want to race much in America.

It was significant that Britain's best scorers in the 1972 John Player Transatlantic Trophy meeting that Easter were Ray Pickrell and John Cooper, neither of whom rode JP Nortons. I followed them on the British score sheet, to finish fourth overall for the series without a win to my credit.

With the new 750cc Norton at Daytona, 1972, I led the race mid-way through and finished fourth, the first four-stroke home. Team manager Frank Perris is on the right.

I next rode the Norton at Imola, in a 200-mile race for Daytona-type machinery held in April. Shortly before setting off, I had a spill at Brands Hatch when an exhaust expansion chamber on a 500cc Suzuki two-stroke I was testing dug in at Druid's Bend. Then, in the first practice at the Italian circuit I was brought down by a slippery painted line on the inside of the Acqua Minerale corner. The little finger on my right hand needed stitches after it was worn to the bone by the road when squashed under the bike's fairing as we slid, and has never been the same since. In the race I collected another fourth place, with the twin front disc brakes I had asked for. A big factory effort by Ducati paid off, with Paul Smart and Bruno Spaggiari taking first and second on 750cc V-twins. It was a milestone moment for Ducati and led to the 'replica' 1000cc Paul Smart Limited Edition being released many years later in 2006. Poor Ago, my new MV team-mate did his best with a fantastic and determined ride on an unwieldy 750cc MV Agusta with shaft-drive until he retired with engine trouble when leading the snarling pack.

At Cadwell in May I had to be satisfied with yet another fourth, but by then my mind was on other things.

That same Sunday that I was at the Lincolnshire circuit, Ago raced MV's new four-cylinder 350cc machine to victory in the Austrian Grand Prix. So things would be happier in the MV camp, I thought. But if I hoped this would help me drive a good bargain, I was sadly mistaken. I found the contract was already prepared, the terms were fixed. Trials were arranged at Modena and Monza, and if they were satisfied with my performances I could sign the contract. If I signed I would race for MV at Imola in the Italian Grand Prix. That was the deal. Take it or leave it. Naturally, I took it but subject to them paying all my expenses. MV, however, did make one concession, allowing me to ride my own 250cc Yamaha and the John Player Norton. Never before had they let one of their riders also ride for another team.

I stood up to go back out to the waiting room, where Madeleine was sitting surrounded by businessmen waiting to place multi-million-pound orders for the helicopters that were Agusta's prime industry. Much to my surprise, the Count indicated that he'd come out with me and with his revolting little dachshund at his heel he strode out to shake hands with Madeleine and welcome her to 'the family'.

Funnily enough, the thought that kept running through my mind was the fact that I'd not been kept waiting for more than half an hour to see Count Agusta. His late elder brother, Domenico, had a reputation for keeping people waiting for days. I was told a good story about Gary Hocking's first meetimg with the dictatorial Count Domenico Agusta. Gary would secretly have been pleased to race the factory MVs for no payment, but the longer he was kept waiting, the higher he pitched his fee and on the third day they agreed an amount which made Gary very happy. If the Count had seen him within hours of arrival he might have signed Gary for little or no payment. But if you are a billionaire money is immaterial: only a means to an end.

I was robbed of Daytona-winning fame by a long 25-second fuel stop and poor brakes that caused me to twice run off into the dirt when leading.

Enzo Ferrari, whom I once met with Madeleine at his factory, was said to consider his drivers as disposable. And it was said the only time he was seen crying was when he was leaving the Italian tax office.

The trials at Modena and Monza went off without any hitches. Friday morning saw me at Imola. But there was no fairytale debut for me on the proud red and silver Italian machines. Far from it. For a start, I was to ride 350s only. Not until I had served my apprenticeship was I to be given a 500 machine. Seems they thought their 500 was super-powerful and I needed more experience. I was only five times world champion, had raced 500cc Gileras and was racing 750cc Nortons. To my way of thinking it was nonsense, and if anything, it should have been the other way round. The 500 was heavier, but more flexible and controllable. And at a time when both machines had to be ridden to the limit against faster Japanese machines, the 500 was the more stable.

Still, I learned the hard way. It's a waste of time trying to make any kind of point to an Italian if he has made his mind up. For Friday morning's practice, my machine was fitted for the first time with a new Oldani front brake fitted with powerful Ferodo racing-grade green linings. Fine by me, if they were properly chamfered at the ends. What I didn't know was that Arturo Magni, the veteran MV team manager, had chosen to ignore the instruction from Oldani that the powerful AM4 linings should on no account be fitted. Signor Magni warned me to be careful with the front brake before my first practice session.

I could tell at once that the brake was unusually fierce, but I wasn't in any hurry on this strange machine and was going to work myself in gently before getting on the limit. By the end of a few laps I felt more like opening it up a bit, touching maximum down the final straight, swooping through the fast left-hander and then sitting up for the right-hand kink before the hairpin. I touched the brake. Zonk! It locked. Before I knew what was happening I was on my backside, skittling down the track at 130mph. Alongside me was the bike, the beautiful, almighty MV, disintegrating before my very eyes. The petrol tank went flying, the fairing shattered and after it hit the barriers, one wheel went bouncing down the track on its own. 'Please, God,' I thought as the world kept changing direction, 'Let me die now.' But he didn't. I came to rest on the muddy grass verge. Which is where Barry Sheene found me. Was my face red with embarrassment! Here was I, Britain's Prince of Speed, lying in the mud, having to accept a pillion ride back to my pits from the Young Pretender. Not only that. What would Magni say? What would the Count do? I clambered off the back of Barry's Yamaha and walked up to Magni, my leathers caked in mud. 'Can I have a dustpan and brush?' I asked.

'A brush!' he said, looking shocked. 'What do you want a brush for?'

'To sweep up the bits of the bike,' I replied.

There were no repercussions, though. I think everyone was simply relieved I wasn't injured. The bike, however, was a write-off. The Oldani brake? It was never used again. Instead of accepting that they'd made an error in fitting the green linings, MV preferred to put the blame for my crash on the brake manufacturers. Another classic example of Italian excuses! To be fair to Arturo, he did say sorry to me later as did Rocci, Count Agusta's son.

The actual race was not my best performance either, by any stretch of the imagination. That day, Agostini was at his brilliant best, and after a short and hectic scrap with Saarinen - at one time their bikes actually touched - he simply wound on the power and roared away from everyone. I just managed to keep him in sight from third spot, but then an inspired Pasolini came storming through to take me, and eventually pass Jarno, to take second spot. I finished fourth, by then a long way behind Ago: not impressive for a five times world champion.

Nevertheless it was early days and the fortnight on the Isle of Man gave me all the time I needed to get better acquainted with my new bike. Not that I had much time to spare. I had a pretty full programme; my own 250 Yamaha in the Lightweight TT, the MV in the Junior, and the John Player Norton in the Formula 750 race. I made the practice leader board in all three classes, too. I was third fastest behind Rod Gould and Barry Randle in the 250, third again behind Ago and Chas Mortimer in the 350cc Junior, and sixth in the F750. And that was with the MV not revving to its usual limits and a JP Norton that stopped several times with its Achilles Heel gearbox problems. In fact, I only just managed enough full laps to qualify for the 750 event on the Norton and *Motor Cycle*'s speed trap clocked me at 134.3mph, compared with the 150mph of Ago's 500cc MV. Race day for the 350s was Monday, and I got off to a good start with a 100mph standing start lap to lie second behind Ago at the end of the first 37$^3/_4$ miles, despite a flooding carb that caused a misfire. Thirty seconds separated us, but the fates didn't allow me the chance to see if I could narrow the gap. On the second lap, the gearbox jammed at Windy Corner, and I had to remove the chain and freewheel down to the pits. Ago, in perfect unison with his MV, made a nonsense of the word race, winning by five and a half minutes from Tony Rutter. Mick Grant was third.

I found the 250cc TT much more to my liking. Moved on by one day to Thursday, because of bad weather, it provided me with my second successive victory in the Lightweight and my sixth TT overall. I led right from the start and held that position on all four laps, taking the flag almost ninety seconds up on Rod Gould, despite the fact that a specially made seven-gallon tank gave him a non-stop run whereas I had to come in for a 25-second pit stop at the end of the third lap. Equally satisfying was the knowledge that I'd obtained maximum points from my only two rounds in defence of my world title.

The F750 race, however, was a disaster, both personally and for the John Player Norton team. Misfiring and gear selection troubles on the first lap put paid to my endeavours, but poor old John Cooper came to an even more ignominious end when his gear-lever fell off.

Whatever my own triumphs or disappointments, though, the ruling emotion at the end of the week was one of sadness and anger. In Friday's 125 race, Gilberto Parlotti, the Italian Morbidelli factory rider and championship points leader, was killed when he crashed off the road at The Verandah, a series of four gentle bends on the Mountain section taken at the highest speed. He was leading at the time. For many international riders, Gilberto Parlotti's death was the last straw. Moves to boycott the TT races gathered strength. Count Agusta was so upset by the accident that he decided MV would never race there as a team again.

As far as I was concerned, my mind, too, was made up at the end of that TT Week. I had raced over the Mountain Circuit for the last time. No longer would I be involved in maintaining a tradition at the expense of friends' lives - and possibly of my own. Some people said I was just scared, that I was a coward. Well, I risk my life every time I ride a bike, every rider does. When you're travelling at speeds well in excess of 100mph, there's no such thing as a safe circuit. But there is such a thing as a dangerous circuit, and there's no reason on earth why any rider should be compelled to risk his life riding on one. In those days, all top riders were under pressure to compete in the TT to collect World Championship points.

As one opponent of the Isle of Man TT said, 'They stopped throwing people to the lions centuries ago.' We're supposed to value human life in a civilised world.

For me, the turning point in my relationship with the Mountain Circuit had been in 1970 with the death of Santiago Herrero. Santi was a lovely little guy; cheerful, friendly, kind, caring and compassionate, a true friend, someone you could respect. It was through him that I had meetings with the Spanish Ossa factory back in October 1969, with a view to my racing their proposed 500 GP racer and supporting Santi in the 250cc class. The King of Bilbao, they called him, and he had the manners and the breeding to live up to the name.

I'll never forget the time Madeleine and I went to Bilbao for talks with Ossa. Santi took us to this really fantastic hotel we'd have never have found ourselves and all the time we were there we had the best of everything. It was superb. But when it was time to leave, and pay our bill, the manager was horrified. Terrified might be a better description.

'Oh, no, no, no! No payment, please! If you pay me, Senōr Herrero, he will be very, very angry with me.'

The way he carried on, you'd have thought Santi was going to stalk him through those dark streets of Bilbao. So we didn't pay, and the only way we could repay Santi was by having him to stay with us and giving him the best of everything. Then, in the 1970 Lightweight TT, he crashed. But he wasn't killed outright. He died a horrible death, and from that day I turned against the Mountain.

So why had I raced at the TT in 1971 and 1972? For any British rider, especially one of my generation, the Isle of Man was an ingrained part of his life. You couldn't throw it aside overnight. I grew up believing that the Isle of Man TT races were the greatest in the world and in earlier times, during the heyday of AJS, Norton and Velocette, they undoubtedly were.

Even in the early 1960s, the magic of the Island was revered worldwide, and to race at the TT was the dream of any ambitious rider. It was the place to meet trade representatives, the press, enthusiasts and organisers from all over the world. If you wanted to make the grade, the TT was an absolute must. For a young Englishman like me, it was accepted without question that you would race in the Manx Grand Prix for club-level riders and then, having done well there, move on to the TT itself.

Leading the 1971 250cc TT at Ginger Hall

I led the 1972 TT on my private 350cc Yamaha TR3 before having to retire.

In those days, when all I wanted to do was race motorcycles, danger was the last thing I would consider. If anything, the thrill, excitement, and even fear of the Mountain circuit was something we youngsters actually sought. The special atmosphere and tradition of the event were like a drug to anyone calling himself an enthusiast. Everywhere I raced it was Phil Read against the elements, and in the Isle of Man that sensation was at its keenest.

You accepted, at first, that riders did get killed and that it was dangerous. But as I grew older and perhaps more mature, and as the death toll rose with my increasing years, I began to harbour doubts about the sense of racing over such a course.

Conditions were rarely ideal for racing. It was either raining, windy, or misty with visibility on the Mountain section down to a few yards. Or it was so hot that the tar melted. And because the circuit was on public roads designed for the needs of everyday traffic and used only twice a year for racing, the dangers were only too apparent; telegraph poles, kerbs, signposts, stone walls, houses, to name but a few.

Continental circuits could be dangerous, too, but when riders asked for a tree to be removed, or a few straw bales placed in front of a wall or post, the organisers, reluctant to do anything more than they were obliged to, would counter by saying we raced on the Isle of Man without question knowing the dangers. So why pick on them?

There was a similar attitude towards start money. How could riders put pressure on other grand prix organisers to offer realistic money if we raced on the Isle of Man for nothing, which is what we did until the early 1970s. In 1972, as a five-times world champion, I was paid only £50 by the TT organisers for my travel, ferry and two weeks living in the Island.

But, even more than money, safety was becoming the major concern of the top riders contesting world championship rounds. Not only at the TT but everywhere. Lives were being lost simply through lack of thought and consideration. When the 1970s brought change, slow but inevitable, the TT dragged its heels.

There was much talk of £100,000 improvements to the Mountain Circuit, but these were merely to the road surface and the shape of bends. Nothing was done about hazards lining the track, and these could have been moved to make it safer for the rider. The trouble is, of course, that the circuit functions as a public road when racing isn't on, and in those days it wasn't set up from a rider's point of view, only from what the organisers thought necessary. And they weren't riders with recent experience. It seemed they didn't even study previous accidents and fatalities in any attempt to remedy the situation.

Gilberto Parlotti's fatal 1972 accident illustrates the point. Manx highway engineers who rebuilt that stretch of road over the winter had taken away a wooden fence on the Verandah section and replaced it with concrete posts. The posts were quite close to the circuit at a place where speeds were high. Where was the regard for riders' safety there? I'll freely admit that the following year the posts were removed and others moved further back. But by then it was too late.

In 1971, and again in 1972, I went round the track looking for the most obvious hazards. There were hundreds of them, yet with just a little effort and expense many of them could have been removed. Some didn't even serve any particular function and could have been removed. And why not take down signposts for the duration of the races? That's exactly what a more enlightened TT organisation started doing years later.

When Count Agusta announced his intention to boycott the TT, many of us felt a great sense of relief. Ago had been unhappy with the place for some years, yet for all that only Mike Hailwood had lapped the Mountain Circuit faster than him at the time. And one of Ago's laps had been at 108mph from a standing start. That answered a few dyed-in-the-wool TT enthusiasts who sneered that he was chicken.

Mike Hailwood wasn't too keen on the place either, 'They should pull out the plug and let the Island sink,' he once said with typical humour. Every year he would say how dangerous the circuit was. It's rough and bumpy, he would complain, and he was no happier than the rest of us about having to race in vile weather conditions.

I was firmly of the opinion that the Mountain Circuit had had its day as a Grand Prix circuit. But that didn't mean I wanted the TT to disappear.

Indeed, as I will explain in chapter 9, I sparked further controversy by returning to race on the Mountain Course in 1977. But that was after the TT, quite rightly, lost its World Championship status and the organising ACU were prepared to offer far better rewards than in 1972, to have me take part in the new-look event.

During the 1970s, the TT grew to be much more than just a race around the Mountain Circuit. It became a ten to fourteen days' long festival of motorcycling, ranging from rallies and vintage events to sprints and motocross. Over the years, the fortnight in June that once heralded the start of the tourist season replaced that season in contributing to the Island's economy.

I often thought a smaller circuit could be the answer for improved safety and to reduce delays due to weather. In 1973 Geoff Duke formulated a plan to move the TT to a proposed new circuit near Castletown in the south of the Island. A genuine road circuit, six to seven miles long in a natural setting, it would have been as safe for its type as any in the world and less subject to the low cloud and mist that plague the Mountain circuit. Plans for pit areas and accommodation facilities were good, and practice sessions wouldn't have interfered with daily life on the Island. It seemed an ideal solution to me and many others.

Yet I'm now pleased this project did not proceed because we would have lost the magic and challenge of the Mountain Course. Despite gloomy predictions and some tough times, like the 2001 cancellation due to Foot and Mouth disease or when the hugely popular David Jefferies was killed during practice in 2002, the TT has survived. Thanks to the Island's dynamic director of motor sport Paul Phillips and his team, great work has been done in recent years to kick more life and commercialism into the TT. Its unique role as the last great road race has been emphasised, efforts made to bring in willing riders from all over the world and top MotoGP racers have been invited for demo laps. And now the same team has addressed the slow decline of the Manx Grand Prix by transforming it into the Classic TT.

By comparison, Britain's MotoGP and World SuperBike championships races are run at soulless Silverstone, a circuit rebuilt purely to suit Formula 1 cars. It just doesn't have the same spectator appeal or atmosphere that the Isle of Man can offer.

I cannot erase my fond memories of the place, and I will admit the 1972 decision not to race there again was tinged with regret.

Even my first Manx Grand Prix provides unforgettable memories and thoughts of unforgettable people, people like a racing scoutmaster who was in my digs. He was in trouble. Three days had gone by, and because of things going wrong with his International Norton he still hadn't completed a full lap. A chain would break, a plug would oil up, there was always something wrong. Also sharing the same digs was a Geordie, George Bell, who'd gone out of his way to befriend me, still a shy lad from Luton, and one evening George and I decided to sort out the scoutmaster's bike for him, new plugs, new chain, valve springs, all sorts of goodies. It was a different bike. And it was a different person who came back to our digs the following day.

'I've done it!' he shouted. 'I've finished a lap! And,' he added in triumph, 'I passed someone!' His best lap was around fifty minutes, I think. But he had the time of his life, and I'm sure his scouts listened in awe to his stories for months afterwards.

Yes, just to ride in the Manx or the TT was a racer's dream come true. But even dreams must change with the times, and the Isle of Man TT had to change too.

At Ramsey Hairpin on my winning 1967 125cc TT ride

7 That fabulous 500 title

I ended the 1972 season with mixed feelings. There was disappointment that I wasn't able to retain my world title, even though I knew that riding for MV and John Player Norton would leave me little time to give full attention to my own bikes.

> Disappointment was tempered by elation at MV's offer of a full works contract that could put me in line for the 350cc and 500cc world titles.

Sad to say, I ended my John Player Norton contract with some relief, for my year with them had been full of frustrations. In my opinion, too much time was given to the team's image rather than to improving the engines and gearboxes. When we should have been out testing, for example, Frank Perris would want me for publicity photo sessions. I felt, too, that Norton was making a big mistake persisting with the Commando twin engine. If only Norton and Triumph had merged earlier (they combined to become NVT in 1973) they might have used an improved version of the Triumph Trident triple engine that had enjoyed great success in 1971 instead. Anyway, the terms of their new contract were the last straw, as they would have precluded me riding any other make of bikes in 1973. With Count Agusta promising the chance of world titles, such a contract from JPS Norton gave me the choice of racing the Ferrari of motorcycles at the prime grand prix circuits or racing a Ford Popular at UK Nationals.

Ther had been another option available to me that year, racing on four wheels. Ken Tyrell invited me to test drive a EldenMk8 Formula Ford at the Brands Hatch short circuit, some British Pathé film still exists and can be seen on the internet.

Phil Read To Drive Racing Cars

It was my first time at the wheel of a single-seater car and Ken Tyrrell rated it as 'a very fine performance'. His timing had me within four seconds of the lap record.

He said to me: 'Give me a call and tell me what other car team has contacted you and I'll tell you who not to drive for'. But signing for MV put an end to that idea of racing cars, starting at the bottom after my years of experience racing bikes. I have no regrets: it's one thing to be brave in a car but to get to the top you need to build up experience from an early age and drive for one of the best teams to have that extra edge to win, perhaps a bit easier in those earlier days.

The man to whom I relinquished my 250cc world title in 1972 was the worthy and fantastic Jarno Saarinen. The 'Flying Finn' also got close to robbing Agostini of his fifth consecutive 350cc World Championship title. Ago, of course, won the 500cc crown in that year. I finished fourth in the 250 and fifth in the 350, notching up my first win for MV with the responsibility of racing their new 350 four cylinder machine, my only World Championship win after the Isle of Man TT, at the East German Grand Prix. As it transpired, this was to be the last major race at the old Sachsenring road circuit which, when you consider that it attracted 300,000 on race day and probably around 100,000 just for practice, was a great pity. The main problem in those Iron Curtain times was currency. Few Western European riders wanted East German currency, yet it was difficult for the East German organisers to provide any suitable alternative. The Czechs had similar problems, too. Mind you, the fantastic trophies they gave out in Communist Bloc countries were quite valuable. I had been presented with two made from the finest Dresden porcelain.

Mention of Czechoslovakia reminds me of a pretty eventful trip to Brno that year. We were driving at night, Madeleine and I in the Silver Cloud with the caravan behind, nearing the end of a long, tiring journey from East Germany. Visibility was poor, thanks to a torrential downpour and the roads were not the best I've travelled on. Occasionally a flash of lightning would show up the surrounding countryside. Then all would be pitch black again but for the car headlights. For a moment we picked up the rear lights of another vehicle, in the next we were past it. I was driving fairly fast, anxious to make Brno as soon as possible.

'That was Derek Booth in that van,' Madeleine said. Derek used to transport our bikes all over Europe for us.

Just then, the lights picked up a road works notice. I touched the brakes as gently as possible to slow down when, suddenly, there was this floating sensation followed by a massive bump. The Rolls shuddered a bit, coughed, I straightened out the swaying caravan, and continued on its shaken way.

Instead of going round the road works, we went right over them. Journalist Chris Carter, who was travelling with Derek, told us later that he'd seen our tail lights disappear and then a flash of lightning had shown both car and caravan flying through the air. I'm sure any other car would have overturned! As a result of our little effort, they managed to go round the road works instead of through them.

There was worse to come, though. Arriving in the paddock at Brno tired and exhausted, all we wanted to do was sleep. We unhitched the caravan and put down the jacks. Madeleine opened the door, then wailed. I rushed round to see what the matter was. Inside the caravan was chaos. Sugar, tea, butter, jam, milk... everything from the cupboards lay strewn about. The carpet was a mess. The whole thing looked like something out of a slapstick comedy.

That was another good thing about joining MV, no more living in a caravan and long drives across the Continent. It was back to staying in hotels and flying to and from meetings. I'd re-joined the jet set from my Yamaha years.

One person, however, was not happy about my joining MV. That was my team-mate, Giacomo Agostini. I can understand how he felt, but it was the Count's plan for me to help him retain the 350 title by keeping back the challenging Yamahas, so Ago should have been grateful. It was clear right from the start that I was to be number two and he number one, rightly so due to his previous great successes, giving him the choice of best bike and choice of equipment, he even used parts that I personally carried from the UK to improve the MV's performance! Only when he had finished testing was I allowed to practise - and then it was his second choice of bike! I could have lost my temper, could have protested. Instead, I bided my time, prepared to see what the coming season brought before making known my feelings. The Rebel tag still hung around my neck, but I wasn't going to give anyone the chance to use it against me. MV would have to see that I was a good team man.

I believe I gave them good value during my years with them. For, as well as my riding ability, I could help on the technical side when the Agusta team were scraping the bottom of the barrel. As the next few seasons would prove, the MVs were no longer the unbeatable bikes they used to be and even at the beginning of 1973 we knew we were in for a hard year from the four-cylinder 500cc Yamahas of Jarno Saarinen and Hideo Kanaya. The team was also worried about the developing König four-cylinder two-stroke's speed, raced by the impressive newcomer, New Zealander Kim Newcombe. Following his unnecessary crash at Silverstone in August 1973, after which he didn't recover, I believe he could have been the strongest contender for the 500cc world championship the following season.

With improving opposition, the MVs had to be ridden harder to their limit, and the result was that faults, not previously apparent, began to hinder their performance against the two-strokes. Valves dropped in the engine and bearings collapsed. The drum brakes and handling needed improving, and there was a constant need for more power.

My greatest value to MV was the extensive list of contacts, both in Europe and the United States, that I'd built up during my many years in the sport. Morris magnesium wheels from America, special aluminium metal-plated brake discs from the London based Pagehiln Company, brake calipers from AP Lockheed and improved front fork internals, I was able to arrange them all. Amazingly, the team sometimes had to be convinced that these improvements were needed. In many cases I even paid for them in advance and when necessary carried them to Italy in my bags. At one time it seemed as if every flight that Madeleine or I made to MV included another delivery from Read Express Parcels Service.

In March 1973, Madeleine was in Guildford, preoccupied with a delivery of another kind, our second son, Roki Marc, at whose birth I was present to witness another miracle of life.

I celebrated by satisfying a years-old ambition, one I'd had since my father taxied me around our disused field in his Aeronca 100 twin JAP-engined monoplane. I bought my own plane, a new single-engined Cessna 172 Skylane, G-BAIW. I suppose it was a luxury, because apart from flying to the English circuits and occasionally to Guernsey, Belgium or Holland, I flew it to obtain my PPL (Private Pilot Licence) and simply to give me another challenge to add to my life's experiences. Flying helped exercise my brain when I wasn't involved with racing. Still, I could afford some expensive hobbies now. They were the fruits of success, and I'd gathered those fruits the hard way. Surely I could enjoy them? Mind you,

I flew my Cessna 172 Skylane G-BAIW into Mallory Park to test the MVs prior to the 1974 Race of the Year. Here I'm seen here in the paddock with race promoter Jim Swift and the MVs under the plane's wing. I flew two white-knuckled Italian mechanics back to my Surrey home that evening.

Count Agusta wasn't at all happy at one of his riders flying about in a single-engine aircraft.

'Well then,' I quipped to him, 'You'll have to give me one of your twin-engine models if you want me to be safer!' But this time, sad to say, he didn't rise to my bait.

Because of Roki's birth, Madeleine missed the opening round of that year's world championship, the French Grand Prix, staged for the first time at the multi-million-pound Paul Ricard circuit at Le Castellet, now owned by one of Bernie Ecclestone's companies, I believe. I flew alone from London to Marseilles where I was met by Rocci Agusta, Corrado's son. The others, including Ago and Magni, still hadn't arrived. There'd been some hold-up in finishing the bikes in Italy.

The hotel MV Agusta team had booked was part of the 'Ile de Bandol' complex owned by Paul Ricard circuit, a small island reached by a five minute boat trip from the seaside town of Bandol. Rocci Agusta expected the others to arrive in time for dinner, so I'd said I'd wait for them.

The bar was deserted, except for a bored barman and a very pretty girl who also looked bored. I chose to talk to the girl. She was French, a model, or so she said, and there was no reason why I should have doubted her. She had that sort of class. I asked her what she was doing on the island. 'I wait for a friend,' she replied.

'Oh yeah,' I said. 'Is he coming for the racing?'

'Oh yes,' she said. 'My friend, he is Mino, he races for Agusta.'

Now that put a different complexion on the matter. Mino was Ago's nickname in the MV team and close friends. If she was his girl, as she implied she was, I'd better be careful. It was bad enough that the man did not like me being in the same team as him. I didn't want bad blood because I'd been chatting up his bird. Still, as time went on, and two drinks became three, there was no sign of Ago and I was feeling hungry. Rocci Agusta appeared.

'They're going to be late as they haven't left Italy yet', he told me. I might as well eat, since he was going back to the airport. I looked at the girl. Perhaps, as Mino wasn't coming and she'd like to have dinner with me. She smiled, stood up, and we followed Rocci out of the bar to the restaurant .

None of us saw the photographer.

After dinner we played cards, and by the time I escorted her to her room, there was still no sign of Mino and MV team.

I bumped into her the next morning after breakfast, and she was still very, very friendly and just as pretty. 'Aah,' she said in her broken English. 'What a pity it was Mino arrived, for we could have been good in bed us two.' 'What?' I gulped.

'Did Mino arrive then?' I asked - anything to change the subject.

Yes, Mino came very late and arrived by helicopter from the factory. She went on to tell me all about it, and later I heard the story again from Rocci. Apparently he had told Ago at the airport that Read was dining with his girl. So Ago immediately got on the phone to the hotel, waking the poor girl up - stupid idea!. If it had been me I think I'd have gone straight to the hotel. But if I had been there, I'd have had plenty of time to get to my own bed before his arrival, yes?

Mind you, the real trouble came the following weekend at Belgium, where we were riding in an international meeting. For what should happen when Madeleine flies in but a fan shows her a newspaper photo of me and Ago's girl together. Worse still, the caption says she's my latest wife! Nor was Madeleine very pleased when this wretched girl kept following her around the paddock, saying, 'what a lovely time Phil and I have together. Ah, such a lovely man!' Things were getting out of hand, and it took a lot to explain just what had happened and what hadn't happened. The only person who saw the funny side of it was Ago.

As far as I was concerned, that was one time I was glad to play number two to Agostini!

Someone who definitely wasn't playing number two to the world champion in the opening rounds of 1973 was Saarinen. Evidence that the 500cc Yamahas were as good as the rumours had made out came first at Paul Ricard, and again at the Salzburgring. In France, Ago had crashed trying to stay in touch with the Flying Finn, luckily escaping with only cuts and bruises, while neither of us finished in Austria. Indeed, Mino's race was really short-lived. He managed just eight laps out of thirty-five in the wet conditions, complaining of a mysterious engine fault and that his visor kept misting up. I kept going, chasing the Yamaha pair, until water in the electrics reduced my four-cylinder MV to a three.

The MV camp was a picture of despondency. After two rounds, Saarinen led with maximum points, Agostini had yet to score. All we had to count was my twelve points for heading off Kanaya-san at Paul Ricard with a second place. We returned to the hotel, knowing that sooner or later Count Agusta himself would be on the phone for an explanation. I made up my mind about what to say if I was given the opportunity.

When Corrado did phone, I let everyone else have their say. Then I had mine. Give me a bike of my own, I told him; not just one of Ago's rejects. Then MV would start winning again. For a moment there was silence. I wondered if I'd said the wrong thing. But no.

'Would I be prepared to ride the new four-cylinder 500?', he asked. Agostini, who had crashed it in practice, didn't like the bike, although I was convinced it was a potential winner. I accepted his exciting offer. 'Yes I will race the new four, thank you Count,' I replied. I was told the bike would be at Hockenheim, specially prepared for me.

Ago blew his top when he discovered that Corrado had sent the four exclusively for me to ride and that he couldn't practise on it. He phoned Gallarate, crying and shouting at the Count that he was Agostini, the world champion, the MV was his machine. But it was all to no avail. Wealthy Italian autocrats such as Count Corrado Agusta do not change their minds and Ago was firmly told that he'd said he didn't like the new model after he had previously practised on it. Therefore, the bike was now Phil Read's. Mino would have to accept the Count's decision.

Team manager Arturo Magni and one of the mechanics worked in Italy all week to have the 500cc four ready for practice at Hockenheim. And I knew when I took it out on the track, that at last I had a more competitive machine to race against our strong opposition. Now I'd give Saarinen a run for his money. There'd be no holding back.

That was the big thing about racing against Jarno, there just couldn't be anything less than riding against him on the limit, since the Finn rode, it seemed, over his and the bike's limit. It's something few riders are capable of... or willing to do. They might go to the limit for a spell and then drop back after some frights. They might even go over the top occasionally and crash. But Jarno, like Mike Hailwood, Ago and Bill Ivy too, would ride to the limit from start to finish flag. That was part of Jarno's genius and something I don't do unless I'm really pressed.

At Hockenheim, racing was again on-the-limit stuff, as anyone who saw Saarinen and me fighting for the lead on that day will testify. No quarter was asked, none given. We swapped the lead more often than I care to remember. Below me, part of me, the MV roared with the pride of an all-conquering lion. Ahead of me, alongside, behind me, was the nerve-wracking scream of the two-stroke Yamaha. It was a battle of courage and of noise, a contest of speed and power in which all glory would go to the winner. It ended as such races never should. With me leading with only four laps to go, the drive chain on the Yamaha snapped. The race was mine. I was sorry for Jarno. It was a rotten way to be beaten and lose points.

After winning the 1973 German GP, Werner Giger (hidden by official) was second and Ernst Hiller (on right) was third.

1973 at work during the 1973 German GP at Hockenheim, once my favourite circuit, it is much shorter now, a bit Mickey Mouse, as we say!

500 MV at Silverstone August 1973

Ago, never in the hunt, retired five laps from home when lying third some way behind us. It was a bad day for him, for he'd also failed to finish in the 350cc race. So had I for that matter, and the fifteen points went to Jarno's young fellow-countryman, Teuvo 'Tepi' Länsivuori. Thanks to my win, MV were now back in the hunt for the 500cc title, but it looked as if Ago and I would have to pull out something special if MV were also to retain the 350 title.

At Monza, the four-cylinder 350s came good again. Or at least Ago's did. Mine went out with a dropped valve after five laps, leaving Ago on his own to fight off Renzo Pasolini on the new Harley-Davidson two-stroke, until Renzo went out in a most infuriating way for him. The zip on his leathers burst open slowing him like a parachute. Second to Ago was Länsivuori, with another Scandinavian, Kent Andersson, third.

Jarno hadn't raced in the 350cc event. Fastest in both the 250 and 500 practice sessions, he was concentrating on getting top points in both for his bid to win a double world title and capture Ago's 500cc crown. Alas, his dreams were never to be fulfilled.

In the 250cc Italian GP, Jarno and Renzo were killed in a terrible high-speed multiple crash on the Curva Grande, the first bend barely half a mile from the start. Several other riders, including Walter Villa, Chas Mortimer and Spanish newcomer Victor Palomo were injured in the melée. The accident was a cruel blow to motorcycle sport and the Yamaha team. Both men were highly talented riders, popular with their rivals and adored by their fans.

Pasolini, a seasoned campaigner, had only recently been given a new lease of life by his tie-up with the Italian arm of Harley-Davidson. Jarno stood on the very threshold of a glittering racing career. His name was on everyone's lips.

Yet it need never have happened, if it's ever possible to say that about any accident. Some say it resulted from oil spilling from Walter Villa's Benelli during the running of the previous 350 race. You'd think track marshals would have enough sense to stop a bike when it was obviously spilling oil, but no action was taken. Forty years later, it is generally thought that the main cause of the terrible 15-bike pile-up was Paso's engine seizing when he was leading the race around this fast curve on the first lap.

It transpired that when John Dodds, representing the riders, tried to get the 250cc event postponed until the oil had been treated, he was threatened with all sorts of action from expulsion to jail. It was the same old story: you're only a rider, so do what you're told. It was yet another case of officialdom overruling common sense. When the leading riders went down, the marshals panicked and if Chas Mortimer, himself injured, hadn't run back to slow the riders who were following, who knows what might have happened?

On a personal level, I was shattered as I'd come to consider Jarno as one of the true greats, a rival to be proud of racing against. Before the start of that fateful race, Madeleine and I had gone down to the track entrance to wish him luck.

'Take it easy, mate,' I said, touching him on the back as he passed, last out of the paddock.

'It's all right,' he replied. 'I'm saving the big one for you.'

Both Renzo and Jarno were old adversaries with whom we'd fought in many race battles over the years, I knew there was no way I could ride in the next 500 race that day, and was fully in agreement with the decision to abandon the meeting.

Agostini, however, wasn't, and, seemingly unmoved by the accident, tried hard to get the Count to have the race run. To me, winning points on the day your chief rival has just been killed was stealing from a dead man. I told Count Agusta so too, while the race organisers were shilly-shallying over whether or not to abandon the meeting. His reply stunned me. 'If Yamaha race, MV race,' he said.

'No way,' I replied, unable to take my eyes off his unblinking ones. 'I'm not racing.'

I couldn't get over it. I'd always considered the Count was a sportsman but now I was sorely disillusioned. I realised that I was just another number to him. Fortunately, and inevitably, Yamaha withdrew, and so with MV's approval, without which the organisers were afraid to act, the meeting was abandoned.

With MV Agusta boycotting the Isle of Man, together with most of the major factory teams, I had to wait until the Yugoslav Grand Prix at Opatija for my next chance to show the effectiveness of the MV four. It was, as events proved, an even longer wait.

Monza, the TT, and other recent incidents had pushed the question of safety uppermost in many people's minds, MV's included. And when the fairing on my bike caught on one of the milestones by the Opatija road circuit that wasn't protected by the hundreds of straw bales lying around the track, Signor Magni, MV's team manager, decided we would withdraw from the meeting. I agreed with his decision, for my brush with the stone seemed to be another case of disregard of rider safety. If a team like MV was now prepared to back up demands for better safety, other organisers would see that the bluffing had stopped. I was prepared to acquiesce. We wouldn't race.

There were no complaints about the Assen circuit, however, and the Dutch TT proved a happy outing for the MV team. Ago won the 350 with me second, although we were made to work hard by Länsivuori. He was back racing, after thinking seriously about retirement following the death of his close friend Jarno. Tepi gave us both a good run for our money until gearbox trouble handicapped him in the closing stages.

I couldn't understand Ago that day. He simply dawdled round, making it very difficult for me, as his back-up rider, to help him win. Even after I'd overtaken Tepi, I had to hang round waiting for Ago to take the lead as planned, and several times I felt like going on and winning myself. But relations between the two of us were strained enough as it was, without my making things worse. I'd already put my foot in it by telling the Count at Monza that I wanted Ago to return the magnesium wheels and metal-sprayed aluminium disc brakes I'd organised and paid for. Mino wasn't happy. Besides, I wasn't interested in the 350 title, my sights were firmly set on the 500. In the 500cc race it was a case of every man for himself. That's just how I like it. But when Ago dropped back, then retired with gearbox trouble, as he reported, that left me with another 15 points to take my championship tally to 42, just one adrift of the flying Kiwi Kim Newcombe. Fifth in the French and third in Austria, Kim had ridden his very experimental König into first place in Yugoslavia and now had picked up another twelve points at Assen. Ago, the defending champion, was still without a point after six rounds, which seemed an incredible situation for him.

At Spa-Francorchamps, however, Ago came good. With no 350cc race on the programme, he was able to concentrate fully on the 500, and he did so with a vengeance, riding that super-fast circuit almost to perfection to win at an average lap speed of 128.50 mph. I'd always thought of Francorchamps as my circuit, but I realised that afternoon that you're never too old to pick up a few tips from a master. They were to come in useful, too, but that's another story for another season. I was second there, with Kim third, so I jumped into top place on the championship table.

Approaching La Source hairpin on the MV triple in the 1973 500cc Belgian GP, where I finished second to Ago after stopping for adjustments. In the following year I took 10 seconds off Ago's lap record aboard the four-cylinder 500.

1973 Czech GP Brno, I came a poor second to Ago's 500 MV.

Brno brought a couple of nightmares, the first right at the start when the MV refused to fire until the whole field had got away. Then, trying to make up for lost time, I went into a frightening ton-plus hundred yard slide through the first village. It was some scare, I tell you, but I managed to keep the MV on the road, despite severe blistering on my hands from fighting my machine around the Brno road circuit. I had good reason to be well pleased with second place behind Ago.

A second in the Swedish TT at Anderstorp was all I needed to clinch the 500cc World Championship; the most coveted prize in motorcycle racing. It was unbelievable. At times I had to pinch myself to prove it really was happening to me. Me, who'd already been written off as too old and being referred to in the press as a 'veteran'. Well, I thought, I'm showing them. At 34, I'm only a race away from winning the most prestigious championship title, and then let them eat their words!

If I was going to make certain of that world crown, though, I was determined to do it in style. Winning this challenge the easy way was never Phil Read's style as history recalls, although that had not been by choice. My 500 battle with Ago at Anderstorp was so terrific that Chris Carter, who was giving the on-course public address commentary, insisted on everyone in the paddock going to the fence to watch the action. It was some race, with the two red MVs locked in battle the full distance. At the flag there was only half a second separating us, and the winning wheel was mine. I'd beaten Ago fair and square, I'd taken his title, which he had won for the last seven successive seasons. Now I was *Campione del Mondo*.

Ago was unhappy, of course, as he had been Italy's Superstar for many years, attracting large amounts of sponsorship money, loads of media coverage and women. More than that, he was in danger of losing his 350cc title as well. The threat was Tepi Länsivuori, whose victories in Czecho and Sweden had put him back into contention. Nor was Ago even sure of runner-up spot in the 500cc class, for Kim Newcombe, with a third in Sweden, was well in the running. My orders from MV were most explicit. Help Agostini to win the 350 title. I couldn't help smiling to myself at the irony of it all.

I had just narrowly beaten Ago and his Yamaha at the Imola International, much to the delight of the *tifosi*.

Phil Read 1974 Race of the Year, Mallory Park

Sadly, because I think Tepi was one of the truly nice guys of motorcycle racing and first to stand a round at the bar, the Länsivuori challenge for the 350cc title came to grief in front of his own countrymen. Battling alone against Ago and myself, he crashed, leaving Ago an easy winner with me backing him. I played the same role in the 500, letting him collect his fifteen points, though this still left him sixteen points in arrears of the fourth-finishing Newcombe. Ago would have to win in Spain, with me preventing Kim from finishing higher than third, if he was to have that runner-up spot. As it turned out, he didn't have to bother with the Spanish Grand Prix.

In August, Newcombe crashed heavily at the Silverstone International, hitting the unprotected wall at Stowe Corner, and died four days later from serious head injuries. He had been in a coma for some time when his life support machine was switched off with agreement of his wife Janeen. It had been a very sad and sobering year for me, with my four sons and Madeleine's future happiness and security to consider.

With Ago deciding to give Spain a miss, it was left to me to fly the MV flag at Jarama. And even though I was looking forward to a comfortable win, I found myself with quite a scrap on my hands when my MV Agusta began firing on only three cylinders and the tigerish Swiss ace, Bruno Kneubühler, swept ahead of me. I was really worried, and had to let it all hang out, scratching and slithering after Bruno. I caught him after setting a new lap record just four corners from home, helped by the exhaust on his Yamaha breaking. That was again a bit too close for comfort, but was nonetheless enjoyable and a good way to set the seal on my successful grand prix season for MV Agusta.

Winning the 1974 French GP from Barry Sheene's Suzuki at Clermont-Ferrand

The only disadvantage of riding for MV was that Count Agusta kept all the trophies his riders had won, which made for quite a number from their many championship-winning years. But they did let me take my 500cc MV home to Britain for some of the end-of-season races. The British fans were really great, giving me a wonderfully warm welcome. At the same time it made me realise just how valued the 500cc title was; not always rightly so in my opinion, because there can be much more effort entailed in winning, say, the 250 world title. But the media like focusing on the big stuff, it is the men who ride the large capacity machines, the superbikes, who became the superstars, especially in Britain. I had some pretty exciting races against one of those budding superstars, Barry Sheene, on the British circuits that year, but the day was still to come when Barry could get the better of me.

Early in 1974, I read in the press:

> **"Even taking all the facts into consideration, the cards were stacked against Britain's Phil Read and his bid to win the 500cc World Championship for the second successive time when the (1974) Grand Prix season opened at Clermont Ferrand for the French Grand Prix."**

I certainly didn't agree. The reason for this speculative judgment was Giacomo Agostini's decision to change teams to Yamaha. Or perhaps I've got it the wrong way round. Perhaps it should be Yamaha's decision to part with a large sum of money (reputed to be £100,000 over two years) for Ago's services in 1974 and 1975: then a tremendous amount.

Albeit unofficially, the Yamaha factory had made their return to grand prix racing towards the end of 1973. In theory, their involvement was tied to the Scandinavian Ardwidson team for which Tepi Länsivuori also rode, to whom they supplied the factory bikes, transporters and mechanics. In 1974, confident that

Riding the 500cc MV up Cadwell Park's Mountain in 1974

the four-cylinder two-stroke that Jarno Saarinen had raced so effectively the season before was competitive, they came out in the open as an official factory team with the very fortunate Giacomo Agostini, as it transpired. When they signed Ago, with Tepi as back-up rider, it was obvious they meant business. The only doubt hung over Ago's ability to ride two-strokes after a career spent almost exclusively on the MV Agusta four-strokes. A brilliant performance to win the Daytona 200 on the new 700cc Yamaha four, followed by a similarly mounted win at the Imola 200 and a victory on the 500cc four at Modena, proved conclusively that Ago was master of these superb new Yamaha two-strokes.

Still, he wasn't having it all his own way in the build-up to the world championship season. The Italian crowd, who were very unhappy at his 'defection' from MV Agusta, booed and jeered him at Modena, and it must have been really galling for him to see his countrymen mobbing me in jubilation after my victory at Misano the week before, when he failed to finish. Finally, only a week before the opening round of the world championships, there was our classic battle at the Imola International meeting, a race that was at the time, described as the best seen in Italy for many a year. I won from Ago by a few feet - the disliked Japanese Yamaha against the Italian MV Agusta, so you can understand why I was mobbed. There at Imola, with me in the pits was Madeleine and my three boys, with baby Roki at home. The fans had become so excited they stormed over the fence into the pits to get to me. Mad and I were so scared for the boys' safety that we lifted them up into the nearest truck to avoid them being squashed. I'm pleased I've never been a pop star!

With Ago getting a much better feeling for his Yamaha and becoming our greatest challenge, we fitted the MV with a new lightweight frame and disc rear brake in an effort to retain superiority over the Japanese 500cc two-strokes. Pre-season tests had shown a satisfying improvement. We had done well in the early-season meetings, but with the first of the grands prix imminent it was imperative to strike a major psychological blow by winning again at Imola. I set out to prove superiority right from the start, jumping into an immediate lead and making Ago chase me. Third away, he took over second place after three laps and the battle was on. Riding right to the limit he took me. There was little I could do except sit behind him and bide my time. My chance came on the second-to-last lap. As we braked, coming up to the hairpin bend, I squeezed ahead, rubbing elbows as I passed him. He came at me again and again, but each time I managed to hold him off. There was never more than a wheel in it, and the 50,000 *tifosi* were on tiptoe throughout, shouting the odds. I powered from the last chicane, across the line, the winner by a bare metre. The battle for the world title was on.

It was inevitable, I suppose, that Ago and I would be rivals from the first day I received Count Agusta's call. Certainly, by the end of the 1973 season, relations between the two of us had been decidedly cool, with Ago complaining loud and often to any journalist who would listen that I had 'stolen' his 500cc title.

To tell the truth, I couldn't understand the man; and I'm sure there must be some people who say the same about me, even now. But Ago was a puzzle, to use that word again, an enigma. He'd give a smile and a wave, yet rarely stopped to talk with his fellow competitors, unless he wanted to know about a new tyre, or some other piece of special equipment. It seemed he was incapable of talking to you face to face about his likes and dislikes, his hopes, his fears, his ambitions. For example, even though the press greatly exaggerated the 'feud' between us, to this day he is still a private man. Ago and I rarely saw eye to eye. Yet we never had an open row, because it was always done through the press. He preferred the newspapers to do his shouting. Perhaps that's the Latin way, I don't know. To me it suggested a devious mind.

With Arturo Magni and 500 MV, 1975

But don't think this was some personal vendetta, that I was jealous or envious of him. Even today, I'd like to get to know him better, to be a closer friend instead of having the superficial relationship that we have always had. But how do you get through to him? He seems to lack compassion, sincerity or generosity. He's not a socialiser unless it involves an advantage to him. Admirers might chat and laugh with him, but do any of them know or understand him?

Because of his willingness to 'confide' in the newspapers, Ago's dissatisfaction with the way things were going at MV soon became common knowledge, and rival factories showed interest in signing him for 1974. As we've seen, Yamaha made the most attractive offer, through Rod Gould during covert meetings in Italy. It must have been a very serious decision for him to leave MV, because he'd raced for the factory since 1965 and his name was synonymous with the marque. Yet, in the end, he was left with little choice. His complaints about me to Count Corrado and to the newspapers, worried the MV chief to the extent that he decided the MV team wasn't big enough for both of us. His problem was who he should ask to step down. In normal circumstances, I'd have been the one to go, for Giacomo was an Italian with a long, proud tradition of loyalty to the factory. But I had won the 500cc world title for the Count when it looked as though Ago had lost it.

Corrado, with a sudden display of democracy, decided to ask team manager, Arturo Magni and the mechanics to cast their vote. Surprisingly, I won the vote. This left Ago with the choice of riding with me as an equal or accepting Yamaha's good offer. That was one time he did have my sympathy, I knew how he must have felt having had a similar response from Yamaha a few years earlier, but because I had won for them against illegal team orders. It was a shame that we all didn't have a round-the-table meeting to discuss a better future for MV Agusta when Ago was still a brilliant rider.

But, Ago could see the writing was on the wall for MV Agusta as they were not in touch with any progressive hi-tech developments and I believe the Count did not see a good future for their road machines, which at the time needed a vast investment they didn't have. The Agusta helicopters were their future. Ago was also helped in making up his mind by the fact that Japanese two-strokes had become more competitive in the bigger classes, there was a big financial incentive, plus he was intent on beating me and MV. That news made sensational headlines in the world's media and the Italian tifosi were upset that their hero had deserted them.

With Giacomo's signature on a Yamaha contract, MV now needed a second rider. My own choice was Gianfranco Bonera, still under 30 and a mere novice with fewer than 30 races under his belt. But for all his lack of experience, he had shown terrific form on the Harley-Davidson in the Czech and Yugoslav GPs, and in a late-season meeting at Misano he'd made me work really hard for victory. In fact, I had to dive under him on the last corner to get past. Shy, quiet, yet nonetheless cheerful, he struck me then as just the type to be a good team-mate.

The MV people, however, wanted someone with a reputation and another rider I favoured and suggested to the Count was Dieter Braun, the reigning 250cc champion. He was a big man and an aggressive rider who would be ideal to fight with the 500 MV.

While skiing at St Moritz with Mad and my two youngest boys, Pip and Marc, (Phil and Roki) as Count Agusta's guests, I arranged a meeting between Dieter and the Count. Much to everyone's surprise, Dieter declined the offer, saying he preferred to race 'factory' Yamahas as promised by Rod Gould in the smaller classes. As it would transpire, his 'factory' bikes were in fact production racers which caused him to be very upset. He felt that he had been conned by Gould.

Years later Dieter told me about his strange physical confusion at that time which he thought would cause him to fail on the MV machines. He would have been a great team-mate for me against Ago and their Yamaha riders. Barry Sheene's name was also mentioned but, as I suspected, he'd already signed for Suzuki, who were resuming factory support for grand prix racing. Again I suggested Bonera, but he was still under contract to Harley-Davidson. We were back where we started. Then up popped Gianfranco with the news that Harley weren't giving him a contract after all. Within hours he was signed up and I had a new team-mate. As the coming season was to prove, this was a mistake.

If I'd thought about it, which I didn't, I should have welcomed starting my world championship defence at Clermont-Ferrand, as it was there that I'd notched up my first GP victory ten years earlier on the factory 250 RD56 Yamaha. But I had too many things to think about without remembering anniversaries. It was bad enough having Ago and Länsivuori ganging up on me, but Barry Sheene, Paul Smart, Australian Jack Findlay, and Italian Guido Mandracci were also lined up against me on very fast 500 Suzuki two-stroke fours. It was going to be one hell of a hard race series.

I had a good morale boost in practice, equalling Mike Hailwood's absolute track record he set back in 1968 on a Honda six, and I reckoned I'd worked out how to take advantage of the two-strokes' not-so-obvious weakness. Due to their thirst they would need to carry more fuel than our MVs. Consequently it would be heavier in the early stages of the race. That was where I planned to strike home my advantage, starting fast and building up the sort of lead that would put pressure on the riders and bikes chasing me.

I managed the fast race start I needed, just beating Sheene to the first corner with Ago and Tepi tucked in behind him, but on that very tight part of this circuit I could not get far enough away. At the end of the first lap, only three seconds separated the first four, and on the fifth Ago swept past me as I knew he might with his better handling machine. Even more than the previous year, the MV was proving difficult to handle under heavy braking, and now the acceleration out of the corners was inferior to that of the Japanese two-strokes. As Ago began piling it on, breaking the lap record by 3.6 seconds and opening up an eight-second lead, I began to long for the fast, sweeping circuits like Francorchamps where the MV would be in its element.

But Ago was pushing too hard, and on the ninth lap he broke his engine. I was in the lead, only to find myself, surprisingly, under pressure from Sheene. Ironically, Barry had only been trying to keep my team-mate Gianfranco at bay when he discovered he was closing up on me. However, I didn't know this at the time until I got the pit signal, and pushed harder to take the flag just five seconds up on Barry, with Gianfranco a close third. I couldn't have asked for a better start to the season, though I knew it was going to get harder to win.

With only a week to the next round, the West German at the Nürburgring, there was no time to sort out the MV's handling problems. I'll just have to live with them, I thought, and hope for the best.

Winter still hadn't left the Nürburgring when we turned up for practice on Friday morning. There was snow on the ground as well as on the mountains, and it was literally freezing. But it wasn't just the weather that upset us. Contrary to expectations and the FIM regulations - the motorcycle grand prix was combined with car races, and the bikes relegated to second place. For example, cars had the best garaging facilities while the bike mechanics were working with thirty machines to a garage. It just wasn't on.

But when we went out for practice and word came back that there were only a few thousand bales of straw scattered around the 22km circuit instead of the ten thousand or so needed to make the Armco-lined track safe, the murmurs of discontent grew much louder. As usual, though, it took an accident to bring matters to a head. There had already been several spills, none of them serious.

When I went out on the 350 MV for my first really serious look at the circuit. I was horrified. The insufficient straw bales they had placed were meaningless around this long circuit which was surrounded by mostly unprotected steel barriers. It's impossible to conceive just how dangerous that is in relation to a circuit like the 'Ring. Or any circuit, come to that.

I was getting really boiled up about it, I can tell you, when I came across a scene that made my blood run cold. A rider lay motionless by the Armco barriers, his bike on its side near him. Standing beside the prone form was Ulsterman Tom Herron. I brought the MV to a halt alongside Tom's yellow Yamaha and ran back.

'It's Bill,' Tom said. Bill Henderson was a friend of Tom's and at the time Chas Mortimer's mechanic. The pair had been practising together when Bill crashed. As a result Bill Henderson suffered a broken spine. I have seen a wide-angle photo of the accident, taken just after Tom stopped to see if he could help. There isn't one straw bale in sight! An additional complaint was the lack of a prompt ambulance service. We had specifically requested an ambulance to be stationed at every three kilometres, yet it took over ten minutes for an ambulance to arrive for Bill. All that time he was lying there in the freezing cold. Little wonder Tom and I rode back to the pits looking very grim-faced, thinking it was time for a showdown.

A meeting of riders followed, after which Ago, John Dodds, and I presented an ultimatum to the organisers. If they refused to put out more bales at the potentially dangerous corners, (a further ten thousand was the figure mentioned although Ago said he would have compromised at half that number) the riders would refuse to race. A further two and a half thousand were promised, but in our opinion this wasn't enough. We went back to the other riders and the following document was drawn up. It was delivered in Italian, so this is a fairly rough translation.

On account of the dangers of the Nürburgring track, and considering that the organizers, in spite of the repeated demands of the riders, have refused to place around the 22km track the minimum number of straw bales necessary for the riders' safety, we the undersigned have decided not to participate in the German Grand Prix, the second round of the World Championships.

It was signed by all the works riders and their team managers. However, when all but a few of the privateers also declared their intention not to race, the organisers realised they had underestimated the strength and unity of the riders. Another unhappy feature of the whole affair, from our point of view, was that the paying spectators could be robbed of seeing the stars perform in these world championship races.

In the event only a few solo riders, mainly Germans in fear of losing their licences, raced, as did the leading German sidecar teams after a good deal of arm-twisting. And because the FIM Jury voted by six to one that the circuit was safe for racing, the other sidecar racers were forced to race or concede valuable points.

Nor was the affair over. Not by any means. The organisers used the track loudspeaker system to lambast the boycotting riders, accusing us of lack of courage and of following the commands of 'the Italian Mafia'. And after the meeting, the German Federation carried out its threats to suspend a number of riders, among them John Dodds and Dieter Braun. They also issued a press statement, saying that the riders had been demanding more money, which simply wasn't true. The fact that we were in the right was proven when the FIM, at a special meeting in May, reprimanded the German Federation, fining them and the race organisers heavily and suspending race chief Kurt Bosch from future FIM duties. But it was just a token gesture. The fine was later lifted, Bosch was later welcomed back into the fold, and the FIM closed ranks again.

At the time it seemed like a great victory; riders forgot their differences and acted together, not for money but for safety. I felt proud to be part of it. Yet what came of it? I'd like to think that our action did, in the long term, do some good. Nowadays we see the MotoGPs run by Dorna on well-organised circuits where safety is paramount.

Ago came back with a vengeance the next weekend, beating Gianfranco by a quarter of a second after a tremendous cat-and mouse battle around the rain-swept Salzburgring. As usual, it was an unlucky circuit for me as my MV tightened on the very first lap and eventually seized on the eighth. But lady luck is a funny old girl, and it was only a fortnight before she was smiling on me again. First, though, I had to shake off a bout of flu which wasn't helped by racing at Misano on the Adriatic coast. Incidentally, it was at Misano that Count Agusta withdrew the unhappy 350 MVs, leaving Bonera and me to concentrate exclusively on the 500cc World Championship with a 430cc engine machine as a spare.

The handling of the big MV was still worrying me at Imola, venue of that year's Italian GP, and the way the front would judder on fast corner approaches was frightening. (Even today teams still suffer from this problem.) Even a week of testing at Misano failed to solve this serious problem, and it's not surprising that I needed physiotherapy after every race after fighting to keep the machine under control and not crash.

My other major concern was my health. I was still feeling weak with the after-effects of that flu, and I wasn't sure how I'd stand up to 115 miles of concentrated effort. We decided it would be better for Gianfranco to battle it out with Ago and Barry while I tried to pick up points by finishing. Even then, I didn't imagine I'd be picking up ten points. But Barry crashed, breaking his ankle. Then, with Ago showing all his majesty, reeling off record laps as he simply annihilated poor Gianfranco, the almost unbelievable happened. Within two laps of the finish, his Yamaha ran out of fuel. The crowd were temporarily stunned, only to break into renewed cheering as Gianfranco hurtled past the stationary Ago to take his first Grand Prix victory. Tepi was second and I was a lucky third.

With the leading riders still boycotting the Isle of Man TT, the 500cc World Championship was in effect at the halfway stage. Bonera led the table with 37 points, followed by me (25), Barry (22), Tepi (20), and Ago (15). It was a good opportunity for a rest from racing and when MV ordered me to go home to England to get fully fit I didn't argue.

Rumours that Ago was going to race at the TT were given some weight by another rumour that a well-connected Yamaha importer had requested an entry from his Amsterdam office for a 500 four cylinder Yamaha in the Senior TT, rider un-named. This worried us somewhat. The closest Ago got to racing on the Island was a trip with the rest of us to the Post-TT international meeting at Mallory Park. There I equalled the circuit's outright lap record in winning the unlimited race and set a new 500cc lap record chasing Tepi in the 500cc Shell Sport final. That was one in the eye for those like Vernon Cooper, then Chairman of the ACU, who were saying I was 'over the hill' because I refused to race in the TT.

On the 1975 German GP rostrum, with Agostini and Länsivuori, I felt very lucky to finish second behind Ago and ahead of Tepi after a long 120mph broadside around Hockenheim's East Curve. Only my high speed forced me back into the saddle.

Leading MV team-mate Gianfranco Bonera at La Source hairpin in the 1974 500cc Belgian GP, I won, averaging 130.50mph.

The bark of the MV Agusta 500/4

About to try an experimental winged fairing at the 1974 Belgian GP, Madeleine is on the right.

Mind you, if my critics had seen me going through my paces at our local gym under the eagle eye of England boxing coach Johnny Barnham, they'd have realised why I wasn't yet over the hill and keen to get stronger and fitter to help cope with the demanding MV schedule that saw me racing almost every weekend. After Mallory, for example, it was back to Misano, where cheeky little Gianfranco blasted Ago and I into the minor placings. I was beginning to feel glad he was on my side. Then we set off for the Dutch TT at Assen with high hopes for an MV one-two. Ago put paid to those dreams, and in fact it was a Yamaha one-two with Tepi, fastest in practice, filling the runner-up spot. Ago was brilliant that day, zipping round Assen in a record lap under three minutes - on the longer old circuit. His race average set a new record, too, and there was no way Gianfranco and I could live with that sort of pace the way our machines were handling with the front wheel judder. Still, I finished third, 30 seconds back, and Bonera's fourth kept him at the top of the table.

We went south to Belgium with our tails between our legs. At Spa, MV showed up with experimental fairings developed at Turin University, for me to try in practice. Small wings fitted on either side at the front of the fairing proved a bad idea. When cranked over into these high speed corners they had the effect of pushing the front wheel away, which is the last thing you need! I only did one lap with these and stopped to ask the mechanics to remove them.

I didn't need aerodynamic help at that round! If the Dutch had been Ago's race, the Belgian Grand Prix was all mine. Yamaha had given us a scare by unveiling a new lightweight slim-line four for Agostini, but as I've often said, Francorchamps is my kind of circuit. It was the MV's circuit too, for the handling and braking problems were by no means as pronounced there as elsewhere, and I decided to answer Yamaha's new challenge with a special one of my own.

Right from the start I left all opposition with the gutsy roar with the MV ringing in their heads. In the pits, Madeleine and the crew were listening for the arrival of the unmistakable sound of the MV being given its head around this super-fast circuit. They couldn't really believe their ears or their eyes - when they heard me changing down into the last corner, the La Source hairpin, and with no other rider in sight or sound we suddenly roared into sight down the pit straight and up the steep Eau Rouge climb out of sight, the MV's engine reverberating around the hills of the Ardennes. They checked the lap time, a staggering lap record of 130.25mph from a standing start! Next time round they had to wait a full thirteen seconds before the second bike came into view. Tepi was already out with a seized engine, Ago was fourth behind Barry and Gianfranco. I could hardly believe it myself. Everything seemed so perfect. It was the race of my life and I hoped I didn't make a mistake to spoil our day.

According to my pit signals I was increasing my lead at the rate of approximately seven seconds a lap. At the end of the fifth, Gianfranco stopped in the pits for a hydraulic fluid top-up, leaving Ago and Barry battling it out for second. But by the time Gianfranco was ready to rejoin me, a lap behind, for a high-speed tow through the tail-enders, Barry was out with a broken gear lever. There was no way now that Ago could catch me, assuming I kept going, so I could afford to slow just a little to help Gianfranco along. And as we came up to the hairpin for the last time, I let him nip through so he could complete the full distance. It gave him tenth place and a single point, but at the end of the season a point can prove most valuable for the championship table.

1974 Belgian GP, chatting with Barry Sheene

Madeleine and I celebrated that evening at the hotel with a bottle or two of vintage Dom Perignon champagne with John Brown, the great journalist. Nothing tasted better on that day.

Now I was back where I felt I rightly belonged, at the top of the World Championship table. I felt on top of the world. I'd never known such a feeling of togetherness and control over my MV's power and speed in a race before. I thought I'd been through it all before, yet it seemed the MV was still able to surprise me. I still look back on that 1974 Belgian Grand Prix with some measure of disbelief, like my first TT win as a privateer, but it's mixed with pleasure and pride that I was capable of such an outstanding ride.

Just to give some idea of my speed that afternoon, my lap record of 133.34mph was the fastest recorded in any motorcycle grand prix at the time.

Awaiting the start of the Belgium GP with Matza holding my 500 MV, during the race Ago and Sheene both retired, I set lap and race records.

My average speed for the full distance was higher than the previous Spa-Francorchamps 500cc lap record, (by Ago!) which that year put me in the *Guinness Book of Records*.

There was no chance of a repeat performance in Sweden, though. Anderstorp's twisty track may delight the fans, but the MV was not as impressive on a circuit like that. Nor were we helped by the fact that the tight practice schedule didn't leave long enough for us to make effective adjustments to my bike, so it was a pretty dejected pair of MV riders who walked on to the grid to claim their bikes from the factory mechanics. Ironically, though, it was disaster day for two of our challengers, Agostini and Sheene. We were still in the process of sorting ourselves out during the first few laps when, at the end of the long back straight on the second lap, the back wheel on Barry's Suzuki slid out on water spilling from its radiator. Seeing him crash, I kept my MV on a tight line to swoop past on the inside, missing him by inches. But Ago made the mistake of lifting his bike and the pair of them, bikes and all, ploughed into the catch fences at high speed, both incredibly lucky to escape with nothing worse than severe bruising and the odd twisted neck or shoulder. Had there been Armco barriers outside of that fast bend, instead of the three rows of catch fencing, they would have been killed for sure.

Länsivuori kept the Yamaha colours flying high with his win, but I was more than happy with my totally unexpected second place behind him. Gianfranco was fourth behind yet another Finn, Pentti Korhonen.

There was no time for celebrating, though. We had to get Barry home to England. As soon as the victory ceremony was over, I arranged for a private plane to fly Barry, Mad and I down to Gothenburg, where we could pick up a scheduled flight to London. We must have looked a pretty funny sight when we pitched up at Gothenburg. Madeleine was still wearing her working gear, the jeans and jacket she'd worn in the pits, while I was in the first clothes I could lay my hands on when I took my leathers off, and Barry was bandaged up in a wheelchair. But even funnier was the look on his face when he suddenly realised that he was careering across the tarmac towards our BEA Trident without me. I'd given the chair an almighty shove and let it roll! But Barry, chirpy as ever, didn't realise I wasn't there. His face was a picture when he noticed he was out of control and he shouted for help.

Tepi's win at Anderstorp had pulled him up into third place in the championship behind me and Gianfranco, so with Ago out of action for the following weekend's Finnish GP, Tepi would be the man to beat. He knew the Imatra circuit of old, as he had shown in practice. Still, I did my bit to keep MV morale high for what could prove the vital round by breaking the lap record in practice.

The fates did their bit for us again, too. Tepi fell on the first lap of the 350cc race when his rear tyre went flat, leaving him battered and bruised for the big race. Nevertheless, he wasn't deterred and he shattered the lap record as he closed in on Gianfranco and me in the last few laps.

I'd got away to a sensational start, but then for some reason I had trouble finding my race pace, riding like an old woman. Gianfranco tucked in behind early on and that was how we spent most of the race. But on the last corner, with Tepi furiously in pursuit, disaster almost struck. Dogged by gearbox trouble during the race, I now missed a gear as I accelerated out of that corner. Gianfranco, right on my tail, came close to hitting me, and while we sorted ourselves out Tepi got to within a couple of seconds of us, but just not enough. The two MVs swept across the line one second apart. I had my 15 points to retain my second 500 world title. But what a fantastic and brave ride by Tepi, who deserved more than he later received from Team Suzuki.

With only the Czech remaining, there was no way I could be beaten. Boy, did we celebrate that night. We drank the hotel out of champagne; hundreds of pounds worth of bubbly! And then, first thing in the morning, we flew home to Heathrow, the most bedraggled party of passengers you could ever set eyes on.

With Tepi in such outstanding form, however, Gianfranco was by no means certain of the runner-up spot, so there was no way of getting out of racing at the Czech GP. Not that I really wanted to, but with involvement in the end-of-season meetings at home on top of an arduous championship campaign, it might have been convenient to have given Brno a miss. Nevertheless, Gianfranco had given me tremendous support throughout a difficult year, and helping him fill second place was the least I could do for him. As it turned out, he left himself with much to do after a poor start. Out in front I did my best to keep Tepi behind me long enough for Gianfranco to catch the Flying Finn, which he did with a tremendous ride during which he smashed the lap record. Once he'd picked up Tepi there was no stopping him until he caught up with me to finish the race the way we finished the world championship series, MV first and second. It couldn't have been more satisfying.

Leading Tepi Länsivuori on his just-visible Suzuki in the 1975 500cc Czech GP, this was my last 500cc world championship race win.

The races in Britain went well, too, with victory in the Mallory Park, Race of the Year, its highlight was racing, as I later discovered from Mr Magni, a four cylinder MV of only 430cc beating some of the best factory riders on bigger bikes. This change of machine from the full 500 was due to my practice crash when losing the front end on Devils Elbow. Seriously damaged, it was not repairable in time.

I had been voted Man of the Year in the *Motor Cycle News* readers' popularity poll.

But what really put the icing on the cake was the news, in November, that It's an honour that had never come my way until then. News of this was phoned to me at Hamamatsu, where I was visiting the Suzuki factory and I was absolutely thrilled. I'd always had a strong core of faithful supporters who'd stayed with me through good times and bad, but the *MCN* accolade meant that a great many more British fans thought I was tops too. And I didn't need to put in hundreds of votes for myself, as someone once told me that another well-known rider did. It made all the effort over the years worthwhile.

I also collected another award from the press guys, being elected Rider of the Year by the Guild of Motoring Writers.

My presence at Hamamatsu, Japan, while Barry Sheene was also there testing for Suzuki, really stirred up speculation about my plans for 1975. 'Read Tests a Suzuki' proclaimed *MCN* in big, bold type. The *London Evening News* hinted at a 'Suzuki Pairing for Britain' and there was speculation about a lucrative contract with the Japanese company, figures of £150,000 being the most frequently quoted sum. Big money at that time!

Yet my trip to Hamamatsu was supposed to be secret and would have been if that other rider in Hamamatsu hadn't tipped off *MCN*. In September, I'd received a letter from Suzuki asking me to consider riding for them in 1975, and to travel to Japan to test their machines. I explained I was still under contract to MV, which prevented me from testing for other factories, and that I would want to consider MV's terms for 1975 first. Yes, said Suzuki. They understood that. But they'd like first option on me as their number one rider.

I often seemed to be visiting an injured Barry Sheene.

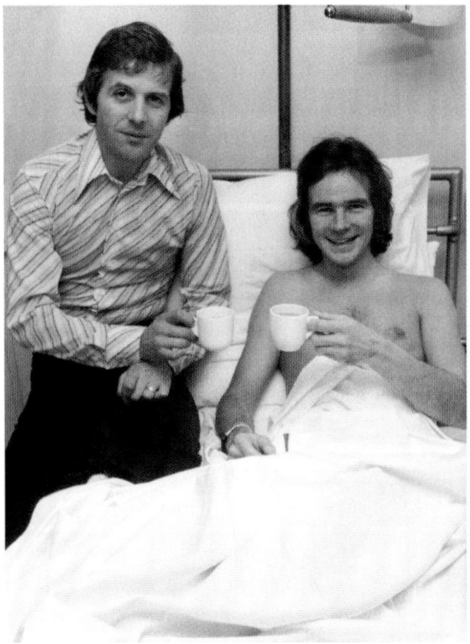

Well, all this interest in me, especially with my 36th birthday only a few months away, set me thinking. A trip to Japan would certainly be worthwhile. In order to stop the press getting suspicious, Madeleine and I planned a 'business trip' around the world, starting off with General Motors in Detroit, where Bill Mitchell, president of GM's design centre, really did us proud, giving a fantastic reception in my honour and taking us on a conducted tour of the automobile development and design complex.

From Detroit, we flew down to Wichita so I could look over the Bede Aircraft Corporation factory, where I intended to order a Bede BD5 single-seater jet to use for aerobatics. Then there were quick stops on the West Coast and Hawaii before going on to Japan. Nothing could have been more natural than going up to Hamamatsu, also the factory base of the Yamaha Motor Co. where we found Barry recovering from concussion after a crash when testing a day earlier. To hear him on the phone to *Motor Cycle News*, though, you'd have thought he'd broken every bone in his body until Madeleine told him to stick to the truth.

He also told them I was there, something I really didn't want made public, as I was still under contract to MV Agusta. Before he crashed, Barry had told the Suzuki crew he thought that the bike was terrific, but I later decided he wasn't so good at analysing technical and handling issues.

When I got my turn on the Ryuyo test track I immediately realised that the bike's front wheel was out of balance and I also suggested some changes to improve the machine's fairing and foot control positions. On my second day out on the track, after these certain modifications had been made, I was able to break the track lap record and hoped I had impressed all the right people with my handling of their latest two-stroke square four in a new chassis. Perhaps it was because I didn't fall off! I was quite impressed by my ride, too.

That evening I learned more of Suzuki's ambitions, and the role I was to play in their plans. They again stressed that they definitely wanted me as their number one works rider, but they also felt I could help them with development, as I'd done for Yamaha in the 1960s and for MV Agusta of late. It was too much to sleep on, so Madeleine and I took off for some Hamamatsu nightlife, with Barry in tow, of course. His latest 'injuries' didn't stop him from dancing the night away.

The third day, however, was a complete waste of time. The bikes weren't ready, and there was so much messing about that I didn't even sit on one all day. As Madeleine kept saying while we hung about shivering, it would never have happened at MV. I felt sorry for the factory directors who'd come down specially to see me put their bike through its paces. They hid their annoyance extremely well, and they were most apologetic and embarrassed for the trouble to which they were putting us. But when they began wining and dining us, presenting Madeleine with expensive gifts, and generally making me realise how much they wanted my signature on their contract, I was the one to feel embarrassed. Already, deep down, I was beginning to realise I'd stay with MV if their terms were right, although the fact that Suzuki could offer a 750cc machine as well as a 500, which MV couldn't, was in the Japanese company's favour. I stalled when the question of a contract was discussed, asking for time to speak with Count Agusta.

As I recall Suzuki were offering an amount which wasn't really enough for my services. But the main reason for deciding against Suzuki's offer was my friendship with Barry Sheene. In a fairly short career he'd already had more than his share of bad luck and I felt he deserved the chance to be a number one rider. Moreover, I valued our friendship at that time. I didn't want to go through another Bill Ivy episode again. No matter how good a friendship, it has to be very strong to withstand the pressures of riding as team-mates throughout a whole season when we were fighting to be Suzuki's first world champion in the 500 class, as Barry was.

I also had to consider MV. They'd been good to me. Their bikes had taken me to two world championships. Now that they were no longer invincible, it seemed like leaving a sinking ship to go off to another factory, like Agostini had done.

And, finally, there were the British fans. The weekly *Motor Cycle* ran a poll asking its readers to help me choose, stay with MV or go to Suzuki. More than 80 per cent wanted me to ride the MV. Having a British rider on that legendary four-stroke meant so much to them.

By December I'd signed a new contract with the Count. I knew, after the trouble I'd had with the bikes in 1974 that I'd have to ride even harder to retain my world title. But in spite of all the known faults in performance, I thought that the MV's superb reliability would give me an outside chance and not give me the dangerous problems Barry had already suffered, painfully.

St Moritz; skiing, biking and bobbing with the GB Bobsleigh team seen holding Union Jack Premier helmets from my Shannon factory

Once again Count Agusta invited Madeleine, the children, and myself to be his skiing guests at St Moritz, where I managed to get in some of pre-season one-upmanship over Ago. He, too, was staying at the exclusive winter sports resort, but while I was doing relatively safe things like skiing and flying around the mountains in the Shah of Iran's private helicopter, loaned to the Count, he was hurtling down the formidable Cresta Run. Not all of it, mind you, just the Curzon Cup course from Junction - a distance of some 970 yards (887 metres) which he covered in just under 52 seconds. The great Italian tobogganist, Nino Bibbia, apparently shot down the same course in 43.59 seconds at an average of around 45mph. Recently Brit James Sunley had pushed the record to 41.3 seconds.

I had no illusions of equalling that record. But, despite the fact that I'd never ridden the Cresta Run before, I was determined to beat Ago's time. Fitted out in ski-gear, gloves, crash helmet and goggles, I felt just like a motorcycle racer - until I had to lie face down on the toboggan, looking into the wall of ice. Nor was there that friendly, healthy roar of the MV as I set off, just the ghostlike swish of the runners over ice and my toe-blades scraping as I braked. Being so close to the surface gave a terrific feeling of speed, but what I hadn't bargained for were the sudden drops. It was like the Isle of Man all over again, and several times along the way I lost my stomach. I kept my nerve, however, and when I learnt that my time was almost two seconds better than Ago's I was really elated. Pathetic isn't it? For all that, though, I didn't tell the Count what I'd been up to!

St Moritz saw another example of the Read spirit of independence - but this time from my son Pip. Out skiing with other children he looked pretty good, so I thought I'd help him along with a few hints. But oh no! As soon as I started showing him a better style he lost interest. Just like his father, he wanted to do his own thing to learn his way: kids!

Looking back on 1975, it obviously wasn't meant to be my year. Things just kept going wrong. For a start, Gianfranco broke a thigh bone when he hit a straw bale in an early-season Modena meeting and missed the first five rounds. It was a terrific blow to my championship hopes, for his replacement, Armando Toracca wasn't in the same league and didn't help me.

That was never better illustrated than in the third round at Hockenheim. We'd fitted new front forks and a modified cylinder head in an attempt to put the MV on equal terms with the Yamahas of Agostini and his new team-mate, Hideo Kanaya. I got away to a lightning start to take an immediate lead. Ago had been left behind, but he soon began making up lost ground and passed Toracca like a dose of salts. Armando didn't actually wave Ago by, but I know for sure Gianfranco would have made our biggest rival really fight to get past. Instead, Toracca simply moved aside and I was soon fighting a duel reminiscent of the one with Saarinen at Hockenheim two years earlier. Just sticking with Ago on the medium fast corners meant riding on the limit of tyre adhesion and sometimes beyond. But when some nasty moments were climaxed by a horrendous 130mph slide rounding the fastest East Curve, which carried me more than a hundred yards sideways, I knew it was time to call it a day and settle for a safe second place. Somehow, I had the MV back under control after being nearly high-sided off at over 100mph, when Ago fought his way back off the grass to pass me, having taken avoiding action to miss my expected almighty crash.

My second bit of bad luck came in the first championship meeting of the season, the French GP at Paul Ricard. A tumble at 120mph during practice at the end of the Mistral Straight further damaged the little finger of my right hand, my braking hand. I'd originally broken that finger in a crash during practice on the John Player Norton at Imola in 1972 and had spent two years trying to get it right. I even used to joke that I had the best two-fingered braking hand in the business. After that incident at Paul Ricard, it was no laughing matter. The MV was difficult enough already without my being unable to exert complete control on the front brake. On today's MotoGP machines the carbon brakes need only a light one-finger touch.

The third twist of fate came in the penultimate Finnish round at Imatra. A spectacular repeat of the previous year's performance at Spa-Francorchamps and a fortunate second to Barry in Sweden after Ago's Yamaha had punctured two laps from home, had put me on top of the table for the first time that season. But though my total points were better, Ago boasted the better performances, with three wins and a second to my solitary win and a string of seconds and thirds. What I needed were more wins when the worst scores were discounted. The championship was decided on the best results in half the races, plus one. I fancied my chances at Imatra, the Finnish GP venue virtually on the Russian border.

Yet it was at Imatra that the MV, a top-three finisher in every round to date, let me down. It was heartbreaking, for we'd planned the race so meticulously, even to having Madeleine halfway round the circuit giving me race signals and times. And it was just nearing this point, when I was leading Gianfranco and Ago by five seconds that my engine cut out as the magneto failed to supply sparks. There were only five laps of twenty-one to go, but there was nothing I could do. Not a single thing. I parked the MV against a little cigarette shop and walked over to where Madeleine was sitting on a tree stump, tears running down her face as she looked at me, I knew just how she felt.

Our only hope now was that Gianfranco could hold off Ago to stop him gaining maximum points from a win. But even he came to grief, when leading by five seconds, with only two laps to go. He crashed while trying to lap Toracca, ex-MV of all people! It was obviously a good day for ironies.

It was also a day when I decided that Barry wasn't a true friend. He patently had the quickest bike and before the race I'd put a proposition to him, to which he said, 'No problem mate'. I told him if we were together and well ahead of Ago, would he let me have the race to clinch the world championship? Suzuki had no chance and it was commercially better for them if MV Agusta won and not Yamaha. His response the next day just minutes before the start was, 'Sorry mate, but Suzuki want me to win'. He did not finish in the race and was in sixth place in the world championship series, plus he lost two good friends.

Ago needed only to finish in the first four at the Czech GP at Brno to reclaim his title, and he'd been around too long to do anything stupid in a situation like that. I was leading with three factory Suzukis behind and Ago in fifth place: during those laps I was world champion. Then disaster happened, one Suzuki after the other retired, leaving Ago time to stop for a safety 'splash and dash' fuel top-up to be in second place a minute behind me.

Later I heard a rumour that MV's new Sports Director, Fredmano Spairari had approached Barry, as well as Braun and Länsivuori, offering inducements to let me win. I don't know if there was any truth in that, but that would not have helped me or MV.

The win took my total points for the season to an impressive 96, but that was academic. Ago, with that second place at Brno, when counting the best six best performances, ruled the roost with eighty-four points to my seventy-six. Kanaya, who'd gone back to Japan halfway through the season, was third, and Tepi, who'd switched to Suzuki for this season was fourth. It was a frustrating year, made even more infuriating by the fact that, deep down, I felt I should have won that elusive third 500cc title. I even began thinking about the Suzuki offer, but I had survived a hard season without a crash caused by engine problems, unlike Barry. As the season progressed I grew disenchanted with the way MV was being run. There seemed to be too many people with different ideas of improving the

1975 500cc Czech GP podium: Phil Read first, Giacomo Agostini second and Alex George third, French rider Olivier Chevallier (right) was fifth.

machine and running the racing team. Take engineering director Luigi Ghisleri. His actual experience of racing was very limited, but he was full of great ideas on promotion and publicity. Team uniforms, boots, even some delectable young ladies were introduced to the MV team in 1974 for promotion purposes. Pleasant though it was to have them around, however, they didn't help us win races. And if Ghisleri thought the young ladies might serve some other purpose, he missed out on the fun we had, as an incident following the 1974 Dutch TT illustrates. I'd finished a pretty disappointing third at Assen that year, but even that was better than poor old Barry, who'd been forced to retire when the Suzuki began making noises similar to those when he was flung off at Imola. Consequently he was well down in the dumps at the way his luck was running. Madeleine and I decided to take him and his girl-friend Leslie, out to dinner to cheer them up. Alberto Pagani, at the time assistant team manager with MV, came with us; so too did Gianfranco, his girlfriend Graziella, and one of the MV 'models'. (The other one had gone off with Ago.) So much for improving MV's image! After dinner we all went back to my room, where we had a few more drinks, and what with the alcohol and the easing off of the tension that always accompanies race days, we were soon all pretty happy with life. Outside in the street, the budding Agostinis and Reads were doing their very noisy thing with burnouts and revving their motors till they blew. It was obvious we wouldn't get much sleep, so we ordered more drinks. It wasn't long before we had a good party going. Some time before midnight, the girls decided to remove the dirty old vest that Gianfranco never seemed to be without, regardless of time or place. They'd been threatening to take it from him for some time, and now they had the opportunity they made the most of it. Quite why they took his socks off first I'm not sure, but they did, and as each item of clothing came off, Madeleine and others flung the removed items unceremoniously out of the open window and over the balcony. Now it so happened that Ghisleri turned up at the hotel while all this was happening. He'd been dining with some of the FIM people and obviously felt it was time he got to talk with me. However, when the receptionist phoned through to my room to say he was downstairs, none of us bothered to pick up the phone. It was more fun watching Gianfranco lose his socks and other garments. The receptionist told Ghisleri that Mr Read had not returned, but as he was walking back to his car, he heard this great roar of laughter and screaming coming from my room. And just as he looked up a pair of ladies' jeans came floating over the balcony, into the street not far from where he was standing. You can just imagine what he must have thought: an orgy in Read's room and he was missing out. After all, it was he who had provided those lovely girls. 'Pheel', he shouted up to the balcony. 'Pheel! Pheel! Pheel Read! Pheel! Pleeze! Letta me in?' Poor Ghisleri, it just wasn't his night. We were making so much noise that we didn't hear his frustrated pleas. In the end he climbed into his car and drove back to his hotel, an unhappy man.

From a racing point of view, though, the promotion girls were a definite disadvantage. When you are riding to win, the last thing you want to have to worry about is posing with models and taking part in publicity stunts. Racing itself occupies all my time and energy at a meeting, and I wait until afterwards to let off steam. Nor do I think all those promotional activities did much good for MV in terms of selling their clothing or their bikes. Another of Ghisleri's ideas was that he could demand large sums of start money from the grand prix organisers in 1975. But as he took an assistant with him on pre-race trips to negotiate start terms, it was costing the factory more money than the few extra pounds he was able to extract from the different organisers. However, I came out of it very well, for when I was negotiating my new contract with MV, Ghisleri, confident of his

1975 Czech GP Brno, 500cc winner Read on 4 cylinder MV Agusta

ability to twist organisers' arms, agreed to pay me a set amount per grand prix. Little wonder, then, that the total cost of the racing year was much more than in the previous year. Despite considerable sponsorship from the Elf petrol and oil company, MV lost a lot of money from their 1975 racing activities. Niggling little things went wrong, too, due to insufficient organisation. For example, we arrived at Paul Ricard for the first grand prix of the 1975 season to discover we'd been allocated racing numbers in the twenties instead of the 'one' and 'two' to which we were entitled. Why? Because the organisers had been kept dangling for so long while Ghisleri was trying to arrange the terms he wanted that they didn't know for sure whether we would even be racing. It's not the sort of thing I should have had to worry about, but I was proud of riding with that number one emblazoned on my fairing - I'd earned it. In the end the organisers kindly gave me a zero. Quite what the significance of that was I'm still not sure. Perhaps they were trying to suggest I didn't exist!

Not long after the start of the 1975 season, Mr Ghisleri, not surprisingly, became deskbound through pressure of work, and MV brought in Fredmano Spairani, who had a background of success at Ducati. He was quite a different character, pushy, go-ahead, but I felt, lacking in sincerity. He was an expert in boosting morale from the lowest paid worker in the factory to those at the top of the managerial tree, a politician who would promise whatever was necessary to achieve his objectives, but who could always forget what he'd said if he had to. He seemed to promise me the earth if only I won the next race... or the next grand prix... or the world championship. An aircraft from the MV Agusta factory at a special low price was talked about at one stage, and though it was never directly linked with retaining the world title, I had no doubts that this was the arrangement. Angered, I told Spairani in no uncertain terms that I didn't need any incentives to help me win. I always rode to win. Still, I'm glad some of his promised deals never came to fruition. I'd won my races and my titles fairly and squarely out on the track, and if I couldn't win the world title that way in 1975, I certainly didn't need to win it any other way.

Then, finally, there was Arturo Magni, the team manager who had come from Gilera many years before to develop the MV into the greatest racing machine the world had seen. The history of MV is just as much the history of Arturo Magni. Yet surprisingly, for a man with 30-odd years of racing behind him, he could never see the need for round-table discussions between himself and the riders to formulate race plans. With Magni, it was every man for himself, and that's a dangerous policy. It's vital that riders know what plan to ride to so that they can help each other throughout the race. Of greater concern to me was that Magni seemed reluctant to try anything new. Perhaps after so many years of success he had begun to take it for granted that MV can win, but 1974 had shown that the MVs were losing their superiority, and 1975 confirmed the fact. In Magni's eyes, though, the problem was that Read and Bonera weren't riding his world-beaters to their fullest potential. He refused to accept that the opposition had caught up and even overtaken us.

Everything came to a head after the Italian Grand Prix. Count Agusta, having seen the electrifying duel between Ago and myself at Hockenheim and the way he powered away from me at Imola, called an emergency meeting. Magni, to try to prove that I was at fault, produced Imola lap times going back fifteen years! His times showed that I was not lapping as fast in 1975 as I had the previous year, and he argued that, with the engine improvements, I should have been going faster. I was beginning to feel that we were getting nowhere, when the Count cut him short. 'Signor Magni', he said, 'The machine is deficient. I will not allow Phil to risk his life like that for MV's sake. So what are you going to do about it?'

Seeing and hearing the bellowing four-stroke MV was a treat for fans at the 1975 Brands Hatch Hutchinson 100 meeting.

I could scarcely believe my ears. The Count, positive and decisive, was on my side. Now, surely, something would be done. But it just wasn't to be. Count Agusta is a busy man, for whom racing is an expensive hobby. He left it to his staff to tell him what was happening in the factory and with the team, and he wasn't always told the truth. When he did discover that nothing had been done to remedy the situation after Imola, it was too late. Had Magni not been so jealous of his reputation we might just have been able to do something to turn an unsuccessful season into a successful one. But his trouble was that he didn't want anyone else to take the credit. It was as if he was so insecure that he felt he'd lose his tight control of the racing team if he allowed anyone to 'interfere'. In 1974, there were two incidents which proved my point. First I suggested MV should call in Ken Sprayson, the frame expert at TI Reynolds, the tubing company, to help improve the handling. Ken made a number of valuable observations, such as suggesting Earles leading-link front forks to stop wheel chatter, but only a few of his recommendations were ever implemented. The rest were conveniently forgotten. Second, one of the engineers in the helicopter plant at Gallarate had asked for and was given permission to design a new frame for the racing machines. With the aid of a computer he designed the frame and had it built. But it was never developed properly. Bad suspension units were put on it, pieces were cut off the frame itself and others welded on. Whatever qualities the frame had in the first place were completely ruined. Who knows? It might have been the answer to our handling problems.

With Suzuki GB team boss Rex White and 750cc triple I raced at the end of the 1975 season

I think rivalry handicapped the Italian engineer, Giuseppe Bocchi, too. He was a brilliant man, a gifted engineer, but he knew nothing about motorcycle racing. He needed help, and Magni was the obvious person at the time to provide that help. Had it come, Bocchi could have done wonders for the MV racer. Instead, it was several years before his influence was felt, when his introduction of a counter-sprocket on the drive chain reduced the jumping effect of the rear wheel on braking.

No, it was all very disappointing. But that's life, Italian style, and there was little I could do about it. Anyway, the more I think about it, the more I'm convinced that 1975 just wasn't meant to be my year. Just look at how my season ended, in October, at the final round of the MCD Superbike series at Brands Hatch. I'd managed to persuade Suzuki GB to lend me a 750cc triple for the big race after Barry Sheene had broken his leg popping wheelies on a trials bike, and I was determined to show prospective sponsors that I was just as much at home on the 750s as on the 500s. Anyone who can remember watching ITV's *World of Sport* that day will know what happened. I was brought down in a first lap multiple pile-up. My race lasted fewer than three hundred yards and I came out of it with four badly broken ribs and a warning from the doctor that if they didn't knit together quickly I wouldn't be fit until February. I didn't believe him, but I should have. I don't think I helped myself much by trials riding around the garden and playing with the children on a mini-bike. All in all, it was a pretty depressing way to end the year. But even then, feeling sore in body and low in spirits, I had no thoughts of retirement.

I was determined to win back my 500cc world title, and I spent the winter months thinking about it and planning it. I was going to do it even if it meant I had to do it on my own.

Chasing Barry Sheene's Suzuki at La Source in the 1975 500cc Belgian GP, I won this race, but Ago won the world championship on his Yamaha.

8 The end of the Grand Prix trail

At the outset of 1976, I believed I had several good years of racing ahead of me.

Moreover, with more outside sponsors climbing on the motorcycling bandwagon, there seemed to be plenty of potential backers for me to run my own team. With MV reluctant to make a firm decision about their plans and news that other major factories were ending their official involvement, I offered to take over all the financial considerations of running the MV factory team, using the existing engines until the new 'Boxer' flat-four motors were available. It would have been expensive, but I felt it would be worth it. However, Count Agusta was lukewarm about the idea and finally turned it down.

Next I approached the Japanese. Kawasaki showed a flicker of interest that soon evaporated, and Yamaha said sorry but they were unable to help. In fact, they admitted privately that they were pleased when Ago turned down their offer of racing the 500cc Yamaha four because spares were in such short supply. But the TZ750 Yamaha was no problem as it was a production machine, and ultimately business contacts in America organised the 750cc that I rode at Daytona and through the remainder of the 1976 season.

What I desperately needed, though, was a 500cc machine, and my hopes rose when Suzuki GB showed interest. I should have known better. I may be wrong, but I suspect that I was being set up as bait to ensure they got Barry Sheene's autograph on a contract. Surely it was no coincidence that Suzuki GB lost interest in me as soon as they got Barry. I'm not blaming them, though I still feel hurt that no-one had the courtesy to give me an official answer to my enquiries after I'd had talks with the top men in the organisation, including managing director Peter Agg.

The first news I had of the Suzuki GB team for 1976 came from the motorcycle press, where I learned that Sheene, John Williams, and John Newbold had been signed. I don't really blame Barry for not wanting me in the same team. After all, what had I done for him apart from telling him how to get on in the racing world, to treat the right people with respect, improve his image by throwing away his scruffy old jackets and jeans and getting some smart casual clothes and taking care to invest for the future? And I'd flown him home a few times when he'd come off and broken something. They are the sort of things I did for a friend, and still would. Let's face it, if I'd had a potentially successful season thwarted through two freak accidents and was trying to negotiate a contract with a major sponsor, I wouldn't want a rider as good as Barry Sheene joining the ranks. It would simply make a difficult job even more of a problem. Besides, Barry, with his cult following, was getting a lot of publicity, some of which would naturally rub off on the Suzuki GB team. He was obviously their number one choice.

A greater disappointment was the collapse of the Professional Motorcyclists' Association International Ltd. The riders' 'union' had been set up that winter through Mark McCormack's sports management organisation, famous for handling top golfers and tennis stars. The plan was to have an association of leading riders, initially Giacomo Agostini, Gianfranco Bonera, Dieter Braun, Johnny Cecotto, Tepi Länsivuori, Victor Palomo, Patrick Pons, Michel Rougerie, Barry Sheene, Walter Villa and myself. The group would be offered to organisers at a package deal rate, and the start money obtained distributed to the riders on a sliding scale. Neither Ago nor myself at the top of the scale would really benefit, since individually we could negotiate similar fees on our own behalf. But we both wanted a strong, well-organised riders' body with a voice. We'd been involved in riders' unions over the years, none of which had worked properly but this plan promised to be the basis on which a viable organisation could evolve. Moreover, the other riders in the PMAI would certainly benefit, perhaps even doubling their previous start fees.

However, when it came to actually supporting the terms of the agreement and facing up to a head-on confrontation with the organisers, there was always too much dithering by some team-sponsored riders and that was the end of it. Without solidarity there was no bargaining power, and it wasn't surprising that McCormack decided to wash his hands of us. He'd already spent a lot of money registering the company in Guernsey, drawing up contracts and opening bank accounts in different parts of the world. He must have wondered just what sort of monkey outfit we motorcycle riders were. The failure of that venture disturbed me a lot. I'd put a lot of faith in it, yet it all came to nothing. It was the same old story; riders looking after their own short-sighted interests. Take Barry Sheene as an example. With his superfast Suzuki, he could see a world title at the end of the road, even if it meant being treated like a performing animal en route. The last thing he wanted was a season possibly punctuated by financial disputes between organisers and riders. To win that world title he needed to ride in and win every championship round he could. Any boycotts of meetings would have been disastrous to his ambitions. I can appreciate that. But we'd put a lot of time and thought into the Association and yet it seemed that, even with a powerful international group behind us, a mere eleven riders couldn't stand together to speak with a strong united voice. It was very frustrating.

Equally disheartening was my brief encounter with the Norton Cosworth Challenge in December and January of that winter. Facing a shortage of machines to race, I was attracted by the prospect of taking on the world with a British company, especially Cosworth with their vast experience in motor racing.

Norton had commissioned Keith Duckworth, chief engineer at Cosworth and brains behind the phenomenally successful DFV V8 racing engine, to design a 750cc motorcycle power unit. The idea was to replace the ancient pushrod engine Norton used in road and race bikes and when the project got under way priority was given to a racing version for the company's Formula 750 team.

Although John Player had withdrawn sponsorship after 1974, the Norton team battled on and the Norton Cosworth Challenge made its race debut at Brands Hatch late in the 1975 season, only to be involved in that same pile-up in which I'd broken my ribs.

However, looking at performance comparisons, I knew we'd have to lose some weight. My 500cc MV Agusta had developed 100bhp and weighed 130kg (285lb), whereas the 750cc Cosworth was developing only 90bhp while weighing about 45kg (100lb) more. Yet the MV was not competitive against the latest 750cc Japanese two-strokes.

I felt I could find the necessary sponsorship to develop the Cosworth engine if I organised my own Team Read. So I approached Dennis Poore of Norton Villiers Triumph (NVT) to obtain one of the Cosworth race engines and a complete chassis for development. Time was short and I wanted to set something up quickly. Poore not only agreed to the idea but suggested that, if I was interested, I could buy the entire Norton competition shop based at the Thruxton circuit for £10,000.

When Norton's team manager Frank Perris heard of my plan, though, I think he thought I wanted to kidnap his baby. That couldn't have been further from the truth: all I wanted was an engine and a chassis, just to get my own team on wheels. If necessary, I was prepared to co-operate with Norton's race shop, but if I was going to race and finance the bike, I wanted it under my direct control. Surely that wasn't unreasonable?

However, the whole thing fell through, mainly I think because when Ferrari won the first Formula 1 GP of 1976, all Keith Duckworth's attention was concentrated on the Formula 1 challenge. He simply could not spare the time needed to develop a Stage II engine for my machine and without his direct involvement I knew there was no way the venture could succeed.

Little did I realise when I reluctantly withdrew from the venture that a storm of wrath and indignation would come down on my head from the motorcycling press. I wasn't surprised, for I've often had the rough end of the stick in the papers when it comes to controversies, but the reactions and bitter accusations hurt very much. For all that I've always stood up and said what I think, I'm a very sensitive person, possibly introverted at heart. I may be positive in the things I do, but that doesn't mean criticism just falls off my back. No, I hurt like other people, and if I'm not showing it, then it doesn't mean that I'm not suffering deep down. The only trouble is that it all has to come out sometime and does so in unexpected ways. The person who kicks the dog or cries is lucky, he can relieve his emotions straight away. I live with mine.

Aside from the antagonism, I was genuinely sorry to be forced to withdraw from the Cosworth venture. I saw it as the British motorcycle industry's last chance to figure in top-class racing. And I don't think I'm being big-headed, when I say that I might have been the man to lead them back on the path to success.

Let me quote from *Motor Cycle*:

'The Norton Cosworth Challenge needs a rider of the calibre of Phil Read far more than he needs the so-far untried and unproven British hope. In fact, if Norton wanted to sign a rider of similar standing to Read it would cost them at least £20,000 - and that's assuming that such a rider is available and willing to chance his arm on a bike which, to be frank, is not at the moment very impressive. It is much too heavy and much too bulky.'

By contrast, look at the four-cylinder two-stroke Suzuki RG500 production machine I bought soon afterwards. Straight out of the packing case all it needed was a change of tyres to be instantly competitive against Agostini, who was back on the 500cc MV for 1976. It was a sad reflection of how Japanese factories had eclipsed the old British industry.

Phil Reads 1976 Suzuki RG500

On the RG500 Suzuki two-stroke four in 1976

At the same time as I was involved with the Cosworth I was busy negotiating to set up my team for 1976; an expensive business. It meant, for one thing, selling my coveted Cessna Skylane aircraft. It also meant hustling around Europe and the States seeking sponsors. But, in the end, the money was found, contracts tied up, a new transporter arranged through General Motors and mechanics hired. People had confidence in me; people like Castrol, who seemed to have supported me for as long as I could remember and for whom I've the utmost gratitude.

The person with most confidence in me in 1976, though, must have been Bob Eccles GM, the pilot in the RAF Red Arrows jet aerobatics team, with whom I flew later in the year. Before we started, the RAF ground crew stuffed sick-bags in the cockpit all around me, thanks, this flight is going to be body wrenching or should I say, 'wretching'. After the group had been through their manoeuvres, Bob climbed away to 10.000 feet when pulling some 6G aerobatics that had my head spinning and my stomach churning. Then he said, You have control, 'Roger', I replied. He not only let me fly his Gnat jet trainer but also let me put it through a basic series of loops, rolls, and spins. For me, being up there at speed with the world revolving around me was the thrill of a lifetime. And I didn't need the sick-bags, thank you, to the surprise of the ground crew after we landed! My pilot, on the other hand, thought the same about riding my Suzuki along the runway at 150mph.

'That was fantastic', he said. Mind you, when it came to telling each other how to handle our respective machines, Bob won hands down for 'what not to do' instructions. I told him not to apply the front brake too hard, otherwise he'd be thrown off, and keep the revs above 8,000rpm. When I was about to perform my first loop, he warned me not to pull too quickly on the controls - otherwise the wings would fall off!

I wasn't neglecting my business interests either, while trying to arrange the coming season's racing. Towards the end of 1974 and in the early part of 1975, the Premier Helmet company whose product I had been wearing since meeting American owner Chuck Tinch, in California, in 1971 went through a bad financial patch. I had the opportunity of buying their factory in Shannon, Ireland for a nominal amount. While the racing season was in full swing there was little time to devote to the business, so the winter had to be spent flying backwards and forwards between Heathrow and Shannon, plus trips to distributors on the Continent. Safety standards and quality had to be checked; solicitors and accountants had to be met. I was almost glad when time came, in the first week of March, to fly to Florida for the 200-mile Daytona classic.

I say 'almost' because Daytona never rated highly for me. The sunshine, the beach, the glamour, the razzamatazz of American showmanship are all very fine, but they count for nothing if you don't win. Even less if, as happened to me, the bike only lasts for six laps, because then it's very expensive. It cost more than a thousand pounds to compete there, and all but a few went home with much more than an unhappy bank manager to show for their troubles. Then, too, there are all those weird and wonderful taxes the Americans specialise in. And on top of everything else, it's a boring circuit: once everyone sorts themselves out, the race becomes a mere procession. Give me an interesting British or Continental circuit any day.

After America, it was straight down to Italy and one of those bitterly cold days you could get at the old Autodromo di Modena: there was snow on the Apennine mountains and an icy wind that cut through normal protective clothing. I was wearing a hooded fur coat I'd bought in Alaska over my leathers but was still shivering. Little wonder that people around the track were lighting fires that sent clouds of smoke billowing all over the circuit.

My first flight with the Red Arrows; RAF pilot, Bob Eccles GM, let me perform some loops and fast flick rolls in the fantastic Gnat jet.

The new Team Read was in Modena for the early-season Italian internationals, trying to sort out my 500cc Suzukis before the start of the grand prix season.

Happily, though, it took more than a spell of cold weather to stop racing at Modena, in the homeland of Ferrari and Maserati. And racing we were. Or at least some people were. My race lasted as far as the first corner. Quite what happened I don't remember: others have since related different versions.

Apparently, my old MV team-mate Gianfranco Bonera went into a slide at the corner, a slow left-hander, and I put my bike down to avoid hitting him. Mind you, I'd have done the same for anyone, but Gianfranco's a special friend; I'd even lend him the key of the Rolls. Unfortunately I didn't account for the riders behind us. Someone ran over me; I remember that. I'm told someone else went over my head. I don't remember that bit, but it was a damned good advertisement for Premier Helmets that I lived to tell the story.

In the pits, Geoff and Jim, my mechanics and Vittorio Fabbri, who looked after my Italian interests, were waiting for me to come around. Their worst fears were confirmed when they heard the ambulance siren, then saw it haring towards that corner. Off raced Geoff and Vittorio, arriving in time to see the ambulance driving off with a pair of red Read International boots sticking out at the back.

I'm told I was in a pretty bad way, even needing heart resuscitation in the ambulance. But I was conscious by the time Geoff and Vittorio arrived at the hospital. The room was already full of Italians, some of whom I recognised, others I didn't even know. In fact, there seemed to be a lot I didn't know; probably because I was still suffering from concussion. For one thing I didn't know where I was, and when Geoff fought his way through the crowd, I kept asking him what had happened.

'It was just like that crash you had at Brands,' he said. 'What crash at Brands?' I asked. 'I've never crashed at Brands.'

'Don't you remember? End of last season, when you broke your ribs.'

'No, never crashed at Brands,' I persisted. 'Where am I? What happened?'

He tried to keep talking to me quietly, but it was hopeless. Confusion reigned; in my head, and around my bed. There were doctors telling me I needed two weeks' rest; other people, ignorant of the medical issues, were telling me I could get out of bed and go back to my hotel. Well, I've never been one for staying in bed longer than I have to, not without some interesting incentive, and encouragement like that was all I needed.

Geoff had brought the fur coat with him, so wearing that, my racing boots, and very little else, I discharged myself. The following day the Italian papers featured pictures of this mad, fur-coated Englishman marching out of hospital. I don't think many of the English papers gave me the same publicity, but maybe I should be glad of that!

Back at my hotel, Geoff and Vittorio evicted some of the camp followers and gradually restored order. We had something to eat as I was starving and then I went to bed and slept long and well. The next morning I drove the Rolls to Bologna and flew home. What was worrying me most of all was whether or not I could race the following weekend in the Imola International. It would be my last opportunity to test the 500cc Suzuki against Agostini's MV before the grands prix. Would my doctors let me race? The answer was a kind of yes, but only if I wanted to badly enough. They wouldn't advise it. What the hell, I thought. I'd been advised not to race before - and yet won vital GPs. It was not as if I had to win at Imola, but I did need to see how competitive my new Suzukis were.

Malcolm Edgar's contribution

Whilst attending the Motorcycle Show in 1975, Phil asked me to work for him as Sales Manager in his Phil Read International business at Hersham, near Walton-on-Thames. I accepted his offer and started work in the office alongside Barbara who was his secretary as well as running the office.

Phil had been associated with Premier Helmets since 1971 and his familiar helmet was known world-wide. The factory in California was owned by Chuck Tinch who had encountered some financial difficulties. At that time, the authorities at Shannon Airport were leasing business units within the International Duty Free area of the airport. Chuck Tinch took one of these units and started to produce Premier Helmets from this address.

Unfortunately for him, it was not easy to run a factory so far from California and quite soon he was forced to put the business up for sale. He approached Phil and together they worked out a deal whereby Phil bought the Premier Helmet rights in return for a nominal sum. Phil also took over the lease and all the debts.

At the factory, Pat Frost was in charge of finance and administration. He was doing a fantastic job within the constraints put on him. It was very evident, however, that Pat could not do everything on his own so I was asked to go over to Shannon in order to take on the job of finding European distributors, gaining all the required approvals in each country, as well as taking responsibility for the day-to-day running of the factory. I accepted this challenge and spent the whole of 1976 travelling between England and Eire as well as setting up distributors in every major European country.

In those days, Premier Helmets were well ahead of the market with their range of designs and colours. Demand was high but production was slow. It should be remembered that each helmet was made by hand from an individual mould. Designs were drawn, masked and sprayed by hand and each helmet was individually assembled and boxed. This was very time-consuming and expensive and it was very hard to increase the production volume. Finance was not easy, because Phil was also actively establishing the Phil Read International business in England. During 1976, sales grew each month and the helmets were meeting 'Type Approvals' and 'Testing' in each country. In the short term things were looking very good.

Unfortunately, the time came when there was not enough finance available to carry on in the ever-developing helmet market and I could not continue to spend so much time in Shannon when my family was back home in England. Ultimately, a decision was made to sell the Premier name to Raymaker of Holland, who was already the largest Premier Helmet distributor and knew the products well. That company made Lookwell Leathers and had manufacturing contacts in Italy as well as other European countries. It was natural, therefore, that they would probably be the best company to source a new helmet production facility. This would almost certainly be in Italy.

Reluctantly, I parted company with Phil, although we have remained friends to this day.

Consequently, the following weekend saw me back in Italy, at Imola. I wasn't feeling great. In fact, there were times when I felt bloody rotten. When I got on the bike for practice, it was a very fragile Phil Read who finished well down in qualifying. Still, I was happy with the bike and when, in the race, I was able to sit on Ago's tail for most of the distance, I almost forgot the crippling pain in my side. At the finish, although I had dropped back a bit among the tail-enders, I was only three and a half seconds down on the MV. I was happy: the Suzuki was competitive.

Physically, though, I was shot. I couldn't even use the clutch to stop the bike and had to stall it in fourth. Somehow I managed to get off and hand the bike to Jim. Back in the caravan I collapsed in pain.

You might say a more sensible person would never have considered riding in the Imola 200 the following weekend. They would have taken a few weeks off to prepare for the first round of the world championships, the French GP at Le Mans in late April. But look at people who get to the top in life: they're the ones who are out there every day, rain or shine. They don't sit on their backsides, living on sick pay or Social Security. I'm a motorcycle racer. It has been my career, my whole life. There was a race at Imola and I was going to ride in it.

Mind you, my body had other ideas. During the week I caught flu, and then it came to light that I'd cracked some ribs in that Modena episode. No wonder my chest was hurting. Nevertheless I was at Imola for the practice sessions, and this time, my body was tired of being torn apart by Read bloody-mindedness and threw down a handful of aces. I had contracted bronchial pneumonia; and that was that. Madeleine put her foot down. We were going back to England: but not before one final aggravation. The organisers refused to pay over any of the money they had promised - a continuing saga in my dealings with Italian organisers.

Back in England the doctors, hiding their 'we told you so' expressions rather well, ordered a complete break. A proper holiday, a family holiday. I was no longer in the mood to argue, and the next five days found us and the boys, Pip and Marc, at Restronguet, near Falmouth in Cornwall. My doctor had advised me it was a good area by the sea where I could rid my lungs of infection. We often walked to the harbour there, fished and bought lobsters from the fishermen to cook back at our riverside cottage. No doubt the doctors were thinking of longer than five days when they ordered me to rest.

We all had a great time but I had to captain the British team in the Easter Transatlantic meeting against the Americans, didn't I? You don't just give up an honour like that because you'd been feeling a bit ropey. That short spell away from the pressures of racing, running a team, and my other business interests, also gave me a chance to sit back and think of one or two other matters. Perhaps because I was now in my twenty-first year of racing, people had been speculating that 1976 would be my last season. Myself, I didn't know. Certainly, at 37, I felt I might have a bit longer to go, but it's a long haul around the Continent in the fight for championship points. Down there in Cornwall, away from the sound· of revving motorcycles and ringing telephones, playing with Pip and Marc, taking time over meals, I began to see what I was missing: a happy family life.

Easter brought the Transatlantic Series against the Americans in which, despite Barry's disapproval, I captained the British side. We won, too, and considering the bronchial patch on my lungs I was most pleased with my performance: fourth best score overall. Barry rode really well, topping the British scorers, helping us to victory, which is why I handed the Transatlantic Trophy over to him, rather than keep it for myself, which I was entitled to as captain.

My production 750 Yamaha didn't perform as well as I needed to be competitive with the other top riders, first with a standard chassis, then a Don Vesco one. But when I had a Dutchman, the great Nico Bakker, make me one, my results improved.

The next Sunday saw the start of the world championship, with the French Grand Prix at Le Mans, where the Suzuki seized. But it was going really well again at Salzburgring and I was leading the Austrian GP there when I cranked over that tiny bit too far and hit my knee on a pavement, forcing me to drop back, and I eventually finished third behind the Suzukis of Barry and Marco Lucchinelli. With a fortnight between Austria and the Italian round at Mugello, we were able to bring the better of our two RG500s to fine racing pitch; the result of weeks of experiment and testing. We improved the suspension, fitted new brakes, a special new ignition system and carried out some engine modifications. Yet, after all that, I was left behind on the grid at the start. All that hard work looked like being to no avail, but I got my head down and began to make up lost ground. By the halfway stage I had caught up with Ago and Barry, who were lying first and second respectively, and when Barry took Ago, I went by as well. From then on, we were really racing. Every time I sneaked past Barry he came back again. Behind us Virginio Ferrari was taking over third spot from Ago, but most of the crowd were gripped by the lead-swapping duel between Barry and myself. The support the crowd gave me that day was overwhelming and was I mistaken, or were some of the Suzuki GB team actually cheering me on as well? At the finish there was only half a wheel in it, but the winner's garland was Barry's after one of the great races of the season. For me, on a production machine against Barry's specially prepared factory version, it was a moral victory and one of the most memorable rides in my long career.

750cc Yamaha, Mallory Park 1976

Back home there were business problems requiring attention, then it was off to Austria again to take a 750cc victory in an international, which augured well for the following weekend's international meeting at Mettet in Belgium. However, the Yamaha gave me innumerable handling problems on that super-fast circuit and I ended up finishing third overall behind the Yamahas of Ago and Takazumi Katayama. Racing at Brands Hatch, Chimay in Belgium, the Post TT at Mallory Park and the Norisring in Nuremberg kept me fully occupied before the Dutch TT. And it left me feeling more and more tired. Days I spent flying to the Premier helmet factory in Shannon would have been better spent in a gym, getting fit and building up my strength. Also, I could have done with more sleep than I was getting. I wasn't the only one suffering from this hectic whirl of business and racing. The children, especially Pip who was now at school, found the constant coming and going of their parents disturbing. Madeleine was advised to devote more time to them, but that was not easy, because I expected her - or should I say, needed her - to be at race meetings with me. She decided not to go to Assen for the Dutch. We argued, and in the end she came, but the meeting was a disappointment. My heart went out of the race once the bike began misfiring, and I knew it wasn't worth struggling on just to finish well down. Some people said later that I pulled out because I knew I couldn't win, but that's ridiculous. The last thing I am is a quitter. If the bike had been fully competitive that day I'd have raced on to the bitter end. But there seemed little use flogging round on a bike that wasn't running right, especially in the middle of the heatwave we had in that summer of 1976. It was just as hot in Belgium, too, the next weekend. We'd flown home from Amsterdam the previous Sunday, so I had to drive from there to Spa on the Thursday, fitting in a meeting with my Dutch helmet distributor en route. Madeleine was due to fly in to Brussels the next day.

Apart from the extreme heat, there was an added hassle at the Belgian GP. Machine noise was restricted to 120 decibels and our immediate problem, and other riders' as well, was an absence of silencers for the exhaust pipes. Madeleine was going to bring a consignment of them, but machines were supposed to be muted for Friday morning's pre-practice scrutineering. Merv Wright, Suzuki GB's team manager, promised to get us a dispensation so I could at least practise on Friday, and then on Friday night we'd fit the silencers for Saturday practice. Madeleine arrived on Friday afternoon just in time to see me record second fastest time to date. Geoff had done a lot of good work on the bike and I ended practice with high hopes of a Francorchamps hat-trick that would put me right back in contention for the title. But while she was as pleased as me about the practice times, Madeleine wasn't so happy after the non-stop aggravation she'd had on the journey from Heathrow. The trouble began when the package of silencers 'blipped' going through the metal detector as they were being cleared. Madeleine, who was by then settling down in the plane, was called back to customs to open the parcel, which she did, only to fall foul of a ridiculous example of Britain's disastrous bureaucracy.

She had been asked to describe what was in the parcel and when she had said 'silencers for motorbikes' the Customs officer was not happy because it said 'mufflers' on the declaration form. She explained that some people called them mufflers, as they muffled the exhaust sound. Our servant of bureaucracy was not easily persuaded, but in the end he agreed to release the parcel, once Madeleine had repacked it. All this had taken thirty to forty-five minutes, holding up a flight that was already running late. Madeleine had to re-board the waiting aircraft, trying to ignore the curious stares of fellow passengers. Then, at Brussels, the car that was supposed to be meeting her never appeared, which meant an £80 taxi fare to Francorchamps. Even then her troubles weren't over. Despite the fact that

Mallory Park and the TZ750 in the colours of my Italian sponsor Life Helmets

she was carrying a Laissez Passer card purchased at considerable cost from the ACU, the marshals refused to let her into the paddock. She had to hustle about, borrowing passes from mechanics, in order to get herself and the taxi driver into the paddock. Finally, Suzuki had their silencers - or was it mufflers? And of those, we needed only four for our bike.

Of all the days of the 1976 season to have to go through such hassle, that Friday must have been one of the worst. It was so unbearably hot and sticky. Even that evening, as we dined in the village, there was no escaping the heat. It was so bad that I couldn't stay inside to finish my meal, going out instead to sit on the steps of the inn, drinking a coffee and watching the crowds pour into the village and down the hill to the camp sites. My head throbbed. I listened to people talking in the bar, the mechanics laughing and swearing at the bar billiards table. Once upon a time the place would have been full of riders, I thought, but now it was the mechanics who enjoyed the camaraderie of the bar. The riders aspired to higher pleasures. It had all changed so much; so much. I watched the non-stop stream of traffic, from mopeds to Honda superbikes, VW Beetles to Alfas and Mercedes. I began to feel very depressed and tired. I wanted to be away from all the noise, all the people.

I needed to sleep. But a message we'd received from Carol, the children's nanny, that things were not going well at home was playing on my mind. It seemed to be the final link in a long chain of events.

Another time it might not have worried me. I might have looked at everything more rationally. Or perhaps I was being rational in deciding that my children came before everything else. Certainly that was how it seemed to me at the time. Madeleine argued that I should honour my racing commitments, but I refused to listen. I had made my mind up. I was going home. I stormed out of the hotel and into the Rolls and went hurtling off through the Belgian night to reach the ferry at Zeebrugge. I had arrived there before the full realisation of what I'd I done struck me, and by then it was too late.

As dawn approached, I sat in a deserted cafe, alone and unrecognised drinking coffee and endlessly smoking cigarettes, watching the black North Sea gradually turn grey. I was waiting for the ferry that would carry me back to England. I had turned my back on the grand prix circus; I had climbed off the merry-go-round.

Not for the first time in my life, I'd acted on impulse. I almost wished someone would come and talk me into going back to Spa. But no-one came, and I returned to England and my sons. My stupid argument with Madeleine had sent me hurtling through the Belgium night to the coast and home.

When the national press found out they had a field day, of course. Well, those who specialise in dragging people's lives through the mud did. But they see only the moment, then they move on to the next target and leave you to clean off the mud they've slung. What they never know, and never bother to find out, is what makes things like my sudden departure from Spa happen.

There were other problems, too, including a split-up between the partners who ran Life International, Italian helmet makers, who were my race team sponsors, which was managed by ex-rider Alberto Pagani, son of former MV team boss Nello Pagani. I was not getting the outstanding 50% of funds agreed so could not afford to continue to finance the running of three bikes, three team personnel and a large team transporter/motorhome. Maybe I could have found another sponsor, but I left Spa in a huff and looking back on everything that had happened, the injuries, the frustrations, the disappointments, I'm only surprised I didn't snap completely. Perhaps, I should have retired from the grand prix scene at the end of 1975, after all?

The trouble is that motorcycle racing's more than just a job, it's a way of life.

You don't ever reach a point where you sit down and say, 'That's it. Give me my gold watch and pension. I'm retiring now.'

But, several days after returning to England, I announced my decision to retire from world championship racing, confining myself instead to the major British races and a few chosen internationals on the Continent. Gradually the phone stopped ringing every few minutes, and by the following week life was almost back to normal. We began work on a swimming pool and there were business matters to attend to. We had family and friends to stay, took the children to the zoo and did other things that normal parents do. In fact, for the first time, we settled down into some form of family life. In time, we became relaxed.

Fortunately, there were still races to run and bikes to be tested. I don't think I could have adapted to not racing at all and I certainly enjoyed the latter part of 1976. I rode well, but even more satisfying was the tremendous reception the fans gave me. The motorcycle papers had been very kind to me when I announced my retirement from GP competition, but I was still apprehensive when I made my first appearance at Silverstone for the Hutchinson 100. I needn't have worried. The fans were terrific and I was overwhelmed by the response when I turned out to race on an MV at Cadwell Park in September.

I was surprised that Count Agusta agreed to let us have the machine but I felt the British fans deserved to see - and especially hear - that tremendous beast in action at least once in the season. Happily the Count saw my point of view, and the Cadwell crowd were treated to the sight and sound of the MV at the end of its racing life. I'd raced my 750cc Yamaha earlier in the meeting, finishing fifth after a really tiring ride. But all feelings of exhaustion disappeared with the noise of the MV being warmed up. I couldn't wait to get out there and put it through its paces again. I didn't really think I could win against the works Suzukis and the Kawasakis in the up-to-1000cc event, but I was determined to go down fighting. For something like the first eight laps I held the lead, lapping Cadwell faster than the MV had ever been round before, and I'm not exaggerating when I say the crowd reacted like fans at a pop concert. Every time I went past they were leaping up and down, waving and cheering at me and the bellowing red and silver machine. I was so moved it's a wonder I didn't lose control, because the brute was still a swine to handle. But it felt so good. And that superb sound. No wonder, after a season monopolised by shrieking Japanese two-strokes, everyone was turned on. Even when Barry Ditchburn went past me on his Kawasaki the crowd still cheered and cheered. Poor Barry. I felt sorry for him, for he'd ridden well to take victory yet was scarcely heralded by the crowd. They were all with the MV, there was a standing ovation as I did a farewell lap of honour. After the race we were swamped by fans wanting to look at the bike and wish me well. Someone gave Arturo Magni a fiver to buy drinks for the MV mechanics. Even when we did eventually get away from the circuit, there was no getting away from the fans. We stopped some distance away for a meal, and fans kept coming up while we were eating to ask for autographs and to thank me for racing the MV that day.

Throughout the week, came the letters and the telegrams. Thanks, thanks, and more thanks. Not just for Cadwell but for everything I'd done for British motorcycle racing in my career. It was as if people had seen something symbolic that day. Phil Read and the MV, two old warriors at the end of a great era of motorcycle racing.

elf
1
GUSTA
1

There was a similar reaction from the Italian fans at Mugello a week later. With Ago rejecting the MV during practice, I was asked to ride it and was only too happy to do so. Once again we worked together perfectly, the MV taking two seconds off its own best time around Mugello. But then I stuck my knee out a bit too far on a corner, hit a curb, and had to fall back because the pain was so intense. In fact, I was lucky not to be ending the season on crutches. That would not have been good, since the end of the 1976 season looked like also being the end of the career of Phil Read, seven times world champion, second only to Mike Hailwood as Britain's most successful rider.

I wanted to walk away on my own two feet with my head held high.

9 Back in the Island

Many people were surprised - and some were even angry - when I entered three 1977 TT races after the criticisms I'd made of the Isle of Man Mountain circuit being further included in the World Championship Series and of the ACU TT organisers, since deciding not to race there again five years earlier.

I was returning to TT racing. Some said I had to eat my words, but in fact it wasn't so much me who had changed, but the TT programme itself.

After 28 years as an FIM world championship venue, the IoM TT event had been stripped of its Grand Prix status. By that time there was a widely held view that the 37$^{3}/_{4}$ miles Mountain Course racing, held on public roads, could not meet the new International Grand Prix safety standards. This kept most of the big names and factory teams on the international scene from racing there.

The FIM and the ACU came to an agreement that gave the event a new identity. It had originated a new race programme to include three TT Formula races for production-based machines which would carry their own FIM sanctioned world titles. Also to give the needed boost to their new-look TT, the ACU were prepared - at last - to pay top riders and race teams much better appearance fees and considerably increased prize money for all classes. They were offering a lot more than the paltry amounts I was paid in 1972.

My worry had always been that the factory riders and top privateers were more or less forced to compete in the TT so as not to lose valuable championship points.

For this they were paid a pittance that would not keep two people for a day. After all, the TT event spans more than two weeks and then there is the cost of ferries to get there. On top of this, riders were expected to risk their lives at the most dangerous event in the calendar for little reward. I had lost three friends and a number of close acquaintances who were killed racing at the TT for championship points.

But finally attitudes towards these complaints from disaffected riders and teams were beginning to change for the better. The ACU realised they needed to be generous in order to attract top names and teams. I remembered a few years before, as five times world champion, I'd been paid only £50 to race and received an insulting £150 for my win.

It was entirely my decision, with the support of Madeleine, to ride there again in 1977. I recognised and accepted that as I had been offered more than enough to cover our expenses to fulfil my ambitions, with the chance of another FIM world title, it was worth making an effort. That was more like it - and it did show a good result for all the efforts that I and others had made since 1972 to improve these things for current and future riders.

Many people on the Isle of Man tended to take great offence at any criticism of the TT and a few over there were not at all happy about my come-back. Some of the marshals even threatened to go on strike if I raced and when I arrived on the Island one fuel station on the TT course childishly refused to fill up my car.

I had three competitive rides to look forward to. The Honda Britain racing team set up by Honda UK's Gerald Davison was keen to contest this first Formula 1 race, the most important of the three new TT Formula championship events. I signed up to ride their special 810cc Honda built to fit the Formula 1 rules. It had a factory-kitted four-cylinder engine based on the latest version of the CB750 road bike fitted in a chassis from one of the RCB fours, purpose-built for racing in the European Endurance Championship.

For the Senior TT, I had arranged the loan of an RG500 four, similar to the bike Barry Sheene raced in the world championships, from Suzuki GB, while for the up-to-1000cc Classic race I would be lent a Yamaha TZ750 four cylinder two-stroke by the recently retired racer and former Triumph factory tester Percy Tait.

Things looked good - until I got to the Island for practice week and discovered that Suzuki GB hadn't taken the promised bike to the Island for me, they only had one of their spare engines to loan me. Luckily we were able to borrow a spare chassis from Irish racer Billie Guthrie, whose engine had been wrecked during his first practice session. By chance I met Bob White, recently a race mechanic with Suzuki GB, in the hotel bar and he agreed to install the engine and prepare it for the Senior race. Bob made some conditions: we should put the name of his new business in Chester, Bob White Racing, on its fairing and if I did well in the race he wanted my TT trophy. I was happy to agree with Bob to benefit from his fine skills. Thank God I did, as you will read.

Once we had a complete bike we did what was not unusual on the Island, I tested it on open public roads, before taking it out for official practice. We used the long uphill Ballamodha straight between Castletown and Foxdale. The bike was warmed up while I got into my leathers, then I set off and it really flew up the hill. We did a plug chop to get the carburation correct for the conditions, but on the next run the Suzuki went slower and the next run slower still. Bob said he thought the water pump was faulty and he was right: a vital Woodruff key driving the impeller was completely missing. Very strange! When he'd fixed that we had another road test and it felt faster than any RG I'd ridden before. This time the cops turned up and were threatening to book us, but Bob talked them round to see sense after promising never to do it again, in that area.

The Honda Britain team were at an endurance race on the Continent, so they sent Ken Hull from their car department to be my mechanic; he did a good job and I was the fastest Formula 1 rider in practice. I realised how seriously Honda were taking this race when Aika-san, the former grand prix team boss and chief engineer, now in charge of the European Endurance racing campaign, arrived on the Island. He took charge, making sure a new primary chain was fitted along with other things needed for a successful race. Now I felt the big responsibility I had and the uncomfortable pressure to win. Gerald Davison, who had been at the European meeting, flew over, also, I had some especially welcome moral support when Madeleine, despite being in poor health, flew over to join me and my team.

The Formula 1 was the second race in the programme, to run over five laps on the Saturday afternoon. I started at number 11, alongside the to-be-great Joey Dunlop, under grey skies. By the second lap it had started to rain. In those days there wasn't much you could do to stop helmet visors misting, apart from a smear of washing-up liquid, and I started having serious visibility problems. I had to flip the visor up so I could see better up over the Mountain but after the Verandah it became unattached from one side of my helmet. In my effort to re-fix it the visor came off in my hand. I was forced to ride 'no hands' to re-fix it . Wow, that was a near disaster as without a visor I could not have ridden fast in that rain. The rain got worse: it was absolutely tipping down. I was wearing red leathers and I can tell you that my whole body was dyed red for a week. There was standing water on the tarmac and every time the big Honda started to slide across the road I thought I'd crashed. I'd stopped for fuel at the end of the second lap and was due to stop again to top up at the end of the next lap, but at Governor's Bridge I got a signal not to stop for fuel. I slowed down on the approach to the pits to see Gerald Davison, waving frantically at me to stay out on the course. I kept going but was a bit puzzled and decided the team may have thought that the race was so slow that I wouldn't need a second stop.

When I got 'last lap' signals, I realised what was happening. The race had been cut from five laps to four, very unusual at the TT then - it had only ever happened once before, in the 1954 Senior.

At the end of the fourth lap I took the chequered flag to win the race by nearly 40 seconds from Roger Nicholls on the Sports Motor Cycles Ducati. His team was very unhappy, because they only heard about the race being shortened after Roger had stopped for fuel at the end of his third lap. Luckily Mr Davison had already asked the Clerk of the Course what he was going to do in these worsening weather conditions and heard of the race being shortened minutes before it was announced on the public address. I was later told my Honda was not only nearly out of fuel when I crossed the line but the oil tank, which was due

Starting the historic first Isle of Man TT Formula 1 race on the 810cc Honda, it would rain heavily and without the benefit of wet tyres it was the most dangerous race of my life. I won at an average of 98mph. Phew!

Well tucked in through Union Mills on the first and only dry lap

On wet roads in the 1977 F1 TT

to be topped up on the second pit-stop, was also nearly dry. We had been very lucky on that very wet day!

I had not only won another TT race, but had collected my eighth FIM world championship gold medal. For this presentation the FIM invited Madeleine and me to their annual conference that year, at Caracas in Venezuela. There we met Barry Sheene and Stephanie who were there to collect his second 500 GP world championship medal. It was a very impressive event, with the usual jollifications up to a high standard.

For our return trip home, Madeleine and I took advantage of this honoured invitation to South America for a stop-off on the Caribbean island of St Lucia for a few days to benefit from sun, sea and surf. It would boost us before the hectic life we faced on our return to the UK.

When the ACU, together with the TT organisers, were negotiating with the FIM to replace the grand prix-status TT events with three Formula 1, 2 and 3 races, they lacked some lateral thinking. The new world championship road racing classes would have been more commendable and progressive if they had included the Dundrod and North West 200 events in Ulster, and maybe included an established Continental road-race event. That would have attracted more manufacturers to participate with roadster-based machines more in keeping with original traditions of the Isle of Man Tourist Trophy. Also this would have greatly reduced the costs of producing special superbike machines, which now have ballistic speeds to make them heart-stopping to race without electronic controls. I am told this did eventually happen to this TT Formula 1 Series in later years, but was not well enough promoted to obtain the deserved international prestige.

Back to the 1977 TT. When I went up to collect the trophy at the Villa Marina prize giving that evening, there were a few cat-calls from the crowd but two days later I got more sympathy and acclaim after I won the Senior race on that Suzuki RG 500 MkI that Bob built, on which I had led from start to finish. We only had to make one fuel stop thanks to an auxiliary tank fitted behind the seat. It began to drizzle with mist over the Mountain and for the second time in that TT, the race was shortened, from six laps to five.

Winning the 1977 Senior TT on the RG500 Suzuki prepared by Bob White

Easing round the slow Quarterbridge corner in the 1977 Senior, which I was lucky to win. Thanks to a lady marshal, I avoided hitting a fallen Alex George.

That victory meant a lot to me because the Senior TT is historically the most important of the Mountain Course races and I'd always felt that I'd under-achieved in not having won this race. Mind you, there was a moment on the last lap when I thought I was going to die. Racing in the mist over the Mountain, I was about to swoop through a fast right-hander before Black Hut when I saw a marshal waving a yellow duster, which is what they used before proper flags were available. Next thing I saw after slowing was Alex George lying in the road on my racing line and by a miracle I managed to avoid him, just. He had started before me on his Yamaha and was threatening to nibble my lead away on that last lap, but he made a painful mistake to miss this corner.

Looking back at this Senior TT race, run in far from good weather and the horrendous conditions for the Formula 1 race, there is a contrast with today's TT, when a race can be called off merely because of some wet patches on the road, as happened with the 2012 Senior after a rain shower around the Ramsey area. I understand that safety is rightly a huge issue today, but a complete cancellation seemed too drastic to me. Apparently the problem was that there were no wet tyres available for the top riders. So why can't a fully prepared team have a set of wheels fitted with intermediate tyres to exchange on the bike if the roads come damp or wet in some sections of the course. We used to race in the wet and ride according to conditions, we knew that the throttle turned both ways,. Before the age of 'Elf and Safety', when mist covered the Mountain during the races, some successful riders would count the seconds between corners, to know when to begin to turn or brake. That was another skill of Isle of Man racing which I believe to be the true spirit and tradition of Tourist Trophy racing on the world's longest and most demanding road circuit.

Back in 1907, TT racing started on the Island because speed events on English roads were banned by law and there were no motorsports racing circuits then. From 1908 motorcycles raced on the newly-built Brooklands high-speed banked circuit in Surrey, but they were specialised track machines far removed from road-going motorcycles. Manufacturers wanted an arena in which to show that their products could be reliable and a viable form of transport in all conditions on normal roads. TT racing competition also helped enormously with machine development, especially when the arduous Mountain Course was adopted from 1911. Stanley Woods, the TT legend of pre-war days, once told me, 'When racing over the Mountain to win, you needed to choose the best of the two ruts in the cart track.'

A third win in Wednesday's Classic on Percy Tait's 750cc Yamaha TZ, which was faster than any other bike I had raced there, would have been fantastic, but that wasn't to be.

I had flown Yamaha race bike specialist Roger Keen over from France to look after that bike for me. Everything had gone okay in practice, except for heart-stopping moments when it wheelied violently in a number of places and when accelerating up Creg Willys Hill. I asked Roger to fit a new chain, tyres and brake pads for Friday's final practice session, to be bedded-in ready to race the full six lap distance. But when I went to our garage to collect the bike from him for this final and important practice, he hadn't touched it - he'd been too busy working on other riders' bikes. I sacked him there and then.

That meant I still needed to get my Yamaha ready for the race next day, and now was forced to miss this last practice session. So, with friends, we did the required work and took the bike out on the Tuesday evening to do some rather illegal testing with slick tyres on open roads. We used the long straight-ish section from Creg-ny-Baa down to Brandish corner to find the best main jet sizes and to settle down the other new parts. On the third run, I cut the engine and was free-wheeling around the Brandish left-hander towards Hillberry, where my helpers were waiting. Suddenly, for what reason I could not remember, I found myself laying on the road and in pain.

The bike and I were quickly bundled into the van and returned to our Douglas garage. I was still sitting in my van in a daze, with my collar bone sticking out of my leathers, when a policeman put his head in the window to tell me, 'You're nicked!'

Apparently, a local trouble-making individual had followed us and tipped off the cops. They threw the book at me, because that year the Manx police were having a crackdown on fans tearing round the course on open roads. Racing slicks are bald tyres, illegal after all, on public roads! Instead of me riding in the Classic race, Mad and I left the Island with my arm in a sling on a private flight to Fairoaks airfield, near to our Surrey home. But before we left I had arranged to meet the lady marshal who had saved my life in the Senior to present her with my winning helmet.

Despite everything it was job done: I had won two TT races, one on a four-stroke and one on a two-stroke. I'd collected more money than ever before from the TT to cover my high expenses and the TT itself was up on its feet again, to start running to a better future.

I had more Honda Britain rides during the following season, including the Bol d'Or 24 hour race at Le Mans where I shared one of the RCB endurance racers with another TT winner, Tony Rutter. We held third place for three hours but then the engine began leaking oil after a cylinder head stud broke. We dropped back to just about last position while the mechanics removed the engine to fix the problem. Then, back in the long race, we worked our way back up the field to finish 11th.

For 24-hour endurance races, riders really need the support of wives or girl friends to help with the team's many requirements, but at that Le Mans event we were told we couldn't take them with us. And yet team boss Gerald Davison turned up with his girlfriend!

When a deal with Honda was agreed for the following season I thought things were looking up for my 22nd year in racing, but as it turned out, 1978 was not a good year. Madeleine had been having real health problems. She had needed a hysterectomy and had some cosmetic surgery, which was not my idea or wish. During that time she had become quite emotionally disturbed, having crashed the Mercedes SL I'd bought for her birthday more than once. I think she was suffering from some psychological problems, could HRT have helped? They may have stemmed from her disturbed upbringing in a Dublin household. A deep-rooted insecurity tempted Mad to have a boob job and then a nose job which left her in terrible pain. She was taking painkillers to help her acute discomfort. While I was away on business in Germany and Holland in February 1978, our very helpful Croatian au pair found Madeleine in a semi-comatose state in bed and called the doctor. He tried to make her to go to hospital to be pumped out, but she refused, he couldn't force her, he later told me. David, my shop manager, and his girlfriend went to the house to help and removed all the pills they could find. When she recovered a little, she went out with a local teacher friend for the afternoon. They returned within a few hours and she went back to bed. But early on the Sunday morning our distraught au pair found her dead in bed.

That day I returned home to find a policeman in the house. He told me 'I have some bad news for you…' I had lost my second wife, my best friend, without whose support I could not have achieved so much or had two great boys. I felt a terrible guilt that I hadn't called home, or the office, on Saturday before I flew back from Holland, which might have somehow prevented her death. If I'd known or been at home then I would have been able to make her go to hospital, which the doctor had insisted she needed to do. Her life could have been saved.

Without Madeleine's help and advice I allowed some good investments to slip through my fingers. But I was in total confusion after her sudden death. I made some stupid decisions and looking back, one of them was getting re-married too soon after Mad's death.

Madeleine had left her two boys, Pip and Roki Marc with only their father to take care of them. My main concern was that they should be well looked after and helped to overcome the tragic loss of their loving mum. I felt empty and very alone without Mad. She was our best friend and I could not handle racing without her, or dealing with my business interests without her keen business instincts.

With my commitment to race in the upcoming 1978 TT, I was seriously worried about being killed on the not-so-competitive machines I was contracted to race for Honda UK. I was also concerned and determined that the boys should be properly looked after should that happen. In the longer term, I faced a very difficult decision, either to stop racing or to change our lives and concentrate on my bike clothing and helmet distribution business interests, including my Premier helmet factory in Ireland.

Angie and I began to see each other on a regular basis before she moved in with me to help with the two boys when my au pair left to return home at the end of her time with us. Angie agreed that she would be their legal registered guardian in the terrible, but possible, eventuality of my death. Later, I thought that if we got married it would be more straightforward for her to be their stepmother. There were some people who found our marriage hard to accept, as Madeleine was so well-known locally and in the race paddocks.

By 1978 I had expanded my business, opening a Honda dealership in Walton-on-Thames and to cash in on my Formula 1 TT win, Honda UK were selling a Phil Read Replica version of the CB750 roadster. Colin Seeley was contracted to re-style this machine to look similar to my TT winning bike, although I had no input regarding its specification or looks. He produced a new fuel tank, fairing and screen, exhaust system and other parts to make it look like my Honda Britain racer and the machines were converted at his South East London workshops. I can't say that I admired the Replica's looks: the seat fairing was ugly and the curve of the screen didn't match the fairing.

The bike was to retail at about £1800 and I was promised royalty payments based on $2^1/2$ per cent of sales. I can tell you that I wasn't pleased to be told later by Mr Davison that the royalty wasn't to be based on the sale price of this Honda Phil Read Replica, but on the price difference between this special bike and the standard CB750. I wasn't due thousands, but only a few hundred pounds. I was very angry indeed, and have never forgiven Honda.

Shell
DUNLOP
RENOLD
NGK

Glorious sunshine for the 1978 Formula 1 TT, Mike Hailwood was catching me, but when he did I wouldn't let him go. We passed and re-passed a few times and it was magic to witness his fast riding.

As well as riding the CB750-based Honda in Formula 1 events, I was entered in the *MCN* Brut 33 Superbike series to ride one of the big RCB endurance racers. I had to contend with the Suzuki GB and Kawasaki UK factory machines as well as legions of Yamaha TZ riders.

The 1978 TT was all about Mike Hailwood's fantastic comeback, which attracted huge record crowds to this second non-grand prix event. My job was to beat him on a 969cc Honda in the Formula 1 and on the 880cc endurance racer in the Classic. In his final practice on the Formula 1 Sports Motor Cycles 900cc Ducati, Mike put in a really fast lap at 111mph which showed his great ability, even after not racing in the TT races for eleven years and now having to change gear left-footed due to his car racing injuries. But that was the Mike of old, goddammit! The late Tom Herron was second fastest on a Honda four entered by London dealer Mocheck and I was third. I realised then that I was really up against it!

This time, the weather was good for Saturday's Formula 1 race. I set off with a clear road ahead at Number 1 with Mike starting 50 seconds behind me at Number 12. As I approached Ramsey on the second lap I could hear the deep note of a twin-cylinder engine behind me and I thought - oh no, he's here! Mike out-braked me into Parliament Square and we rode over the Mountain together - what a fantastic race it was. Spectators were five-deep at the Bungalow, I'd never seen so many before. We pitted together and set off again with me just behind Mike and his Ducati. My idea was to push him so hard for so long that he'd over-rev his engine and it would break. But that wasn't to be, yet, as I found on our last, and fourth lap. I had a couple of slides through the Glen Helen section when chasing hard.

With my bike for the 1978 Classic TT, on which I was a slow fourth following a row with Honda UK boss Eric Sulley.

1978 Formula 1 TT, 750 winner Hailwood, Ducati, rounds Governor's Bridge. I'm chasing him on the Honda.

Then I was on the Cronk-y-Voddy straight, tucked in behind the flying Ducati when Wooosh!: Myself and my screen were covered in very hot liquid. The union bend of the oil cooler fitted behind the fairing had sheared off. Oil was pumping out all over me. I slowed to a stop before the 11th Milestone. My race was over and all I could do was to sit and listen to a spectator's Manx Radio race commentary on Mike's progress round the course, over the Mountain, through the Creg, to Signpost corner, around the tight Governor's Bridge and over the finishing line. Mike had won and the fans got their fairy-tale result. We all cheered and a big lump came to my throat when I heard this great news of Mike's successful return to the Island.

What most didn't know until much later was that Mike's Ducati engine had broken, never to run again, a few hundred yards before he rode under the chequered flag.

A terrible thought crossed my mind when I considered that if my bike hadn't failed, due to the oil cooler not being fitting correctly by a Honda employee, Mike's engine could have blown sooner. If I had won because of that, I would have been the most unpopular TT winner ever. But Mike got his popular and well-deserved victory. But I doubt whether he was paid what he deserved for the ride of a lifetime or got much out of the Ducati factory to whom he gave the most incredible sales boost for a marque that wasn't considered a TT race winner. Mike was too easy-going to make such demands.

For me, things went from bad to worse. I was staying at the Golf Links Hotel near Castletown with Angie. We were on our honeymoon, although that was not generally known until the *Daily Mirror* blew the story open in the Island. When we got back to this hotel after the race and were shocked to find we'd been moved out of our en suite double room to be moved to a room with twin beds and not en suite. Our room had been given by the late Eric Sulley, boss of Honda UK, to one of his favoured dealers. I was furious. If your team isn't supporting of you, especially at the TT, it's very demoralising. I had a blazing row with Sulley, and the hotel manager. Angie and I walked out and stayed at a boarding house in Douglas. We flew back home the next day just for some peace and sanity, threatening not to return.

Common sense prevailed so I was back on the Island for Friday's Classic race, but I must admit I'd lost my enthusiasm to ride as hard as was needed to win. The big endurance Honda handled so badly I couldn't keep it flat out over the bumps on Sulby Straight and I ended up fourth behind Mick Grant, John Williams and Alex George. Mike Hailwood's big Yamaha holed a piston on the first lap: at least that was better than having it happen on the last lap, after he'd had to do a lot more work.

The mainland races with Honda were frustrating. I had clutch trouble in the first Superbike round and the bikes really needed sorting out. Power wasn't the problem, but handling was and they should have looked closely at how the Honda dealer Mocheck had carried out worthwhile chassis developments. If only I had been allowed to run the Honda UK team we could have got some better results during that period. I believed that Formula 1 racing had a bright future. In the 1980s Honda could boast of 16 F1 TT race wins in a row and eight more TT F1 championships to add to mine, mostly thanks to the late great Joey Dunlop.

Relations with Honda deteriorated further during that season. Part of my contract was to ride in a TT Formula 1 round held at the Ulster GP in August. I missed practice because Angie and I were in Spain where we got delayed in Marbella due to a Spanish air traffic controllers' strike. The Ulster GP organisers wouldn't let me race after we eventually arrived on Thursday afternoon, too late for practice. That's when I got the sack. John Williams, who had been second to Mike in the TT on a Honda Britain bike got my bike for the F1 race, but the day ended very sadly after he crashed in the 1000cc race on a Suzuki and later died from his injuries.

Honda UK's attitude then was that they felt superior and knew best about racing. (I'd only been racing for 22 years to win eight world titles.) One did things their way, or not at all. One day when I had visited the Honda UK headquarters to discuss the soon-to-be-launched Phil Read TT Replica bike, I was told the race team was tyre testing at Goodwood. No-one had told me. 'Thank you,' I thought. I was very upset that was all they thought of my input. I believe that if a rider wants some changes made in order for him to go faster - even having a photo of his kids stuck on the windscreen - he should have it done to keep him happy. Especially in the Isle of Man where the dangers are greatest. There have been more recent examples, such as when Valentino Rossi was racing for Honda. They treated him like a commodity and expected too much of his time for publicity exposure. He felt so bad about this that in 2004 he went off to race for Yamaha, the 'Happy Team', to make their average race bike a great championship winner.

I switched to the South London Mocheck Honda Team for late-season UK races of 1978 and found that their chassis handled well. It certainly helped their team of Ron Haslam and Tony Rutter to win the championship.

Leaving Buckingham Palace in the revolutionary Quasar after receiving my MBE

A high point of 1979 was being awarded an MBE in the Queen's Birthday Honours and I went to the presentation at Buckingham Palace on two wheels, of course, riding the revolutionary Quasar feet-first roofed machine developed by Malcolm Newell and Ken Leaman.

After two years of running the Honda dealership I closed it down. The clothing side had always been good but I had never liked selling bikes, a cut-throat business which required much socialising to become a favoured dealer and get the best deals on new bikes. I would have done better to have invested into the property business and had less aggro.

Along with Mike, who had set up a Honda dealership with Rod Gould near Birmingham's Spaghetti Junction, we had been given one of Honda's six-cylinder CBX1000s for customer demos and to use generally. We were told we could pay for them if and when we wanted. In other words, we understood that they were payment to keep in return for our extensive national advertising campaign. But no, suddenly Honda refused to supply us with spare parts until the CBXs were paid for. The case ended up in court and Mike had written a letter to support my case, but by then he had been killed in a tragic road accident so it wasn't admissible in court. In the end I had to liquidate the business and, of course, Honda UK was my only big creditor, for which I don't think they've ever forgiven me. Only a few years ago I was told at Donington Park by Bob McMillan of Honda UK, that if I wanted to parade a classic factory Honda at the TT, I'd have to re-pay them a large amount first. In my view, we had contra-obligations which balanced each other out.

In 1982, to be honest, at that point in my life I was feeling I'd lost direction and my new wife Angie was not comfortable living in Madeleine's home with the two boys, now her stepsons. So, to give us a new start away from the memories of Thatched House, I was lucky to find at a bargain price a ten-bedroomed manor house with a big barn and stables in three-and-a-half acres near Reigate Heath in Surrey. It was very impressive and offered us great potential on which to maximise. We did some modernisation and made the second floor into the boy's playroom and bedrooms. We held some charity events and some great parties there, with guests including Damon Hill and his widowed mother Bette, Mike Hailwood, Paul Butler, then the Dunlop competitions manager, Frank Perris, ex-Suzuki and Norton, James Hunt and his friends plus various TV personalities, and it seemed all was going well. Guests would ride the boys' motocross bikes and a Honda ATC around the grounds and some into the pond. Damon, speeding in the semi dark, rode into a deep gully and was lucky he wasn't hurt, too much.

Angela felt she needed us to have a child to help her feel she was part of a complete family, so I obliged with this pleasurable task, and in less than a year Esme was born. A few months after her birth she was christened in the village church with Bette Hill agreeing to be her godmother. An associate who had visited my manor house for a party made me an offer I could not refuse. So, within two years of purchasing the property I sold it to him for a nice profit and we moved to Pine Glen, a smaller home but with a swimming pool, in seven acres near Newdigate in Surrey, just two miles away, as it happened, from Barry Sheene's manor at Charlwood. But we were not on speaking terms at the time.

Angie helped me promote new motorcycle products including a sensational promotion for the Phil Read RX15 motorcycle fairing. She even sportingly appeared nude in the publicity photo of us both sitting on a bike fitted with the fairing, quite risqué in those days. The slogan said, 'Who needs more with an RX15?' That certainly attracted a lot of attention and sold all the fairings, but the image was still appearing in magazines and at bike shows decades later.

I was happy that the boys seemed to love Angie, but one day, when Esme was no more than a year old, Angie announced that she would be leaving us the next weekend and was now moving into the spare room. I was shocked and upset and didn't understand her reasons for this life-changing move away from us until much later.

A man can't change a woman's emotional, irresponsible and unrealistic thoughts when they are set in their minds. Any pleading, or trying to make her realise she was destroying a family, her irresponsible and selfish actions would be to the detriment of the children's happy future, nothing would change her mind.

She moved into the guest room, but strangely continued to share my bed till she left with Esme. I believe this made sex seem illicit and more exciting for her. I now think that perhaps her needs had not matured since her freewheeling single days and I have since realised that her craving for sexual excitement was the basic reason for her move to pastures new.

Angie and Esme were collected by her girl-friend and they went to stay with a friend in a bungalow at Cliffe in Kent. I visited her there, mainly to see Esme and came away the last time with a 'dose'. Angie was now having it off with the local farmer whose bungalow she was renting. Funnily enough that wasn't such a bad thing, apart from being uncomfortable for a couple of weeks. As many divorced men will know, the accusations in the petition from the ex-wife-to-be are sometimes exaggerated to make the court believe one is a cruel sex maniac. My condition helped clinch this divorce case in my favour and Angie's petition was dismissed from Court. I became a single father again.

It transpired that Angie and Esme left the farmer, John Filmer, because he would not move them into the main farmhouse, so she initiated an affair with another farmer and moved into his cottage on the adjoining farm. It seems that to get Angie back, Mr Filmer built a tennis court for her, in the middle of his farmyard. She moved in with him to the main house. From reading about these events one can understand that I had no chance of a long and happy marriage with Angie. Sadly the boys and I have lost contact with Esme, who now is married.

Something else that happened in 1982: my mother Doris died. My dear Mum who had done so much for me, even helping me buy my first racing bike, a 350cc BSA Gold Star that started my racing career at Mallory Park on 13 May 1956.

Yes, it was a sad time, but Phil Read never gives up and I had high hopes that things were going to take a turn for the better.

GS1000
PHIL

10

Never give up!

It wasn't just my life that was in upheaval in the late 1970s and early 1980s: the racing scene was changing, too.

The two-stroke takeover of grand prix racing was complete. The once-avowedly four-stroke Honda company had switched to two-stroke power and even the sidecar class had joined the move, while the growing Formula 1, Superbike and Endurance classes were based mainly on four-stroke production machines. At club and national level, Yamaha's over-the-counter 250cc and 350cc TZ twins and Suzuki's RG500s had come to monopolise the full-race classes, great for giving everyone a fair chance on well-matched machinery, but it did mean they all tended to look and sound the same - ear-splitting.

Racers who owned 'obsolete' machinery and those riders and fans who looked back at what they saw as a more interesting and varied past, got together to establish classic racing. Britain's Classic Racing Motorcycle Club started up in 1979 and within a few years historic sport was booming in Europe, America, Australia and New Zealand.

> I have to thank those guys who built up the international historic racing movement, it allowed me to continue competitive, on-the-limit racing.

The great thing about classic racing is that you can have fun without the sort of pressures I'd had to cope with during my grand prix years. But it is important for me do well and my confidence was really boosted by an early classic ride at an international historic race in America in 1986, even though I didn't win. The event was staged within a two-day US national Superbike meeting on the Laguna Seca circuit, so there was a decent-sized crowd of spectators, though I don't know how many would have even heard of Phil Read, only a few I guess!

I was offered a ride with Team Obsolete, a historic racing outfit based in New York, then jointly run by Robert Iannucci and Jeff Elghanayan. I had ridden one of their Matchless G50s at a French classic event but this was my first visit to the fine Californian track, which is hilly and more interesting than other American circuits like Daytona and Indianapolis.

The bike Rob had given me to race was a Matchless G50 for the 500cc Premier race. People have asked me what it's like to get on an old single cylinder bike of the type I raced way back in the early 1960s, after my experience on much more powerful machinery like MV, Suzuki and Yamaha fours. My answer to that is simple; 'To me, a bike's a bike and they all have their limits'. One thing I did find with this historic scene was that there was a lot more spanner work and general sorting out

'Never, never, never give up', Winston Churchill.

required. It's not like a factory team with plenty of technicians around to look after everything when the bikes arrive, already mechanically sound and fully prepared. Then it's down to the rider to decide on the final settings of suspension, gearing and jetting. In MotoGPs this is mostly done automatically or from telemetry, using computer data from every corner throughout a whole lap, recorded from a GPS unit on the bike.

At Laguna Seca, Team Obsolete's regular rider Dave Roper, America's top classic racer, had another G50 and clearly it had a much more powerful engine than mine: I made the best start but he was a good 100 yards ahead of the field by the first corner and disappeared out of sight to take a convincing win. Getting a feel for the circuit, famous for its blind snaking downhill 'corkscrew', I set my sights on the guy ahead, American rider Russell Paulk. He was on a Honda twin prepared by Eraldo Ferracci, who had been a race mechanic with Benelli before he had emigrated to the US and had made his name as a top tuner and later the Ducati and MV Agusta importer, known as 'Fast by Ferracci'.

I could have done with some more speed from that old Matchless, but I eventually caught the Honda rider and managed to pull away from him to take the flag in second place.

Robert Iannucci admitted that he should have given me 'a bit more motor' as he put it: he said my bike had one of his old standard AMC made-in-Woolwich engines. That was when these period engines were still being used for serious historic racing, not something you'd see much today, although the UK Lansdowne Classic Series commendably puts strict limits on out-of-period modifications. Nowadays, competitive 'classic' racing bikes from the 1960s and early 1970s are built with entirely new materials and higher specifications from the ground-up to produce considerably more power. The fastest ones have one-piece crankshafts and shorter strokes which allow much higher revs - perhaps up to 10,000 rpm - to give 10 to 15 more brake horse power. They also use modern ignition systems, some triggered at the crankshaft and with components concealed in a traditional-looking magneto housing. Some have twin spark plugs for better fuel burning, although that feature was employed by Bill Lacey on Mike Hailwood's 500cc Manx Norton to help him win the 1961 Isle of Man Senior TT race at over 100mph. Bill did not have access to electronic ignition, titanium valves and superior coil valve springs. He had to use the traditional hairpin valve springs which effectively limited revs to around 8,000. However, a feature of that Hailwood engine that was not widely known about at the time was a radically non-standard plain bearing big-end in place of Norton's usual roller bearing.

My first classic race win came at Scarborough in 1991. Dear old Syd Lawton, whose bikes I had first raced more than 30 years before, had been the UK's Aermacchi importer in the 1960s. He still had one of the 350cc Italian singles that he wasn't currently racing and thanks to Pete Hillaby, the enterprising organiser of races at Scarborough's hilly Oliver's Mount circuit, I was entered on Syd's bike in a 350cc *Classic Bike* championship race at the July Cock O'the North meeting. While the Aermacchi could have been better than it was, we got it sorted and I won the race by a clear 20 seconds with a lap record thrown in. My team of Syd, Jan Eaton and myself were all amazed, together with many others including some championship regulars who were upset that this 'old boy' could still ride faster than them! On the way home we treated ourselves to a very well deserved steak supper.

At the time Janet Eaton was my partner and we stayed with her folks in the North of England on the way home to Surrey from Yorkshire. Jan and her two children lived with me at Chobham, but our relationship fell apart when I lost my house after the failure of my golf project. She is still involved with bike racing these days and I believe her busy Surrey physiotherapy clinic clientele includes Gino Rea of Moto GP2.

Replica WW1 SE5A

Together with Chris Garville, a good friend involved in military and commercial aviation, we visited the world's biggest home-built and experimental aircraft show in Oshkosh, Wisconsin, USA. I had the plan to import ultralight home-built aircraft that at the time in Europe did not need a special licence to build and fly.

We were impressed by the WW1 Squadron Aviation biplanes, the SE5A, Spad and Fokker D7 aircraft. I arranged to buy a British SE5A kit as a test. It took months to build this interesting and exciting project ready for its first test flight.

I took it to a friend's farm near Gatwick, fitted and rigged the wings, started its small 2-stroke engine and took off to Brands Hatch. About ten minutes into my flight over the M25 I looked around to re-check the rigging. I was alarmed to notice that an aileron nylon cord was being snagged by a unprotected steel rigging joint. I did a 180 turn and prayed it would hold till I landed. It parted just as I touched down in the field. Phew, that was a near one.

My plan was was to help clubs around the Continent to form squadrons of these English, French and German WW1 replicas to stage mock dog-fights with laser guns. I managed to sell four of these kits before more restrictive regulations were enforced on lightweight, home-built aircraft.

Currently I'm keen to help develop the market for a hi-tech, enclosed two-seat, high-performance gyrocopter. The ArrowCopter, built in Austria, cruises at 120mph for five hours and needs only the length of a tennis court to take off and land. Twenty per cent cheaper than a small helicopter, its running costs are no more than a medium-sized car, a great solution to ever-worsening motorway jams.

Quieter than helicopters with no ground effect, gyrocopters offer a cost-effective platform for aerial media coverage of sporting events.

Getting engaged to lovely Melanie in Trafalgar Square during a double umbrella promo shoot

Before my relationship with Jan I had lived with my lovely fiancée Melanie James, but that did not last for more than two years, mainly because of our age difference. She wanted to have children but I didn't feel I needed any more than the five I already had. So she decided to go back to live with her parents and move on to greener pastures. I heard she even employed detectives to make sure I didn't appear on her wedding day at our local Chobham village church. That was during a difficult time in the 1980s when I was taking whatever temporary work I could get. Her leaving did upset me and the two boys, I thought that together we could make a good future to progress out of the motorcycle game into something good for us all.

I was bitter about the loss of the house at Chobham, which was thanks to a business venture that went badly wrong. I joined two partners in a consortium to develop a sizeable 120 acre patch of disused farmland in West Sussex as a top-class golf course. I spent a lot of money on laying out plans, talking to specialist construction companies and was consulting with a famous golf commentator, Peter Allis. I had inadvisably put the house up as collateral against the successful completion of the project and it was called in after my fellow directors pulled out. They didn't lose out, of course. They just walked away.

To tide me over tough times and help my two younger boys get started in racing, I placed my FIM world championship medals as collateral with the village Mercedes dealer, whom I knew from his brother's bike racing, on the understanding that I would eventually buy them back. But when I wanted to re-pay the loan he told me that their value had increased. He wanted more than £10,000 - nearly three times his original loan. Luckily I was able to get replacements to display from the FIM, but, this was not the same as the originals.

I got back on my feet and continued classic racing, of course, and back into the world into which I'd been born. Another very satisfying race win came in 1995, but it wasn't in a classic event. The Triumph Speed Triple Transatlantic Challenge Trophy at the Mallory Park, Post TT meeting was a real confidence builder for me. The American celebrity guests were top classic riders such as David Aldana, Gary Nixon and Jay Springsteen. They were invited to take part on these fine sports bikes supplied by Triumph's selected dealers.

There was no prize money, just the prestige of taking part, but the British team's determination to beat the American Team was paramount . We were keen to make it a good and close race for the very sizeable crowd, with no crashes. So I suggested that it must be 'a last lap to count' race, asking the clerk of the course to black-flag any rider who led for more than two laps or was making the race look boring. I narrowly won the first race after some last lap late braking to squeeze past inside leader Griff Roberts into the hairpin. In the second race, after some close dicing with the Yanks, I was surprised to be leading the bunch on the last lap, but shut off rounding Devil's Elbow to allow one of the Americans to win this second leg, so everyone was happy. Production racing specialist Griff Roberts, on his home track but not well-known to the fans, fancied his chances and couldn't resist trying to win the second race, especially after I had just pipped him in the first race. But he was black-flagged as he was running away in this last race on a damp track. Sorry Griff, but that was the agreed plan. We had made this Anglo-American Triumph Speed Triple event so close and exciting for the spectators that three of my sons who were at Mallory told me it was the best racing they had ever seen. Everyone was happy, especially the Triumph dealers as we had all 'kept it on the rubber', to return their undamaged bikes to them.

In 1998, I decided to race one last time on the Isle of Man in the Manx Grand Prix. Since the early 1980s former MGP winners and TT riders were not barred. But riders over 60 were (temporarily), so I decided that at the age of 59 it was my last chance. I entered the 500cc Classic race, but had no illusions about returning to a highly competitive event on the Mountain Course, on which I hadn't raced for 16 years. My simple aim was for a top-ten finish or better and to turn in a couple of 100mph laps. The 500cc classic lap record, then held by veteran rider and helmet visor manufacturer Bob Heath, was a little over 106mph. My best lap in the 1961 TT had been just short of 100mph, so speeds hadn't improved dramatically over those thirty seven years, even with uprated classic engines producing 20 per cent more power over a circuit made faster by the easing of corners and the smoothing of the worst bumps.

My bike was a Matchless G50 owned by Peter Lockwood, a real enthusiast. Its rolling chassis was from well-known racing sponsor and G50 specialist George Beale, with an engine built by the highly-rated tuner Fred Walmsley, plus an oil-free belt primary drive and a five-speed gearbox made by Manx Norton specialist Summerfield Engineering. From what I knew about classic racing, it looked like a great package. After all, Bob Heath, nine times winner of Classic Manx races, had set the 500cc race and lap records in 1997 using a Walmsley G50 engine.

Peter Lockwood, the rider who offered me this spare G50 was there to help as was my helpful supporter, Alan Seeley of *Classic Bike* magazine. But I was in for more than a week of disappointments and hard work. The chassis needed a lot of tuning and tweaking to get it to handle better, which involved changing the front forks. Then I was forced to adjust the front wheel spokes to get the rim to run true. What a laugh it caused in the paddock to see me working as a wheel-builder. All I'll say about the engine was that in practice loads of riders passed me on the fast stretch leaving Union Mills and by the time we got to the Highlander a couple of miles or so further on, they'd all disappeared. All I wanted was a race bike equal to those of the other competitors, but this was a joke.

I told Fred Walmsley what I thought of his engine, in public. He said I'd got his best one, so I suggested that his top man Bob Heath should have it, and I'd settle for his engine.

We sorted out the over-rich carburation with the Gardner carburettor with a few clicks of the adjuster, not needing to change jets with this great flat-slide racing carburettor. By Friday I'd completed the five laps needed to qualify. That was the good news at least. The bad news was that the engine seized its piston, so when I returned to the pits it was chuffing out thick white smoke. We removed the engine and gave it back to Fred to fix, but it wasn't ready for Saturday's last and most important practice session. To make a point, I pushed the engine-less bike through the scrutineering bay for the last practice - that didn't go down too well, I can tell you. One of the officials told me in all seriousness that it hadn't passed inspection and couldn't practise without an engine, what a prat! I left it in the *parc fermé* with a sign on it saying; 'One good engine needed'.

We got the engine back in time for testing at Jurby airfield on the Sunday and were as ready as we could be for Monday's race. But my expectations had really been lowered as the engine still didn't feel good and didn't want to rev as I knew it should. After delays while the organisers waited for mountain mist to clear our race got under way, but was shortened from four laps to three. I came in 16th out of 88 finishers with an average speed of a pathetic 94.5mph, enough to secure a Replica trophy. I guess it could have been worse, but it would have really helped if we hadn't had such unnecessary hassles during practice week, during which Wendy Markey threatened to go home if I didn't show her some of the Island's wonderful sights and 'not just work on that bloody bike'.

'When you come to the end of your rope, tie a knot and hang on', Franklin D Roosevelt.

Wendy Markey-Amey

With an invitation from Bernie Ecclestone I rode to the Silverstone F1 event in July 1982. I was invited by my daughter's godmother, Bette Hill to the Dog House Suite, overlooking Woodcote Corner. Ex-racing driver member, the chirpy Wendy Markey was hosting. I suggested it would take forever to leave the circuit in her car on the grid-locked roads, so I offered her a lift on my motorcycle.

'OK,' she said, 'if you get me a helmet, jacket, gloves and arrange to return my car to Surrey I'll come with you.' We had a great ride as she was a natural passenger. During that year we met up a few times. Over the following few years I divorced Angela and Wendy remarried, had a son, Robert, then divorced the controlling little squirt. We met again when I rode my BMW K1100RS to meet her and her son when they were staying in a cottage near Cordes in the South of France. On the long ride down I remember sleeping under the trees by the Le Mans circuit. When I awoke there was a black and white rabbit sitting by me. Was this a good omen?

After her divorce Wendy was left with a large semi-empty house with 12 acres in a small Hertfordshire village. Her ex had left and taken most of the furniture and things. In October 1996 I moved in with Wendy to help her put the house to rights and give her moral support and to stop her ex taking more of the house contents.

We soon were taking my BMW to many events and I don't believe Wendy realised how fast we were riding at times. On our way to Scarborough, cruising at over 100 mph on the M1, we stopped for fuel. She asked why we had been going so slow! It was good for me to have such an enthusiastic passenger without a fear of speed, although I resisted fitting intercoms to our helmets.

As young Robert was in need of more space to play his music and have his school friends to stay we considered converting the large roof area into a studio apartment. Quite a big task for us but I had some experience from building extensions in previous houses. Two years later I managed to have Robert's suite finished and signed off by the building inspector for the one bedroom with two upper sleeping galleries, a large sitting room with two of the largest floor-to-ridge Velux windows, with a bathroom and WC and a storeroom. This addition considerably increased the value of Wendy's property, much to the resentment of her ex.

Some years later one of her elder sons, Simon, was in financial trouble so we agreed to convert the large triple garage to a living space and photographic studio, from which we hoped he could make a good living! At that time I was using this garage to stock new MV Agusta bikes and special parts.

In 2003 Simon and I had a disagreement so I moved in with my sponsor Francis Wallis in North Devon. We had much fun and success around the Continent and together we produced the replica of the Duke BSA which I had raced in my teens. We won the famous La Bañeza 500cc race twice in the blazing sun.

In March 2014 we go to Australia for me to race and parade at Eastern Creek's anniversary event and stay some days with her daughter and family near Sydney. We plan to stop for a few days in Hong Kong with a friend and petrol head, David McKirdy. We look forward to it all and who knows, Wendy may buy me another tailor-made suit there.

Directly after our return from Oz we rush down to a big bike show in Limoges, France.

Wendy's enthusiasm is always good for me - she'll always fight my corner and we make a great team.

At least as a valued long-term friend and partner Wendy has given me moral support in difficult times. We met in the early 1980s at the Formula 1 British GP. Wendy had raced cars in the 1970s and as a beautiful racing star she had been sponsored by *Penthouse* magazine, for which she refused to be photographed topless! I was at Silverstone with future world F1 champion Damon Hill. I had known his father, the late, great Graham Hill through us both being involved with the Springfield Boys Club. I had taken Damon to the Earls Court motorcycle show when he was just 16 years old. We were looking for a 50cc bike he could use for transport and he chose a sporty-looking Puch Grand Prix bike. I negotiated the best deal I could for his Mum but although the final cost was more than they had budgeted for, I made up the difference without a second thought. It was probably not generally known then that the Hill family were in difficult straits after Graham's untimely death in a plane crash in 1975. He was trying to land at Elstree airfield in misty conditions with many of his F1 crew on-board. This dreadful accident not only lost us a great sporting hero, it cost the family everything.

Wendy and I have remained good friends ever since our Silverstone meeting and in recent years she has given me tremendous support by running the Phil Read merchandise stall at events all over Europe. We celebrated 30 years of friendship when I sprang a surprise party for us at the 2012 Mallory Park Festival of 1000 Bikes, with many bottles of Pommery champagne I had picked up in Reims for all our racing friends and a bouquet of flowers for her.

At the end of the 1990s, the French ex-GP rider Eric Saul had the great idea of starting up the International Classic Grand Prix (ICGP) series for 250cc and 350cc two-stroke pure racing machines dating from pre-1984, which effectively meant mostly Yamaha TZ250s and 350s. I joined the fun with a relatively early TZ350 with drum brakes and twin-shock rear suspension. Some riders were surprised at me choosing that, since most top classic racers usually go for the latest eligible specification of disc brakes and a cantilever chassis to get the best performance and handling.

Eric was also involved, as a consultant, for the Madeira TT, organised by Patrick Degryse and the local Moto Club, a new event run in 2002 just as winter was settling in over Northern Europe. All the riders and helpers were happy to be in this beautiful, mountainous and sunny island to race on a public road circuit, which was also very hilly and twisty. The only flat part ran along the coast road where the start/finish line and stands were set-up.

Wendy Markey-Amey

After my years of road racing on the Adriatic, Isle of Man, Southern 100 and Scarborough I was happy with the challenge of this difficult circuit. But it transpired that the enthusiasm of a number of riders at this new and exciting event overcame their abilities. Several crashed in the first practice session, causing a few to be unfit to race. It became obvious that this circuit needed to be made as safe as was possible. So Eric and I inspected it with the local officials, who had never run a road race before, to identify the most dangerous places which needed more straw bale protection. With this done, I suggested that I lead all riders around in the next practice session in order for them to better learn the safest racing lines and braking points on this tricky road race circuit.

Pauline Hailwood, Mike's widow, had been invited as Guest of Honour to present the podium garlands. Classic specialist Phil Sharpe rode like a man possessed in a couple of classes to be voted Man of the Meeting and during the evening prize giving he was delighted to be presented by Pauline with an expensive watch, donated by Patrick Degryse. After a faster, nearer-the-limit, race than I wanted, riding my TZ350 against Eric Saul and John Weedon, I managed to win by a wheel and to receive on the rostrum the traditional kiss on both cheeks from Pauline Hailwood. I was thankful not to have crashed and so was able to enjoy the rather drunken celebrations that evening in our hotel's garden. Also, late the next day, I had an amazing tour of this lovely island in the sun with Wendy and friends and we enjoyed the expensive high tea at the famous Reed's Hotel to round off the day.

The following year we raced on the resort island of Porto Santo, the smaller island adjoining Madeira, for another ICGP event where we enjoyed daytime temperatures of 20 degrees centigrade and more. There was a golden two-mile long beach by our impressive hotel, along which, I noticed from our room window, some keen riders took an early morning exercise run. I thought a long walk alone was better.

All the race bikes came by ship in crates to be unloaded on the quayside of this small island, which had a military aerodrome that allowed some local flights from Madeira. We all unpacked our bikes on the dock and rode through the town to a large garage workshop we had been allowed to use alongside the proposed start line at this new racing venue.

During Saturday's first unlimited race on my TZ350 I had a good fight with my fast riding son Graham on a Yamaha similar to mine, and the late John Loder's 500cc Nourish Weslake four-valve twin, to just lead them over the finish line.

In the second event I rode my Duke BSA to come third behind John and Graham, not able to match their speed with my 500cc single-cylinder engine.

On Sunday, I let Graham beat me in the Grand Finale to keep him ahead of hard-riding Loder, who sadly was killed in the 2005 Manx Grand Prix. When it came to the prize giving, it transpired there were no prizes for the Saturday race winners, so whilst Graham was happy to collect the fine trophy for his Sunday win, I got nothing!

The replica Duke BSA I built and raced in that period was based on the original 350cc bike I'd bought from Alan Rutherford to race when I was 19 years old. The BSA factory built 350cc and 500cc bikes for Geoff Duke at the factory, with similar features to his factory Gileras and he sponsored Alan. This project of mine originated at a Thundersprint event held at the Three Sisters circuit in Lancashire in 1999. Frank Melling, the organiser, promised to provide me with a good bike. It turned out to be an oily old Triumph that seized on the first corner. This really pissed me off, I can tell you. Fortunately for me, at the event I met San 'Pepino' Millan from Santander, who agreed for me to share his tuned BSA B50 single-cylinder special. He won the Pre-1972 sprint class and I managed to be third fastest on the same bike which I took care not to crash. Pepino invited me over to the

'Phil has been a large part of my life for over 30 years, during which there have been 'highs and lows', but through it all his kind and generous nature always surfaced! He is stubborn but can often be cajoled out of this. He is extremely compassionate which was aptly shown when I was working in a school for disabled children in the nineties. I asked Phil if he could bring a bike in, to show to the children. He not only did so, but lifted one child from his wheelchair and placed him on the bike, much to the headmistress's consternation!

'The look of joy on that boy's face will remain with me always. Phil has enormous compassion for anyone who is disadvantaged and because of his almost childlike trusting nature, has been taken advantage of by many unscrupulous people purporting to be 'friends!' These people all eager to trade on his name and bask in his reflected glory! He is still trusting and sadly often disillusioned. However, he also has many good and true friends!

'I treasure the fantastic times we have had together over the years, and am so glad to have been part of this great Champion's life.'

Zoe Frances Hayes

I met Zoe after splitting from Wendy, while I was living with my millionaire sponsor, Francis Wallis, at Tiverton, North Devon.

Zoe was an attractive lady whom I felt was in need of some tender loving care although she was sharing a cottage with an ex-partner, or so she led me to believe. We had a sensual and disjointed relationship in and around Devon, but when we travelled to events and meetings in such wonderful places as Rome, the Italian Lakes, Belgium, Germany and La Rochelle, most of the time she seemed emotionally unsettled and reserved until after one or two glasses of red wine which helped her to forget her unspoken troubles.

When we were staying around the Italian lakes we taked about being married on Lake Garda with a promise from Agostini to be best man. I believed that with her freedom from her 'life in a rut' with her latent intelligience and abilities, we could develop into a dynamic duo. But after an altercation with the man she shared the cottage with and her finally admitting she still shared his bed I soon left Devon to relocate in Kent which at least was much nearer to the ferry ports, which I often took to the classic motorcycle events throughout the Continent.

Spanish TT classic race at La Bañeza, a medium size town about 150 miles north of Madrid in the middle of nowhere. It was crazy there. Crowds lined the streets with no regard for 'eff'n'safety' issues. They just jumped back out of the way as riders came through. Pepino's engineer built another bike for me to race at this crazy annual event. In this race, when trying to win, I found myself dicing with Pepino for the lead between the houses, shops, kerbs and the waving fans, mostly on the pavements, until my loaned BSA dropped a valve, allowing him an easy win, as he had done several times before, to be known as the 'Star of La Bañeza'.

The iconic event held in this Spanish town gave me the idea of building my own race-winning BSA single. The club's President did not allow Manx Nortons, Matchless G50s, twins, four-cylinder race bikes or Japanese two-strokes.

Through the Madeira event I had met Francis Wallis, who kindly provided me with some sponsorship and we discussed the potential of my building a replica 500 Duke BSA. It would be fitted with a newly-made 500cc Gold Star engine from ABSAF, the engineering company in Appingedam, in North East Holland, run by Jan de Jong and his English wife, Chantal. The frame ABSAF provided was based on the Seeley pattern, also Dutch-made and nickel plated. Francis helped me with the project and I had the Duke replica head-fairing, fuel tank and seat made in the UK from my old photos. A Manx dual-sided front brake was made for me by Norton wizard Ken McIntosh in New Zealand. We returned to La Bañeza the following season (2003) with the new Duke BSA replica and after some last minute adjustments on the line by Mike Jones, my helper, I managed to win the race. They treated me like a hero at the prizegiving and then we were taken to a restaurant which, to my relief, was in a cool converted wine cellar. But after I had taken one mouthful of my steak I suddenly felt ill. Without realising, I became dehydrated during the race in the very hot weather. I was laid low for a couple of days. I had never felt so ill before. The best and only way I could get some relief was by sitting in a cold bath and then sitting in my VW Kombi with the air-conditioning full on. When I had recovered a little, Mike drove us to Santander to catch our ferry home the next day. The local Piston MC Club had arranged a party with a fantastic barbecue for us and many of the club members that night under the stars, where we were very happy to get well pissed thanks to their kind hospitality with local vino, all of which helped me to full recovery, apart from a hangover which the warm sea air overcame during our return 24 hour ferry trip back to the UK.

The latter-day 500cc Duke BSA at Chimay, Belgium

Sophie Smith-Melcion and her husband Tony Smith with the 500cc Duke BSA replica I built to win the unique La Bañeza Spanish race. Sponsor Francis Wallis loaned it to the France-based pair to race and they like it so much he let them keep it.

The Duke BSA was later lent to a fellow classic competitor Tony Smith and his wife Sophie to race, as I was then mostly riding the faster 500 Moto Paton. I was very upset and disappointed that they and Francis Wallis did not co-operate when I asked to have the machine back. It seems the laws of possession are very complex in some parts of France.

I was thanks to sponsorship from Jean-Jacques Hennequart, a famous French architect and designer of the Airbus construction hangers, and many of his clients that I was able to raise the funds to have the Italian Moto Paton factory build for me a twin-cylinder four-valve GP racer that has really enlivened 500cc classic racing. Giuseppe 'Pepe' Pattoni designed with Lino Tonti and built the first 500cc Moto Paton GP machines in the late 1960s and acquired financial help from the Liverpool car dealer, Bill Hannah, to race as the Hannah Paton team. A number of well-known riders including Fred Stevens, Virginio Ferrari and Roberto Gallina raced the twins with success. Angelo Bergamonti won the Italian championship for Paton in 1967, beating multiple world champion Giacomo Agostini on the MV Agusta. In 1969 the British rider Billy Nelson finished fourth in the world championship.

Decades later, Pattoni's son Roberto built new versions to produce a fast and reliable machine eligible for historic races. While not as powerful as 500cc MV Agusta or Honda fours, the Paton has the edge over the Manx Nortons and Matchless and Seeley G50s, producing around 75bhp at 10,000 rpm. The Paton has had outstanding success in Manx Grand Prix races, where owner Roger Winfield and his rider Ryan Farquhar have won five Classic Seniors. The enthusiastic Italian funder and partner behind Roberto Pattoni's racing efforts is Giovanni Cabassi who always supports the father and son team of Steve and Olie Linsdell with their Paton at the MGP.

Moto Patons are usually painted in their traditional bright green. But as I have a superstition about this colour and which to my eyes is not a nice-looking green anyway, I had mine finished in Ferrari red.

Some good wins on my red Paton stand out in my memory, some at Austria's Österreichring. My first was in the short-lived series staged by the International Classic Association (InCa), run by long-time racing sponsor George Beale. I arrived after my 1000-mile drive from the UK in the VW Kombi with only 100 euros in my pocket and with no helper. The race was held in very wet weather, with streams of water running across the track. That caused me some exciting slides around the high-speed track and I won on standard sports tyres, not racing wets. To put the icing on the cake, the prizes were presented by my ex team-mate, Giacomo Agostini.

My other Österreichring win was in the following year, in really hot weather. It was quite a tough race and I was grateful that my Dainese leathers had knee-sliders, since I had to use them for the first time ever to keep my lead. My secret weapon there for the Paton was the brilliant German engineer Dietmar Fette. He is from the same town as my fantastic dentist Dr Stephan Elisat, who has also done great dental work for Wendy, Jim Redman, Ferry Brouwer and his wife Margriet, as well as my former sponsor Francis Wallis. Stephan's work is fantastic - and painless, thank God.

Dietmar has a dynamometer test bed at his work shop. As well as supporting some top riders, he completed important development work for Harley-Davidson on its V-Rod engine, resulting in 50 per cent more torque. He would be my choice to carry out re-mapping and specialised work if I needed to get optimum performance from a current top-level racing bike.

One thing he did to help me for the warm weather Austrian race was to switch the Paton to a Shell Racing oil used by the Ducati GP team. It made the engine run cooler and faster, as was proved when Dietmar told me my last lap in each race leg was my fastest in that hot event, and that was without fitting an oil cooler.

Dietmar offered useful advice to Paton, helping overcoming problems with magnesium cylinder barrels. When they expanded in the heat of racing, the camshaft drive gears were squashed together. He also suggested the best ignition system, and arranged for more oil to reach the big-end bearings through holes in the two connecting rods, since they are not fed through the centre of the crankshaft.

In 2008, I raced the Paton in a special historic race held during the French MotoGP meeting at Le Mans to commemorate the late great Australian grand prix rider Jack Findlay. Latterly a FIM Safety Officer, Jack had made France his home, originally with his Parisienne partner Nanou Lyonnard, a formidable fighter for riders' rights in the 1960s and 1970s. She supported him at all his races for twenty years. That's why I made sure she was mentioned in tributes, despite this apparently causing some embarrassment, as Jack and Nanou had split up. He then married Dominique Monneret, who was from a famous French racing family.

Waiting on the line minutes before the start, my heart sank when it started to rain. I knew that our classic bikes would look even slower in a wet race, especially as wet tyres were not allowed. I'd calculated that I had the fastest bike so decided to stay with the leading riders, if I had a choice. After a good start I found myself leading, but despite care powering out of the hairpin, I ran too wide and six riders shot past. I followed in their spray and watched, as best I could, during the following laps as one by one they slid off or ran off the track. Shit! This looks dangerous, I thought. Then I found I had an empty track ahead and was leading again. During the last few laps when I was trying to keep my lead, the Paton twice slid sideways. I thought I was going to crash, but as I kept the throttle open to keep a little power on, the bike picked itself up on the outside of the track. As this was happening, Tony Smith was chasing me on his Seeley G50 and when he saw sparks from my grounded footrest as I slid across the track, he must have thought, 'Goodbye Read'. Wrong! I just beat him to the chequered flag. Later, after the champagne spraying on the MotoGP rostrum, a long time since I had stepped on one, I enjoyed congratulations from the Yamaha Team and Valentino

Winning a difficult historic race on the Paton at Le Mans in 2008, I lost my young female helper to Valentino Rossi after his GP win.
He still owes me!

Phil Read with Moto Paton 500 grand prix bike

'Look at life through the windshield, not the rear-view mirror', Byrd Baggett

Rossi in their hospitality unit the next night after the star's great win. As a gift, I made it easy for him to pull my beautiful Hungarian helper Virag, with whom I had spent a few day's sight-seeing in Paris before arriving at Le Mans paddock to set up my stall of regalia by my caravan. Vale didn't return her till the next afternoon, lucky boy. She was star-struck, telling me that she'd be going to other GPs with him and they were in love. I told her to wake up to reality and enjoy what she'd had, it was only a 'one-off'. 'That's not true, take me to the airport', she replied. So I did, but was proved right as the season progressed! Everyone in the grand prix circus knows about and accepts these situations.

When I hear someone sigh, 'Life is hard', I am always tempted to ask, 'Compared to what?' For me, classic racing is a chance to enjoy the competitive atmosphere and to work on improvements to my machines without taking risk to the levels I might have entertained when world championships were at stake. But some of the younger riders are prepared to really push it. An example that comes to mind is when I was racing the Paton on the Chimay circuit in Belgium. I was contesting the lead with Chris Swallow, son of the veteran classic racer and Isle of Man specialist Bill Swallow, and Phil Sharpe, both on fast Manx Nortons. I could just pull ahead of them down the very long straight but when we came to the third gear corner at the end of this fast straight, Swallow Junior tried to out-brake me, shot past with no chance of rounding this corner and disappeared through the straw bales. I thought, 'that's one out of the race', but no, he ended up riding round the outside of the bales lining this corner. To my surprise, he re-appeared at speed over the grass and came back onto the track. Then he ran wide across the grass exiting the Chicane on the last lap! When we had caught several backmarkers along the fast final section, he kept on the gas to dive down the grass verge and fly past them at about 120mph, still in the lead. I couldn't believe his bravery, skill - or desperation - to win! It was a fantastic last lap of dirt riding but I didn't feel I needed to challenge him in this highly dangerous style. After the race we had a chat in the paddock. I congratulated young Swallow for taking the win after his over-the-limit riding. I suggested he didn't need to scare off or beat his challengers this way if he wanted to enjoy many more years of racing to victory. He now lives and races in New Zealand. Tragically his brother David, also a classic racer, was killed by fumes when sleeping in his van.

The end-of-summer Goodwood Revival has to be the most prestigious motor sport event in Britain for historic car and bike racing, with top stars from different eras competing against each other. Drivers, riders, pit crews and most spectators add to the atmosphere of these great historic Revivals by wearing period dress of the 1930s and 1940s. For the Revival in 2001 when the New York 9-11 cloud still hung over us, I was back with Team Obsolete, now run solely by the American, Robert Iannucci. He had shipped over an ex-factory MV acquired in the 1980s and to suit the Goodwood rules for that year it was an older-type 500 four cylinder of 1954 specification. During the first practice session the MV felt faster than all the other bikes so I felt confident of some good results. On the Saturday race day as Rob was warming the engine there was a disturbing noise and it suddenly stopped. On lifting the cylinder head we found a valve had dropped and bent by the piston as the retaining collets had been forced out. With no spares and few tools due to frustrating 9-11 freight restrictions on flights out of New York, we were in trouble. Our race on this potential race winner was over. So Rob substituted a Matchless G50 to race. Colin Seeley had ridden it the day before in practice. He had complained that the carburettor had been flooding a bit but it was otherwise okay. I tried it in the race warm up lap to find it was impossible to ride so we stopped. I stripped the float chamber later in the pits to discover that the float chamber's fuel valve was seized in the body. Obviously, this was the cause of flooding so it was a complete waste of effort for me to race. I rectified the problem in 30 minutes, but too late and I am surprised that Colin, with his vast racing experience, hadn't got on top of it earlier.

On a 1954-type MV four at the Goodwood Revival with helper Steve Wynne (left) and Nobby Clark, potentially the fastest bike there, unbeknown to us it dropped a valve in practice and retired from the race with a loosened distributor.

> 'Failure is only the opportunity to begin again, only this time more wisely', Henry Ford

Tragically, Barry Sheene died in March 2003 at the young age of 52. I have read that he had been diagnosed with cancer of the throat only months earlier. His passing was to be marked by a tribute parade at that year's Goodwood Revival, at which event he had previously raced and won on a Walmsley Manx Norton.

I had known Barry well since he was a cheeky ten-year-old kid and I first rode for his dad in the 1961 TT on a 125cc Sheene Bultaco. Barry started to show his great riding ability on British short circuits where, on a faster machine, I let him mix it with me till the last lap to keep the fans more excited. This certainly helped Barry get some early media exposure, like 'The Cockney kid chases the Champion' during his early days of racing. Later we went through so many ups and downs together on the world championship scene. The annual Goodwood Revival bike races are now titled the 'Barry Sheene Memorial Trophy', a well deserved tribute in his memory.

I've always enjoyed the other Goodwood event organised earlier in the summer by the Earl of March. It's the finest assembly of iconic racing cars and motorbikes in the world, located in the most imposing South Downs setting in the English countryside. The Goodwood Festival of Speed, in the grounds of the stately home, is centred on the hill-climb. There one can mingle with some of the top names in MotoGP, World Superbike and BSB as well as rubbing shoulders and chatting with great past and current Formula 1 drivers. It's an impressive affair for which everyone thanks the generosity of his Lordship, his family and helpers.

The second time I raced an MV Agusta at the Goodwood Revival it was a 1954 model owned by the Auriana brothers, stockbrokers from New York. Our mechanics were Nobby Clark, who had spannered for riders including Jim Redman, Mike Hailwood, Giacomo Agostini, Jarno Saarinen and Kenny Roberts, along with Steve Wynne, formerly in charge of the Sports Motor Cycles crew behind Mike Hailwood's 1978 TT Ducati win and now based in New Zealand.

It took a long time to get the engine and suspension sorted, but in the end this old four was really flying and I was thinking to myself, 'We've got this one in the bag!' But then it never seemed as fast again and we had to pull out of the race when the ignition distributor cap came loose, the one thing these famous mechanics forgot to wire-lock! When Steve Wynne and the MV were back in New Zealand he removed the exhaust pipes and out dropped an exhaust valve head, so it had only been running on three cylinders before we stopped. I think they were so concerned trying to stop the engine oil leaks that they overlooked testing the cylinder compressions and the odd lock wiring. With the fitting of a new valve and a little more attention my young New Zealand partner rider and I could have finished on the rostrum. Yes I know, there are so many ifs and buts in the racing world. Remember, to gain success one must be well prepared for all these little problems and when they are overcome they make all the previous work on the machine and travelling by the team well worthwhile.

Having seen the success of historic races included as support races at major modern bike events, I put together a plan for the 'Continental Circus', consisting of classic bike races to be held at five rounds of MotoGP, undoubtedly the First Division of motorcycle racing. I agreed with my old track rival Chas Mortimer, who runs a successful international trucking company specialising in bike shipping, to provide the necessary transportation.

I approached Formula 1 magnate Bernie Ecclestone, who said he could not help with finance but supported me by calling Red Bull, the energy drink company that runs an F1 team and has a generally high profile as a multi-sports sponsor.

Colin Seeley's contribution

Within a week I could not believe my good luck. I was invited along with my 'team' for talks with Red Bull near their base in Salzburg on the ski slopes of Kitzbühel, Austria. After a two hour discussion in a snow-covered chalet overlooking the ski slopes we agreed terms and I was offered a tight budget to cover the team's expenses to set up this project around the Continent, at five agreed MotoGPs. Later my team and I put arrangements in place to get started with this major venture. For the Continental Circus paddock facility to measure up when placed near the multi-million Euro transporters and motorhomes of the top MotoGP teams and riders, we needed a big marquee to display and prepare our classic bikes. Also, we needed plenty of other equipment such as a tractor and trailer, bike benches, banners and flags, etc, Sleeping accommodation, food and beverage for the riders, helpers and staff who didn't have caravans or motorhomes were also needed. From my experience I knew at these prime events any odd caravans, small motorhomes, vans and tents would be forced to park or camp well out of sight of TV cameras and the viewing public.

I had just arrived at the Race Retro Show at Stoneleigh Park two months later when I took a call from Red Bull. I was shattered. They had pulled out of our agreement, because, they said, Bernie Ecclestone was not putting any money into this project. I knew Red Bull had understood that since our first meeting. Their real reason for this pull-out we will never know, but I expect it has to do with money. We were all very disappointed and out of pocket from the time and money spent preparing equipment and vehicles. These days, I support the rival Monster Energy product, now the main sponsor the the Yamaha GP Team.

As long ago as 1979, the Isle of Man TT organised a historic parade lap as a part of its festival programme. In that year I rode a disc-braked 500cc MV four from Signor Elli in Italy in company with John Surtees and we lapped at a steady 96mph. Tucking in behind him, I could see that John, then in his mid-50s, was still a great rider, but I suspected he had forgotten sections of the circuit. No problem, I was happy to see the old master at work and happy reactions from the race fans. We were having fun riding together at the head of the parade - until Percy Tait overtook us on his 750cc Triumph triple and started to pull away. 'That's not in the plan' I thought. I could not let Percy be the first back to the Grandstand, so I chased after him, passed and was first back to the finish line. Whatever that proved I can't imagine, except that we were still 'racers' at heart, regardless of age.

Chasing Percy Tait on his works Triumph, I beat him to the flag in a 1979 Isle of Man TT 'parade'.

Phil began racing in May 1956 at Mallory Park. I was a late-comer when I began, aged 24, in 1960. We were to cross paths many times and had several tiffs, but always managed to get over it and carry on. As the years rolled by, I witnessed some really exciting races and saw Phil gain success upon success. His business and private life had its ups and downs, but I'm glad to say we are still friends.

When my first wife, Joan, died of cancer in 1979, I set up The Joan Seeley Pain Relief Memorial Trust, many celebrities including Phil Read, Striling Moss, Mike Hailwood and Murray Walker were most supportive, (pictured above with Dr Frances Sorrell). Phil has continued to assist in raising funds, most recently at The Donington Park Festival in 2013. As well as donating his racing leathers for auction, he worked tirelessly all weekend to promote our cause.

So I would like to say a huge thank you to Phil Read, MBE, our most successful living British GP rider, for his tremendous support.

Thanks Phil!

March 1981, Charity Trust Boxing Night, London v Wales, Cats Whiskers, Streatham.

1998 Assen, 500cc MV Agusta

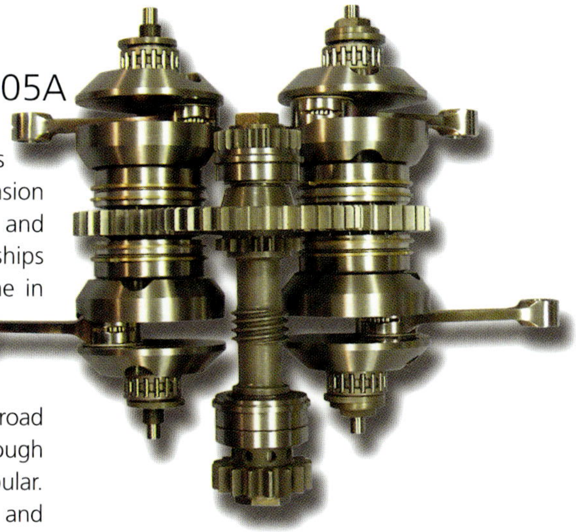

Crankshafts assembly for the 250cc Yamaha RD05A

A Parade of Champions by ex-racers and racers on outstanding machines on similar lines was run at Brands Hatch in 1981. That was a unique occasion when I shared the grid with John Surtees, who'd organised the event, and Giacomo Agostini, all three of us on MV fours. That was 29 world championships lined up together! Another early example of a 'past masters' display came in 1982, albeit against a very sad background. A star parade was staged at the newly-opened Donington Park circuit in memory of Mike Hailwood, who had been so tragically and needlessly killed by another driver's illegal action, along with his nine year old daughter Michelle in a road accident that year. Fans showed up in their droves and it was clear that with enough big names present, non-competitive historic parades could become hugely popular. These types of event have now become a regular feature of race meetings and historic events all over the world and attract many thousands of spectators.

Surely the most ambitious of them all was the Assen Centennial Grand Prix, organised by my former mechanic Ferry Brouwer who was by then CEO of Arai (helmets) Europe. After he sold the Arai company he returned to his passion of preparing and renovating classic bikes to develop the Yamaha Classic Racing Team (YCRT) for which many past top riders rode fine bikes at near their maximum racing speeds, including myself. That Assen meeting was like a who's who of racing with so many champions and other racing names present, as well as a mind-blowing selection of machinery.

There in the Yamaha camp I was delighted to meet guys who had been my mechanics in the championship years: Makita-san, Matsui-san, Seki-san, Suzuki-san and Takasaki-san. And I could barely believe my eyes when I saw fabulous works bikes from the 1960s, including a 250cc RD05A four-cylinder machine in perfect ready-to-race condition. I felt honoured to be the first rider to take this out on a track since my 1968 world championship and when I took it out for practice it ran like a dream. For the race (sorry, I mean fast parade!) Ferry, re-living his past glories, was on hand in Yamaha overalls, but could not get the engine to run on all four cylinders. A coil had gone dead in a new CDI ignition system, so finding a replacement then was impossible. We were all heartbroken about that.

I had some consolation in being in a parade with John Surtees, Giacomo Agostini, Gianfranco Bonera and Alberto Pagani, all of us on 500cc MVs. I negotiated to ride a 500cc four owned by Ubaldo Elli, an Italian hosiery manufacturer who acquired the largest number of ex-factory MV bikes and parts in the world at a bargain cost in the 1980s. He has consistently provided them to be paraded at events by various riders, including Ago. During our parade I overtook Surtees when braking into the first corner, I nearly crashed when the front wheel pattered out of control, due to the front forks being in need of a service. I don't think John was impressed!

I would ride an MV from Scuderia Elli again at Vallelunga near Rome, but although I offered to spend time sorting and correctly adjusting his many machines to make them safer for guests to ride, the offer was rejected in a most off-hand manner.

I love to take part in such events, provided a worthwhile machine in safe condition with good tyres is available. It's great when you have a quick or interesting classic bike to ride for some fast laps: like the four-cylinder RD05A Yamaha 250cc bike of Ferry Brouwer's Yamaha Classic Racing Team, so nice to ride once seizure problems it had in 2011 were overcome. He was lucky I had a fast clutch hand or the bike would have been wrecked a number of times, and I would have been hurt.

'Difficulties strengthen the mind, as labour does the body', Seneca

Talking to the camera at Assen where I was re-united with Yamaha's fabulous RD05A world-beater

A message from Phil Read

In 2011 my parade ride in Yamaha's 50th TT anniversary was most embarrassing. I was just starting to enjoy riding flat-out down Bray Hill and aiming to get a wheelie over Ago's Leap, the crest that follows, when the engine seized. Instead of stopping, I free-wheeled a few hundred yards down to the Quarter Bridge pub, where I was sure someone would buy me a pint if I asked. Also stopped there, on another YCRT machine, was Dieter Braun, whose gear lever had broken off. So together we drank the time away, thanks to the generous TT fans watching there.

It is in the proper spirit of these historic events that our fans can see the iconic bikes and riders that belong together. Obvious examples would include these pairings: **Jim Redman** (Honda), **Giacomo Agostini** (MV/Yamaha), **Phil Read** (Yamaha/MV), **Tommy Robb** (Honda), **Chas Mortimer** (Yamaha), **Wayne Gardner** (Honda), **Dieter Braun** (Yamaha), **Heinz Rosner** (MZ), **Charlie Williams** (Yamaha), **Kenny Roberts** (Yamaha), **Graeme Crosby** (Suzuki), **Christian Sarron** (Yamaha), **Eddie Lawson** (Yamaha), **Bruno Kneubühler** (Yamaha), **Freddie Spencer** (Honda), **Mick Doohan** (Honda), **Wil Hartog** (Suzuki), **Gianfranco Bonera** (MV), **Tepi Länsivuori** (Yamaha).

These are the guys people love to see on their fabulous classic ex-factory machines, riding at near racing speeds.

For a press launch on the track at the Sachsenring MotoGP I was aboard the 1960s Yamaha 250cc four with Cal Crutchlow on his 990cc Yamaha M1 MotoGP machine lined up alongside me for the photo call. The plan was for a short 'drag race' on the new circuit. The large crowd loved it as I left Cal behind. I was gone like a shot, even though his M1 had launch control technology.

Cal's father Derek is an ex-racer and when we were talking at a Silverstone MotoGP, he reminded me that, years before, his tent had caught fire in the paddock. He remembered that I was the person who grabbed an extinguisher to help put it out, no messing.

The MotoGP bikes with up to 250bhp could not be raced to the current levels of cornering speed and lap times if it wasn't for on-board computer controls, like rear tyre traction control, slipper clutches and gear quick-shifters etc. As it is, riders just open the throttle and leave the traction control to do the rest, keeping them on the track. Having said that, electronic assistance surely doesn't detract from the skill, fitness and endurance of the riders on these super-fast 210mph bikes when racing to the limit in close company. They have skill and bravery to the ultimate degree.

Thanks to Yamaha Motor I was given a most exciting opportunity to try the M1 on the Imola circuit as part of their 50th anniversary celebration in GP racing. No-one told me that this fine MotoGP machine had no wheelie control operating. After a short run out of the crowded pit area, when I got to understand the feel of the powerful front brake and gear shift controls, I accelerated out onto the circuit, only to find that if I opened the throttle to the 17,000rpm redline the front wheel shot up to the sky. So all I could do was short-shift at around 14,000rpm to keep the front wheel on the track. Finding the machine a bit heavy to turn into corners, I understood why all current riders shift their weight around so much when turning into corners. At some time I'll also start hanging out my leg to find if that also helps, as some riders now do in MotoGP. I wonder what Geoff Duke thinks when he watches the antics of current GP racers.

Checking over Yamaha's latest YZR-M1 MotoGP machine at Imola in 2011, when the company marked 50 years in GP racing.

I lapped Imola three times on Yamaha's YZR-M1 MotoGP at their anniversay event. Its power and track performance blew my mind.

My ride on the Yamaha M1

As part of the celebrations of Yamaha's 50th Anniversary it was my honour to ride their factory GP M1 race machine for two laps at the Imola 200 Revival. On Friday before this event the Yamaha Classic Racing Team and I were invited by Yamaha team boss, Marco Riva, to the impressive racing headquarters next to the famous Monza Autodrome, the venue of their first world title in 1964.

From the moment I received the invitation I had been dreaming of its 240bhp and the fool I would look if I crashed or looped it when powering this rocket-ship out from the chicane in front of the pits!!

I was really impressed to find the Yamaha pits fitted out to GP standard, with a blue carpeted floor and four smart factory mechanics. Wow! I thought, this is being taken very seriously to allow this old fart to ride their prized GP machine.

After a few laps on my 1968 championship winning 250 Yamaha, the RD05A four-cylinder machine, built and maintained by Ferry Brouwer, custodian of the fabulous Yamaha Classic Racing Team, during which time my old team-mate, Agostini, had warmed up the M1's slick tyres, I was handed this lastest world title winning machine on which to do my worst.

As I'd just been told that the wheelie and traction controls were not connected I was even more worried as I short-shifted down the pit road to keep the front wheel on the tarmac as the torque was delivered in a relenless surge. After a touch or two of the front brake to get the feel of it, I opened the throttle out onto this famous track to feel its arm-stretching acceleration. Too frightened to redline this bellowing engine I shifted up at 15,500rpm, the limit being 18,500rpm, I was rocketed at a speed up to the tight Tosa bend. It was a new experience. This was the fastest and most valuble bike I'd ever ridden so I had to stay out of the gravel. There was little engine braking due to the selective slipper clutch but the most powerful, one finger, front brake did all I needed to slow and hit this bend's apex in good shape to accelerate up the hill, only daring to short-shift to keep the front wheel just pawing the air. I really admire the professional racers who can use full throttle on these powerful factory bikes.

As I flew down to the Acqua Minerale corner I realised my mistake, I had removed my knee sliders. The slick tyres of the M1 allowed such an amazing angle of grip. But no one was expecting me to break any records, just remind everyone of Yamaha's glorious 50 years in GP racing. After all, I'd been there in their first five full seasons.

The M1 rocketed me from the Rivazza down to the tricky chicane at the end of my first lap right by the pits and past most fans and Yamaha officials. I thought I had overshot it as I had never before arrived there so fast. When straightened up on line I pulled the brake lever with two fingers and changing down with my left foot, (I've always had a right gear-shifter), I decided I could make this tight chicane with some curb hopping to not look slow and unimpressive. The M1 wheelied out in good shape onto the straight. I was exhausted, terrified and elated as I sped back into the pits to the cheers of my fans and smiles of relief on the Yamaha mechanics faces. My last flying lap will always be branded in my memory.

Thank you Yamaha.

Andy Roberts' contribution

'Never meet your heroes,' as someone once said, you may be disappointed.

After following Phil's career for many years, I finally lost interest in Grand Prix racing in the mid 1980s, and didn't go to another meeting for about sixteen years. Having watched the Goodwood Festival of Speed on TV in 2000, my wife and I decided to go to the Revival Meeting in 2001. Phil was down to ride an MV triple, but I think it bent a valve in practice, so he rode a reserve machine. During the race, you could see that he had lost none of his style. After racing had finished, I went looking for an autograph, something I had never done before. I had no pen, but Phil said he would swap me a pen for a cigarette. I left with a souvenir pen, a handshake and a programme signed by one of my boyhood heroes, and Phil had a half a dozen cigarettes to see him through.

My next significant encounter came at Mallory Park. I was going to find a vantage point from where I could watch a BSA Gold Star race. As I walked past Phil's van, he looked like a man who had too much to do and not enough time to do it, so I asked if he needed a hand. 'Will you help me?' he asked. 'Of course', I replied, so we connected the battery and fuelled up the bike, then pushed it down the paddock to fire it up. He rode round in an arc, came back and said, 'OK, jump on and keep it running.' After warming up the bike for a few minutes, Phil went out, and I think he finished second that day. When he came back he said, 'We nearly won that!' When he said that, I felt as if we were part of the same team. I felt chuffed to bits. Phil thanked me for my help, and we went our separate ways, but we kept in touch with the occasional phone call or text.

Imagine my surprise when I got a phone call from him asking, 'Do you fancy a trip to Italy? I could do with a hand.' What could I say? We had a fantastic trip through France and Italy that I will never forget.

I have to say a massive thank you to Phil for that amazing trip and the opportunities to see and experience things that I would never have had a chance to see and do, had I not met him. I am proud to call him my friend.

So, if anyone ever asks if you would like to meet one of your boyhood heroes, say YES, you might not be disappointed.

Agostini starts MV Agusta 500 at Imatra in 2008

I like to keep in close touch with the MotoGP scene and since 2002 I have been honoured with the status of Grand Prix Legend by Dorna, owner of the series, to be given a permanent worldwide VIP pass.

Ago and MV Agusta are a good example of having the right rider on the right bike, even though he's had strong ties with Yamaha since 1974 when he left MV. So in order to become free of borrowing old MVs from Sig. Elli, he has a replica of his beloved old 500cc MV three cylinder machine on which to parade (subject to being offered the minimum fee, of course!) It is one of half a dozen manufactured with MV's blessing several years ago by Ezio Mascheroni, his son Maurizio and former MV technician Enrico Sironi. They comprise HRT, who also carried out design and development work on MV Agusta's F3 675 road bike. I understand an edition of at least six replicas was made and sold for an incredible 220.000 Euros (about £190,000) each. I fear there was insufficient dyno testing of the engine, as I know Ago had a piston seize on one of his first outings.

Ago's MV and my Paton at Limoges show 2012

That is loud! Giacomo Agostini fires up his 500cc MV triple replica at Imatra in 2008. Teething troubles saw it seize a piston after only two laps, but no-one will forget that reverberating sound.

In 2012 I was lent an ex-Randy Mamola factory Suzuki to ride at Imatra in Finland and Marco Lucchinelli, 500cc world champion in 1981, came up to me after we'd been on track and said, 'Phil, you are too fast!' That's good for the spectators, too. It's a matter of putting on a good show without being stupid. Every rider has his own way of doing it. I've got Ago sussed, he'll usually do a few quick laps and then back off and take it easy.

I attend up to 10 non-racing classic events each year, mostly around Europe and including the UK Festival of 1000 Bikes at Mallory Park.

Even though I enjoy travelling around Europe, there is the matter of expenses: it's no use pretending that travel, food and accommodation don't cost money. And if you can't ask a premium when you're a multiple world champion, when can you? On the whole I find organisers fair, although there have been occasional unfortunate exceptions .

It's worth remembering that while parading with other top stars may not be all-out like real racing, it can be hazardous as we are trying to show who of the ex-racers can be or look the fastest on similar machines. I remember having to stop suddenly at Spa when I came round a slower corner to find veteran racer Dave Bedlington lying on the track under his Yamaha. The track marshals were doing nothing to help other than waving flags. I parked my Suzuki against the Armco and ran over. I managed to lift the bike off him and dump it aside.

Imagine the sound! Ago, Bonera, Surtees and me on MVs, sandwiching John Cooper on his BSA triple

Thanks Peter Jones

I would like to thank Peter Jones for the many rides on his Magni MV Agusta and the use of his barns for my bikes and regalia storage. I only crashed once on his bike, at Brands. Thanks also go to Steve Wheatman and his support crew for the loan of a Read replica 1976 Suzuki RG500 in recent times.

At my age I need an even faster Suzuki to keep up with Barry Sheene's son Freddie on his later model.

He was unconscious, so I moved him into the recovery position and loosened his helmet so he could breathe better and waited for the Paramedics to arrive. Not one other rider stopped to help which I found very upsetting.

Even seasoned old hands like Sammy Miller, Michelle (formerly Mike) Duff, Mick Grant, Dieter Braun, Tommy Robb and even Giacomo Agostini have been injured from spills when parading. Touch wood, I've been lucky, with a fast clutch hand. 'Courage is going from failure to failure without losing enthusiasm'. Winston Churchill famously said.

I still get a real kick from the enthusiastic response of fans, whether it's in England, on the Continent or Down Under. It's part of the deal that you spend time signing autographs and I never cease to be touched by the memories so many fans treasure from those championship days. I learnt long ago that we should look after and pay attention to youngsters, and signing programmes and giving them stickers is simple enough. Being sensitive and shy in their youth, they remember kindness all their lives, and stay one's fans.

I've made many new friends during my travels throughout Europe, too. One such is Belgian banker Francois Lambert, his wife Fabienne and their three daughters Caroline, Hélène and Pauline. Francois bought a Phil Read helmet at Chimay in 2000 and told me how he remembered my great battle with Barry Sheene there in 1976, when both of us were on Suzuki RG500s. Since then we have met at various times and circuits. After they had visited me in England, Francois and Fabienne kindly invited me stay with them during the winter of 2005. I was made to feel completely at home and did my best to repay their hospitality by cooking dinners, mowing the grass and doing some hard labour to help Francois with his farmhouse renovations and extensions. The year before, when I crashed in race practice at Bremerhaven road circuit in northwestern Germany and woke up in hospital, an hour later Francois and Fabienne were there. I only felt fit enough the next day to drive to the nearest airport and fly back to the UK. Fabienne agreed to tow my race trailer back to their home in Belgium while Francois rode his Honda VFR back in the pouring rain. They are a tough couple.

On my way to stay with them over the winter, I stopped off in their nearest village of Beaumont to buy Fabienne a small gift. Needing a coffee I looked in on an impressive-looking restaurant to be met by its owner who turned out to be a great fan and a keen motorcyclist. Michel and his charming wife Benedicte would not let me pay for a thing and I was very pleased and grateful to eat there often.

The following year I arranged to obtain two pit passes for the Monaco Formula 1 GP when passing through the South of France. I called Michel, who drove down from Belgium to meet me at a mountain hotel along the coast from Monaco, which didn't charge inflated prices because of the F1 races. It was perfect to drive down to catch the train running alongside the Med all the way to central Monte Carlo, with free parking at the station and regular half-empty trains.

We stood by the start-line to watch the race and walked to some prime viewing places. Then we ate oysters and drank champagne by the Red Bull hospitality swimming pool in the harbour, admiring the money Mecca of Europe.

Francois helped to organise a Paton-only parade at Chimay in 2008, which he was most thrilled to ride in along with me aboard his Honda VFR in order to learn the racing lines. That was a great showing for Paton bikes as the four-strokes were joined by grand prix two-strokes Roberto Pattoni has built over the years. But my 500cc twin was not invited into the big marquee with all the Patons because it is red and not the traditional bright green.

Phil Read on Phil Morris

We agreed to become the first joint UK importers of MV Agusta special parts and to import a number of new MV Agusta F4s from France to sell in the UK.

I worked really hard at shows and events around the country, promotions and selling our products. I took all orders, processed payments and posted most parts. Also I did conversions on standard MV F4s to which I fitted carbon wheels, sports exhausts, my huggers and the MV special and carbon parts.

After some months of running this business I was contacted by Mr Morris who told me he was sending a potential customer who was interested in a new fully converted F4 so he would like a test ride.

The customer arrived by car with a friend and looked at the machine. I agreed to let him test ride it as he seemed keen to buy one. He left his friend in the car, but I made the mistake to offering him a cup of coffee. As I went in the house he drove off. Wendy said, 'He's stolen your bike and they won't be back.' She was right! She phoned the police to report the theft while I tore around the area in my car, trying to find them. About an hour later Phil Morris called to say he had my bike and if I wanted it back I had pay him the balance of our contra-accounts, which I had never refused to do.

Some days later I had Mr Morris arrested and questioned but released on bail. Wendy and I then suffered two years of worry and legal charges to get my prized MV Agusta F4 special freed by Mr Morris, which I was forced to collect 'Up North'.

The UK launch at Mallory Park of the first to be seen MV Agusta F4 Oro, a fantastic experience, I suggested some improvements, but the factory acted too late.

Two decades after leaving the MV team, I found myself involved in the marque's revival as a motorcycle producer. There was a big festival at Scarborough's Gold Cup meeting in 1996 with many famous names present, including Barry Sheene and Carl Fogarty. I was riding a historic MV, owned by my good friend Peter Jones of Regency Flooring, Canterbury, as was Ago. He arrived late, landing at the circuit by helicopter, because he had been at the launch of the reborn MV 750cc F4 four-cylinder road machine in Italy. As soon as he saw me, he said, 'The new MV is so fantastic, you wouldn't believe it!'

There was a UK launch of the new machine at Mallory Park the following year, where Ago rode an old grand prix 500 and I rode the top-specification version of the F4, the limited-edition Oro with magnesium and carbon fibre components that make it 12kg lighter than the base model.

I called MV boss Claudio Castiglioni, the industry veteran whose Cagiva Research Centre (CRC) at San Marino developed the new four. I told him I thought his machine was beautiful, but there were two main problems with it. The air intake tubes in the inside of the fairing tended to squash my thumbs on full lock so I couldn't work the throttle properly when manoeuvring in the paddock. Also, I was disappointed to discover it sounded like an LE Velocette, not like the Ferrari of motorcycles. (The LE was a small, slow British utility motorcycle of the 1950s with a very quiet exhaust.)

I was given my own F4 at the factory by MV's designer Massimo Tamburini, formerly of Bimota and Ducati fame, designing the latter company's iconic 916. But I realised that it had the same problems as the one I'd ridden, without the suggested improvements.

Also, various serious technical problems had become apparent from the experience of MV dealers. Gearbox selectors would break, the cams would wear out thanks to a faulty hardening process, the front springs were too soft and the single radiator would start to boil its water on a hot day or in traffic. It seems incredible that there hadn't been enough testing to fix these things in the two years between launching this fabulous-looking machine and starting production.

I set about making my own quite costly improvements to my F4. I had a hugger made for the rear wheel, to stop water and dirt being flung up off the road. I fitted a new ECU chip, a nice carbon fibre exhaust can to improve the sound, and replaced the front air tubes with carbon ones that didn't foul my arms. I took the bike to the racing wheels specialist Dymag and asked them to fit a set of carbon fibres to replace the cast alloy ones. With lighter wheels and therefore less gyroscopic effect, it handled like a 250.

Then I went down to CRC at San Marino and showed the modified bike to Tamburini. He looked it over and said, 'Now it is not beautiful.' I replied by asking if he was the kind of man who liked to receive pain from a beautiful woman!

Later, I was amazed when MV's new three cylinder F3 bike was launched before it was properly shaken down. Press tests by *MCN* even advised readers not to buy one until the problems, mainly concerning the injection/ignition mapping, had been corrected.

MV Agusta worked for many weeks testing various CDI mappings but could not solve uneven running at low cruising speeds. In fact it was a mechanical problem caused by fitting unsuitable shock absorbent cush rubbers in the clutches of the new three-cylinder sports machine. When I was visiting the MV factory I was shown how this unfortunate thing was simply solved by one of their workshop engineers, he changed the rubbers for harder ones, problem solved! I wish I had been contacted to be their test rider, I could have saved them much time and money.

Tamburini said I should go to the factory to get upgrades. They were rectifying problems that I'd told them about earlier, like difficulties with bleeding the front brakes and oil filter canisters that fell off, sometimes causing crashes. I was there for three days while my bike was being sorted and when I spoke to the export manager he said, 'Don't go around saying our bikes are good or bad: please just go away and leave us alone.'

MV built up massive debts and they were lucky to survive. If they had been less superior and employed me to complete lots of circuit and road testing and development I could have saved them two hundred million Euros. The debt MV incurred due to the F4 faults. They were helped out by the Malaysian company Petronas, then owned and invested in by Harley-Davidson for two years from 2008 to 2010 before Claudio Castiglioni was able to buy the marque back for just one Euro. He died in 2011, since when his son Giovanni has been in charge.

Phil Morris on Phil Read

It was at a show in Shrewsbury where I was displaying a Phil Read Honda Replica that I met Phil. He asked if I would be interested in sponsoring Roki in the 1999 BSB British Superbike Championship, which I did for one year. At the end of 1999 Phil asked if I would be interested in importing MV F4s into the UK for resale. We visited Varese and met Claudio and it was agreed that we could bring F4 750s into the UK. According to Phil, Claudio later asked if we would be interested in opening an MV dealership in Oswestry.

Our agreement was that on each sale Phil would pay the cost of the machine and send 50% of the profit on to Morris Holdings within five days of the sale, keeping 50% of the profit for himself.

While I was on holiday Phil placed a very large order for bikes and spares without my knowledge. After repeated requests for payment I was advised by my solicitor that I could execute a lien (a right to retain possession of another's property, pending discharge of a debt). I did so, as Phil explains in his account. After the motorcycle was collected from Phil I informed the Royston Police of my actions as per my solicitor's instructions.

However, two weeks later I was arrested, accused of the theft of a motorcycle. The resulting court action at Stevenage County Court ruled there was no case to answer.

Phil Jnr and Roki

Phil Jnr has done very well in business. He achieved an MBA in his spare time. With Roki we set up a race team with Yamahas, a 600 for Phil and a TZ350 for Roki, with an Iveco transporter/motorhome with help from Letraset, where Roki worked. He went on to become Advertising Manager for *Motor Cycle News* to give them a return of around two million pounds. With his fiancée he bought a house near Peterborough, but when he decided to start a Ducati Sports dealership in Northampton he needed to borrow a great deal which would have caused them to live on a very tight risky budget so she left him. A good move for him I believe.

Phil has become the UK Marketing & Promotions Director for Piaggio and has been head-hunted by a number of top and exciting motorcycle manufacturers and soon may move to the Continent. His 2014 plans include racing the hub centre-steered Alto Performance Rage, developed from the Vyrus he previously raced with amazing success. I'm always delighted to watch him fight his way through the pack to win through fantastic on-the-limit riding.

Roki Read, named after Rocci Agusta, is married to Christine and has two fantastic daughters, Madeleine and Ellie. They are all keen mountain bikers. After some good successes on his TZ350 Yamaha he is now dedicated to mountain and road bike racing and travels to some top Continental events. Also he spends fortunes on his bikes and their special Hope parts, as he does for his three ladies.

He is the southern area manager for Sanderson special windows.

My personalised MV was sold, but then I was fortunate in picking up a Brutale, the unfaired, 'streetfighter' version of the F4, in boxes and at a good price. Ben Shaughnessy of Alto Performance, the brilliant engineer and sponsor of Phil Read Jnr on their extraordinary Vyrus in Thundersport racing a couple of seasons ago. This revolutionary Italian bike with a tuned Ducati V-twin engine in a radical chassis featuring hub centre steering was built by a small Rimini-based outfit.

In the knowledge that Phil Jnr was eager to race their latest Rage version, with a redesigned chassis, similar to the Vyrus, but now fitted with a 1098 Ducati engine. Then we will see if this revolutionary chassis can compete with the BSS Superbikes.

During 2012 Ben sold me a dismantled MV Agusta Brutale in boxes, with a repaired chassis and new sub-frame and forks. I rented a garage and built it up. There was a hiccup with the exhaust system - I couldn't get it to fit because Ben had given me a stock F4 system by mistake. We eventually found the right pipes and got it running nicely after I had taken it to the MV factory for professional help from the service department.

After riding Ben's futuristic and much modified Vyrus/Ducati at the 1000 Bikes event at Mallory Park, I'd say that telescopic forks have surely had their day. Grand prix riders have struggled with front wheel patter for decades and still haven't solved the problem. But the Vyrus does not suffer any patter at all and has rock-steady steering, without any dive under braking.

Looking back, my dream has always been to be able to set up and run a stable of outstanding machines complete with full workshop facilities. But with having moved house so often, my first divorce and then Madeleine's death, it has not been possible for me to get too involved with the development of revolutionary sports and racing motorcycles.

The first innovative bike design that I became interested in was the feet-first bike I rode to Buckingham Palace to collect my MBE. It was the Quasar, designed and built by Malcolm Newell and Ken Leaman near Bristol. Malcolm took me out into the country to a good testing area. My road machine at the time was a Moto Guzzi Le Mans on which I struggled to stay with him as the cornering speed was just amazing. This was due to a low centre of gravity thanks to the rider sitting only 18 inches or so above the ground with his or her legs stretched forward, protected by a windscreen and all-in-one bodywork, with a steamlined nose over the front wheel. The rider had plenty of wind and weather protection from the body with air heating directed to the hands, a windscreen wiper and luggage space behind the passenger seat. Another big advantage in the event of accident or side impact was the fact that the rider was protected by the base body shell. It only had a 38bhp Reliant car engine but still could reach over 100mph. With open sides there was no feeling of claustrophobia and as you stopped, you just placed both feet on the road to maintain balance, as on a normal motorcycle.

If only a progressive manufacturer had become interested in the Quasar's potential, especially if carbon fibre mouldings could have been devised for it. I believe the basic bike could have been developed into a 'must have' sports and touring motorcycle.

Cartier Mumbai concours, 2013, spot Sir Stirling Moss

More recently I have received details and video of an American motorcycle which is out-of-this-world. It's electric powered and totally enclosed in a smart-looking aerodynamic carbon fibre body. The most dynamic advantage to the user is that it won't fall over when parked or even when hit by a car. This is achieved by two on-board gyroscopes which provide 1,300 lbft of torque. When in production it promises to exceed 100mph and cover 220 miles without a recharge. It goes from 0 to 60mph in 6 seconds while offering the efficiency and safety of a car. At the time of writing, this high technology, comfort and safety come at the full production cost of $12,000 (about £8,000) a unit. A perfect utility bike, especially for places such as China or India where production costs are lowest and where there is the greatest need to reduce air pollution? After my recent very interesting visit to Mumbai in India I saw for myself the incredible pollution and traffic congestion there. From my hotel window I could not see further than a quarter of a mile out to sea and it took us nearly 90 minutes to drive seven miles.

I should mention that one of the high points of my visit to India was being introduced to Prince Michael of Kent, who said that it was me and my racing activities that had inspired him to take up motorcycling years ago.

My grandchildren left to right:
Madeleine, Ellie, Daniel, Lauren, Holly and Courtney

Graham and Mike Read

Graham Read, I tried to help him in his first years of bike racing and he had some good results, especially at Mallory Park. I was upset when I read in the motorcycle press that he thought I treated his racing like we were at a GP. I think he preferred to have more fun in the race paddocks with his friends and was not serious enough with machine preparation to make a name for himself on the track. This showed when he retired from a TT race with crankshaft failure after making no attempt to service it after many short circuit races. The TT Mountain Course is an engine killer even to fully serviced motors.

Gray has now progressed to the prestigious work for the Dunlop Race Team for Moto2 and Moto3 series during the worldwide MotoGP events. But I never get a post card!

Mike Read, when I carried him onto the TT rostrum in 1965 I never imagined that around 25 years later he was flying a fully armed Tornado over Iraq during the Gulf War. I am very proud of his achievements in the RAF. His fine flying experience and cool head have led him to become a 1st Senior Officer for Cathay Pacific flying Jumbos and 777s to the Far East. His first marriage to Mandy produced three lovely daughters, Lauren, Courtney and Hollie. Now he has returned to Guernsey where he married Toni and produced my first grandson Daniel, who is now a keen biker around their garden.

I see on facebook that I am about to have my seventh grandchild, from my daughter Esme Markham, and I'm hoping it will be another (my second), grandson.

2013 FIM Gala

Something unexpected happened at the end of 2013 that I found very rewarding and quite moving.

I arrived at Nice airport on my way to the Monte Carlo FIM Gala Ceremony, held every year world-wide to honour the new world champions in various classes of the sport from enduro and trials to motocross and road racing.

A new Mercedes was waiting to take me to the 2013 Gala venue at the five-star Monte Carlo Bay hotel and resort.

On the Sunday all the new champions and Legends were seated on a stage to be interviewed en masse. The star of this part of the show was 12 year old Aiden Tijero from the USA, the new 65cc Junior Motocross world champion, who stood to give a great speech thanking his family and helpers.

At the Gala dinner I found myself seated with the sensational Marc Marquez, winner of the MotoGP championship in his first year in the class. Along with him were his Repsol Honda team manager Livio Suppo and Marc's parents. Talking to them revealed many interesting things.

To my surprise I was asked to join the new roadrace champions at the rear of the Gala stage. I was soon ushered out to an introduction by Matt Roberts, who hosts BBC TV coverage of MotoGP. During his interview I pointed out that he had omitted to mention my 51 GP wins and 121 podiums, to which he replied that he didn't have that much time!

Then, I was most humbled when Vito Ippolito, the FIM President, appeared holding a magnificent Legends Trophy with my name inscribed on it, what a wonderful moment!

Totally unexpectedly, I was asked stay on stage to present the road racing Gold Medals to Sam Lowes for World Supersport, Tom Sykes for World Superbike, Maverick Vinales for Moto3, Pol Espargaró for Moto2, and finally the phenomenal Moto GP rookie, Marc Marquez. I mentioned to him that 15 crashes this season was pushing his luck too far and that he should have slowed a little to give the Yamahas a better chance. He just smiled and bowed his head so that I could place his first MotoGP Gold Medal around his neck.

How good it felt to be involved at the heart of the grand prix scene, where I experienced so many highs and some lows in a long career that I now look back on with pride.

Yes, love him or loathe him, Phil Read world champion and rebel is very much still around!

Great moment for a new champion - and an old one, with Marc Marquez at the 2013 FIM Gala Ceremony

FIM world championships: top-three race finishes

1961

Isle of Man TT	1st	350cc	(Norton)

World championships: 4th 350cc

1962

Dutch TT	3rd	350cc	(Norton)

World championships: 3rd 500cc

1963

West German GP	3rd	350cc	(Gilera)
Isle of Man TT	3rd	500cc	(Gilera)
Dutch TT	2nd	500cc	(Gilera)
Belgian GP	2nd	500cc	(Gilera)
Japanese GP	3rd	250cc	(Yamaha)

World championships: 4th 500cc, 10th 250cc

1964

United States GP	2nd	500cc	(Matchless)
Spanish GP	3rd	250cc	(Yamaha)
French GP	1st	250cc	(Yamaha)
IoM TT	2nd	350cc	(AJS)
Dutch TT	2nd	125cc	(Yamaha)
	2nd	250cc	(Yamaha)
Belgian GP	2nd	500cc	(Matchless)
West German GP	1st	250cc	(Yamaha)
	3rd	500cc	(Matchless)
East German GP	1st	250cc	(Yamaha)
Ulster GP	1st	250cc	(Yamaha)
	1st	500cc	(Norton)
Italian GP	1st	250cc	(Yamaha)

World championships :
1st 250cc, 3rd 500cc, 6th 350cc, 8th 125cc

1965

United States GP	1st	250cc	(Yamaha)
West German	1st	250cc	(Yamaha)
Spanish GP	1st	250cc	(Yamaha)
French GP	1st	250cc	(Yamaha)
IoM TT	1st	125cc	(Yamaha)
	2nd	350cc	(Yamaha)
Dutch TT	1st	250cc	(Yamaha)
Belgian GP	2nd	250cc	(Yamaha)
East German GP	2nd	250cc	(Yamaha)
Czech GP	1st	250cc	(Yamaha)
Ulster GP	1st	250cc	(Yamaha)

World championships: 1st 250cc, 10th 125cc

1966

West German	3rd	125cc	(Yamaha)
French GP	3rd	250cc	(Yamaha)
Dutch TT	2nd	250cc	(Yamaha)
	3rd	125cc	(Yamaha)
Belgian GP	2nd	250cc	(Yamaha)
East German GP	2nd	250cc	(Yamaha)
Czech GP	2nd	250cc	(Yamaha)
Finnish GP	1st	125cc	(Yamaha)
Ulster GP	3rd	125cc	(Yamaha)
Isle of Man TT	2nd	125cc	(Yamaha)
Japanese GP	2nd	250cc	(Yamaha)
	1st	350cc	(Yamaha)

World championships: 2nd 250cc, 4th 125cc

1967

Spanish GP	2nd	125cc	(Yamaha)
	1st	250cc	(Yamaha)
West German	2nd	250cc	(Yamaha)
French GP	2nd	125cc	(Yamaha)
	2nd	250cc	(Yamaha)
IoM TT	1st	125cc	(Yamaha)
	2nd	250cc	(Yamaha)
Dutch TT	1st	125cc	(Yamaha)
East German GP	2nd	125cc	(Yamaha)
	1st	250cc	(Yamaha)
Czech GP	1st	250cc	(Yamaha)
Ulster GP	2nd	125cc	(Yamaha)
Italian GP	2nd	125cc	(Yamaha)
	1st	250cc	(Yamaha)
Canadian GP	2nd	250cc	(Yamaha)

World championships: 2nd 250cc, 2nd 125cc

1968

West German	1st	125cc	(Yamaha)
Spanish GP	1st	250cc	(Yamaha)
IoM TT	1st	125cc	(Yamaha)
Dutch TT	1st	125cc	(Yamaha)
	2nd	250cc	(Yamaha)
Belgian GP	1st	250cc	(Yamaha)
East German	1st	125cc	(Yamaha)
	2nd	250cc	(Yamaha)
Czech GP	1st	125cc	(Yamaha)
	1st	250cc	(Yamaha)
Finnish GP	1st	125cc	(Yamaha)
	1st	250cc	(Yamaha)
Ulster GP	2nd	125cc	(Yamaha)
Italian GP	2nd	125cc	(Yamaha)
	1st	250cc	(Yamaha)

World championships: 1st 250cc, 1st 125cc

1969

Italian GP	1st	250cc	(Yamaha)
	1st	350cc	(Yamaha)

World championships:13th 250cc, 13th 350cc

1970

Dutch TT	2nd	250cc	(Yamaha)
	3rd	350cc	(Yamaha)
Italian GP	3rd	250cc	(Yamaha)

1971

West German GP	1st	250cc	(Yamaha)
IoM TT	1st	250cc	(Yamaha)
Dutch TT	1st	250cc	(Yamaha)
	2nd	350cc	(Yamaha)
East German GP	3rd	250cc	(Yamaha)
Spanish	2nd	250cc	(Yamaha)

World championships:
1st 250cc, 16th 350cc, 19th 500cc

1972

IoM TT	1st	250cc	(Yamaha)
Yugolsav GP	3rd	350cc	(MV Agusta)
Belgian GP	3rd	250cc	(Yamaha)
East German GP	1st	350cc	(MV Agusta)
Czech GP	3rd	250cc	(Yamaha)
Swedish TT	2nd	350cc	(MV Agusta)

World championships: 4th 250cc, 5th 350cc

1973

French GP	2nd	350cc	(MV Agusta)
	2nd	500cc	(MV Agusta)
West German GP	1st	500cc	(MV Agusta)
Dutch TT	2nd	350cc	(MV Agusta)
	1st	500cc	(MV Agusta)
Belgian GP	2nd	500cc	(MV Agusta)
Czech GP	3rd	350cc	(MV Agusta)
	2nd	500cc	(MV Agusta)
Swedish TT	3rd	350cc	(MV Agusta)
	1st	500cc	(MV Agusta)
Finnish GP	2nd	350cc	(MV Agusta)
	2nd	500cc	(MV Agusta)
Spanish GP	1st	500cc	(MV Agusta)

The 500cc Italian GP was cancelled
At the Yugoslav GP, the MV Agusta team withdrew on safety grounds

World championships: 1st 500cc, 3rd 350cc

1974

French GP	2nd	500cc	(MV Agusta)
Italian GP	3rd	500cc	(MV Agusta)
Dutch TT	3rd	500cc	(MV Agusta)
Belgian GP	1st	500cc	(MV Agusta)
Swedish TT	2nd	500cc	(MV Agusta)
Finnish GP	1st	500cc	(MV Agusta)
Czech GP	1st	500cc	(MV Agusta)

The West German GP was boycotted by leading riders on safety grounds

World championships: 1st 500cc

1975

French GP	3rd	500cc	(MV Agusta)
Austrian GP	3rd	500cc	(MV Agusta)
West German GP	2nd	500cc	(MV Agusta)
Italian GP	2nd	500cc	(MV Agusta)
Dutch TT	3rd	500cc	(MV Agusta)
Belgian GP	1st	500cc	(MV Agusta)
Swedish TT	2nd	500cc	(MV Agusta)
Czech GP	1st	500cc	(MV Agusta)

World championships 2nd 500cc

1976

Austrian GP	3rd	500cc	(Suzuki)
Italian GP	2nd	500cc	(Suzuki)

During the Belgian GP, Read went absent for personal reasons

World championships: 10th 500cc

FIM TT Formula 1 world championship

1977
IoM TT 1st in race and championship (810cc Honda)

Non-world championship TT races

1977 1st 500cc Senior (Suzuki)

Manx Grand Prix

1958 3rd 350cc Junior Newcomers

1960 1st 500cc Senior (Norton)

ACU Star

1961 350cc

British Road racing Championships

1963 1st 350cc Junior

1964 1st 250cc

Mellano Trophy, Brands Hatch

1968 1st (Yamaha)

World championships: 500cc: 2, 250cc: 4, 125cc: 1, TTF1: 1 (total 8)

Italian internationals

1970

Rimini	1st	250cc	(Yamaha)
Cervia	1st	250cc	(Yamaha)

1971

Riccione	1st	250cc	(Yamaha)
	2nd	350cc	(Yamaha)
Imola	1st	250cc	(Yamaha)

Evening News Trophy, Brands Hatch

1970 1st (Yamaha)

Evening News Race of the South, Brands Hatch

1972 1st (Norton)

UK long-distance Production events

1962

Silverstone	1000 Kilometres	1st Overall
	with Brian Setchell (650cc Norton)	
Thruxton	500 Miles	1st Overall
	with Brian Setchell (650cc Norton)	

1963

Oulton Park	1000 Kilometres	2nd Overall
	with Brian Setchell (650cc Norton)	
Thruxton	500 Miles	1st Overall
	with Brian Setchell (650cc Norton)	

1966

Brands Hatch	500 Miles	2nd Overall
	with Percy Tait (650cc Triumph)	

John Player TransAtlantic Trophy

1972 (Norton)

Brands Hatch	Race 1	3rd	Race 2	4th
Mallory Par	Race 1	4th	Race 2	5th
Oulton Park	Race 1	6th	Race 2	6th

GB team's second highest score with 50 points

1976 (Yamaha) GB Team Captain

Brands Hatch			Race 2	4th
Mallory Park	Race 1	7th	Race 2	6th
Oulton Park	Race 1	9th	Race 2	7th

Top ten riders, all time in all classes

	victories	2nd places	3rd places	pole position '74 to 2013	fastest lap to 2013	World Championships
AGOSTINI Giacomo	122	35	2	9	117	15
ROSSI Valentino	106	46	28	59	88	9
NIETO Angel	90	35	14	34	81	13
HAILWOOD Mike	76	25	11		79	9
DOOHAN Mick	54	31	10	58	46	5
READ Phil	52	44	25	5	36	7
PEDROSA Dani	47	41	29	44	56	3
LORENZO Jorge	47	36	20	53	24	4
REDMAN Jim	45	33	20		35	6
STONER Casey	45	17	27	43	33	2

Index